D0418801

what's that bird?

what's that bird?

A quick reference guide to the most common European garden birds

Dr Paul Sterry

Bounty Books

First published in Great Britain in 2006 by Hamlyn,
a division of Octopus Publishing Group Ltd

Thsi edition published in 2007 by Bounty Books,
a division of Octopus Publishing Group Ltd
2–4 Heron Quays, London, E14 4JP

ISBN-13: 978-0-753715-16-1

ISBN-10: 0-753715-16-3

A CIP catalogue record for this book is available from the British Library

Printed and bound in China

Contents

Introduction

To people who have not watched birds seriously before, the pleasures of it can seem a bit of a mystery. However, if you take a little time to watch them in the wild you will soon be captivated by their behaviour and want to see more.

Above Many bird species, such as this robin, announce their presence in the garden with distinctive, and often diagnostic, song.

Fortunately, beginners don't necessarily have to go far to pursue their new pastime because, whether we realize it or not, most of us live surprisingly close to birds. Even the most unpromising of suburban gardens is probably regularly visited by 30 or more different species.

Getting started

For many people, an interest in birds starts through noticing them while doing something completely different, such as relaxing in a chair or gardening. One of the main aims of this book is to cater for both casual birdwatchers and beginners with a developing interest. However, because observing birds and learning more about them are likely to kindle an interest that grows and expands, it also includes details that will guide you as your horizons expand beyond the realms of your garden, to the countryside beyond.

Taking it further

Much of the pleasure that many people get from watching birds comes from simply looking at their antics. However, many observers gain an additional thrill from being able to identify the birds they are

Above Our avian fauna is rich and varied, including species that spend much of the time on the wing, ones that are secretive, nocturnal species and birds that are unbelievably colourful.

watching. This provides an extra dimension to the experience and allows them to make a fuller interpretation of the comings and goings of the birds in the garden, so that eventually they will be able to build up a clear picture of the nature and habits of the birds that live around them.

The aim of the book

Many advanced field guides contain bewildering amounts of technical information that beginners and casual observers do not need and include species that most people with a casual interest are unlikely to come across. This book, on the other hand, aims to introduce people to the pleasures of birdwatching, without putting them off with a daunting array of rare possibilities. At first the book may sit on your windowsill and be used from time to time when something of interest attracts your attention. Hopefully, however, the more you use this book the greater your interest in birds will become and you will find yourself referring to it after trips in the car or on returning from holidays to other parts of the region.

Above Birds such as the kingfisher are instantly recognizable.

Above All woodpeckers have feet adapted for climbing and use their tails as props.

Above Predatory birds, such as this merlin, have sharp claws and hooked bills.

How to use this book

This book has been organized to suit the novice birdwatcher. The basic principles of birdwatching appear first, followed by species descriptions; the birds are arranged so that superficially similar species appear close to one another in the book.

Identifying birds

The information on pages 10–17 provides a basic guide to learning how to identify birds, starting with the names of the parts of a bird's plumage and then explains how to get clues to their identity from their shape and behaviour, both on the ground and in flight, their songs and calls, and what features to look for on a bird to make a correct identification.

Bird biology

This section (pages 18–21) looks at key features of birds: their feathers, wings and flight, nesting habits and eggs, bills and feeding methods, feet and tails and how these reflect the species' means of obtaining food, breeding habits and way of flying.

Time and place

Different species have adopted different strategies in order to succeed: some stay in more or less the same place the whole time, while others migrate. In addition, each species has evolved to eat particular foods and to live in particular habitats. This section (pages 22–25) explains how understanding what you are likely to see, where and when, makes narrowing down the possible identity of a bird far easier.

Optical aids

This section (pages 26–27) looks at binoculars and telescopes and offers advice on what the different sizes and magnification levels can offer.

The bird-friendly garden

Across our region, life is getting tougher for birds. If you encourage them into your garden by providing a good environment for them, you will also be helping in conservation. This section (pages 28–45) looks at the provision of supplementary foods and how to garden in ways that will attract birds, ensuring there are good natural nest sites as well as examining the various types of nest boxes.

Above The scarce marsh warbler relies on neglected vegetation for nesting. Beds of stinging nettles are ideal.

Common name

Scientific name

Details of:

- Where and when the species may be seen
- How large it is
- What it eats
- Its call and song
- Plumage differences between male, female and juvenile birds
- What to look out for when they are in flight
- What the nest looks like

Other birds seen in the area that resemble the main bird on the page, but are less likely to be seen in gardens

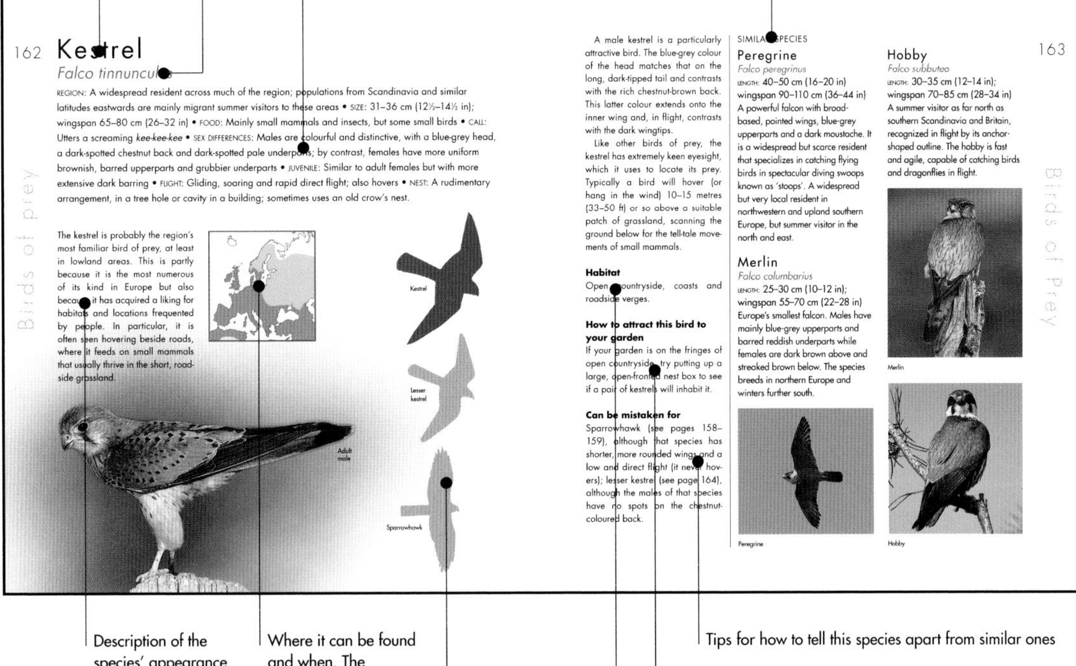

162 **Kestrel**

Falco tinnunculus

REGION: A widespread resident across much of the region; populations from Scandinavia and similar latitudes eastwards are mainly migrant summer visitors to these areas • SIZE: 31–36 cm (12½–14½ in); wingspan 65–80 cm (26–32 in) • FOOD: Mainly small mammals and insects, but some small birds • CALL: Utters a screaming *kee-kee-kee* • SEX DIFFERENCES: Males are colourful and distinctive, with a blue-grey head, a dark-spotted chestnut back and dark-spotted pale underparts; by contrast, females have more uniform brownish, barred upperparts and grubbier underparts • JUVENILE: Similar to adult females but with more extensive dark barring • FLIGHT: Gliding, soaring and rapid direct flight; also hovers • NEST: A rudimentary arrangement, in a tree hole or cavity in a building; sometimes uses an old crow's nest.

Birds of prey

The kestrel is probably the region's most familiar bird of prey, at least in lowland areas. This is partly because it is the most numerous of its kind in Europe but also because it has acquired a liking for habitats and locations frequented by people. In particular, it is often seen hovering beside roads, where it feeds on small mammals that usually thrive in the short, roadside grassland.

Kestrel

Lesser kestrel

Sparrowhawk

Adult male

A male kestrel is a particularly attractive bird. The blue-grey colour of the head matches that on the long, dark-tipped tail and contrasts with the rich chestnut-brown back. This latter colour extends onto the inner wing and, in flight, contrasts with the dark wingtips.

Like other birds of prey, the kestrel has extremely keen eyesight, which it uses to locate its prey. Typically a bird will hover (or hang in the wind) 10–15 metres (33–50 ft) or so above a suitable patch of grassland, scanning the ground below for the tell-tale movements of small mammals.

Habitat

Open countryside, coasts and roadside verges.

How to attract this bird to your garden

If your garden is on the fringes of open countryside, try putting up a large, open-fronted nest box to see if a pair of kestrels will inhabit it.

Can be mistaken for

Sparrowhawk (see pages 158–159), although that species has shorter, more rounded wings and a low and direct flight (it never hovers); lesser kestrel (see page 164), although the males of that species have no spots on the chestnut-coloured back.

SIMILAR SPECIES

Peregrine

Falco peregrinus

LENGTH: 40–50 cm (16–20 in) wingspan 90–110 cm (36–44 in)

A powerful falcon with broad-based, pointed wings, blue-grey upperparts and a dark moustache. It is a widespread but scarce resident that specializes in catching flying birds in spectacular diving swoops known as 'stoops'. A widespread but very local resident in northwestern and upland southern Europe, but summer visitor in the north and east.

Merlin

Falco columbarius

LENGTH: 25–30 cm (10–12 in); wingspan 55–70 cm (22–28 in)

Europe's smallest falcon. Males have mainly blue-grey upperparts and barred reddish underparts while females are dark brown above and streaked brown below. The species breeds in northern Europe and winters further south.

Peregrine

Hobby

Falco subbuteo

LENGTH: 30–35 cm (12–14 in); wingspan 70–85 cm (28–34 in)

A summer visitor as far north as southern Scandinavia and Britain, recognized in flight by its anchor-shaped outline. The hobby is fast and agile, capable of catching birds and dragonflies in flight.

163

Merlin

Hobby

Birds of Prey

Description of the species' appearance and behaviour

Where it can be found and when. The distribution maps give wintering areas in blue, summer areas in green, areas where the bird occurs all year round in purple and migration areas in yellow

Relevant silhouettes. Note that, under most circumstances, silhouettes are more use when it comes to assigning a given bird to a family rather than for specific identification. While a few species are immediately identifiable by silhouette alone, most warblers, for example, look confusingly similar to one another in silhouette. So use these silhouttes as potential short cuts to rule out superficially similar species rather than as descriptive artworks.

Tips for how to tell this species apart from similar ones

Tips for providing food or nest sites that will encourage this species to your garden if you live within its range

Whether it prefers farmland, woodland, high ground, water or the coast

Identifying birds

It is worth spending a bit of time becoming familiar with some of the key names associated with bird plumage because these are included in many of the descriptions of species later in the book. Knowing these names will also make it easier to tell similar species apart because you will be comparing like with like.

Bird topography

This is the technical term for the way that birds' feathers are arranged in defined areas, such as primary, breast and flank. In many species they are quite easy to spot because the feathers are different sizes and textures (see page 18).

At rest

When a bird perches or stands on the ground, many of the feathers overlie one another. Nevertheless, if you look closely, it is possible to distinguish between all the important parts, as shown on the red kite below. Patterns on the head, breast and wings give important clues when it comes to identification.

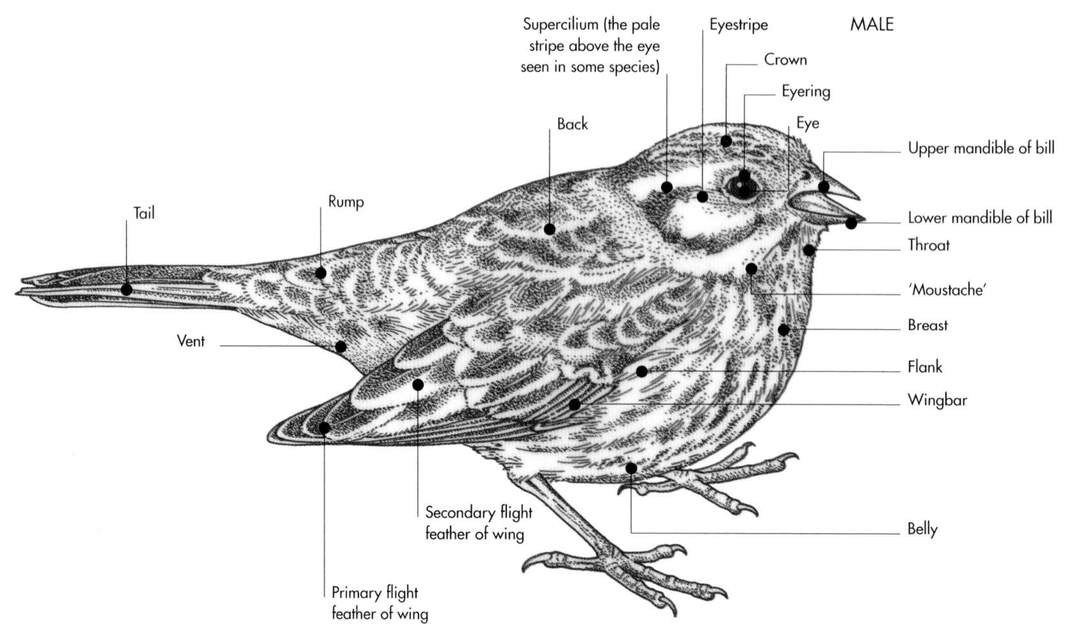

In flight

In flight, the wing feathers are easy to see since they are spread out for much of the time. In many species, striking patches or wingbars that are more difficult or impossible to see when the wings are closed (dark or light, depending on species) are revealed. The shape of the wings and the tail also give important clues for identification, as detailed on the bunting below.

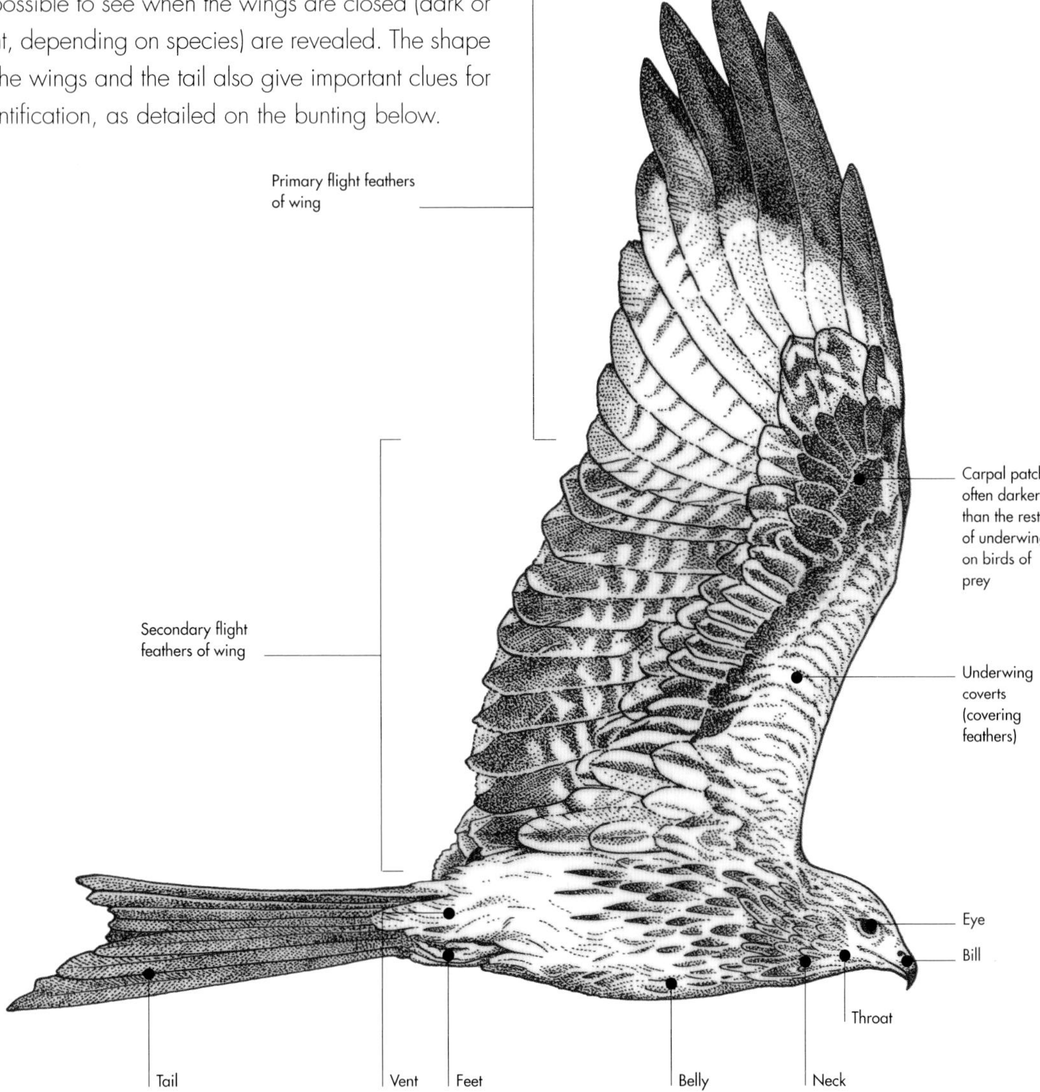

Narrowing it down

Identifying birds is not just about looking at their plumage, although of course this is a key part of the process. With just a little experience, you will find that you are able to narrow the identification down to a family or group of birds, even before seeing their plumage in detail, simply because you have learned to recognize their outline, the way they move about on the ground, the way they feed or the characteristic way they fly. Within a few months or so you will be able to identify the majority of bird species that visit your garden and live in the surrounding area.

Silhouettes

Birds seen in silhouette are, naturally, not as easy to identify as they are when you can see their plumage clearly, but the groups and families do have characteristic shapes. For example, most tits have rather rounded bodies, short tails and stubby bills, whereas finches and sparrows have proportionately longer tails, thicker bills and more elongated bodies. Woodpeckers are often seen in silhouette as they cling to, and climb up, the trunks of trees, while birds of prey can be recognized by the hooked bill and very short necks.

Perched, resting and standing silhouettes

Tits have a dumpy body, thick neck and, in most species, a pointed bill

Finches and buntings have a rather stubby bill, thick neck and dumpy body

Owls have proportionately large and rounded heads and a dumpy body

Pigeons and doves have small heads relative to body size and rather dainty bills

Birds of prey have a hooked bill and almost no neck. Their feet have sharp talons

Ducks and geese have elongated bodies and their bills are broad and flattened

Storks and herons are huge birds. Note the long neck, large bill and long legs

Woodpeckers have a characteristic climbing pose and dagger-like bills

Birds in flight

In harsh light, or against a cloudy sky, all you can often see of a bird in flight is the shape of its silhouette, but with experience you will still be able to detect many of the key features that will help you to work out what it is. In particular, look at the shape of the wings (are they rounded or pointed at the tip?), the shape of the tail (forked or rounded, short or long) and the overall size and proportions of the bird. Some larger birds hold both their legs and necks extended in flight, whereas other species may hold the neck in a 'V' shape.

Above Seen in flight, a raven reveals a distinct and diagnostic wedge-shaped tail.

Flight silhouettes

A magpie has broad, rounded wings and an extremely long tail

Most birds of prey have rather broad wings and a relatively long tail

Woodpeckers have broad rounded wings and a proportionally large head

Large water birds have a huge wingspan and trailing legs in flight

Geese and ducks have broad wings and fly with the neck extended

Swifts have a horseshoe-shaped wing outline, short necks and a rapid flight

Mastering the basics

When you're just starting off, the prospect of being able to identify birds may seem daunting. But don't be put off. Get to know some of the key bird features to look for, familiarize yourself with the most common species in your area and you will have made a great start. You will soon discover that the more you see and learn, the easier it is to detect unusual species, simply because they are different to the ones you are used to seeing. Eventually, you will be able to spot the unusual ones quickly. Some of the keys to identifying birds are listed below.

Size

The size of a bird is useful in the process of bird identification. To start with, however, it can be surprisingly difficult to gauge the size of a bird, especially at a distance and if you're not sure what size a bird *should* appear.

An approach that many people find works, until they have more experience, is to try to compare a mystery bird to another bird nearby of which you know the size. If you are using other birds for comparison, then the more familiar you are with the species, the better your chances of success. So use species such as the chaffinch, blackbird, woodpigeon and mute swan as benchmarks.

Colour and plumage patterns (see page 16) are obviously vital for accurate bird identification. You will learn these in time. However, do bear in mind that your mystery bird may not match the pictures in books exactly.

Sometimes the ambient light can play tricks on your eyes. Features that look obvious in books may be

Above The woodpigeon is the most familiar medium-sized bird that you will find.

Above Down the size scale are the blackbird (above) and chaffinch (below).

hard to discern; for example, the reflective dark sheen of a rook's feathers may look pale and silvery if seen against the light.

In addition, in many species, males and females have striking differences in their plumage, as do adults and juveniles. Some species moult into different plumage patterns at different times of the year, and just before a moult their feathers can be worn and sometimes look less bright.

Calls and songs

It is well worth learning the calls, songs and other sounds that birds make, as they are extremely effective aids to identification. Start by learning the songs of the birds that are commonly in your garden, such as robins, chaffinches, wrens, collared doves and song thrushes. Once you know the basics, it becomes easier to notice a novel song or call. And, of course, there are other sounds that can help the birdwatcher. For example, a loud drumming sound is a sure sign that there is a woodpecker nearby and loud, clattering wingbeats indicate that a woodpigeon has been startled.

Behaviour

Watch out for the way a bird is behaving. A small bird that pumps its tail up and down is certain to be a wagtail, while a tiny, rounded bird that cocks its tail upright is sure to be a wren. A small, mouse-like bird that climbs up a tree trunk in a spiral fashion is a treecreeper, while a small, dumpy bird that climbs down a trunk head first is a nuthatch. Distinctive behaviour that can help to identify a species is mentioned in the species section (pages 46–249).

Above White and pied wagtails have a distinctive call and pump their tail up and down.

Above Even if you cannot see a golden oriole you can determine its presence in an area by its fluty song and weird cat-like calls.

Plumage details

You will soon begin to recognize family ties among the birds in your garden. Before long you will be able to discern characters and features that are shared by, for example, all members of the tit family, or all of the finches. Some members of these families are immediately identifiable and present few problems for the observer. However, others can be trickier and you need to concentrate on the differences – that can be very subtle – in plumage to help with identification. (The photographs here are presented to show the body part in question.)

Ten key questions

1 Does the bird have an eyestripe and, if so, what colour is it?

2 Does the bird have an eyering and, if so, what colour is it?

3 Does the bird have a 'moustache' stripe?

4 What colour is the crown?

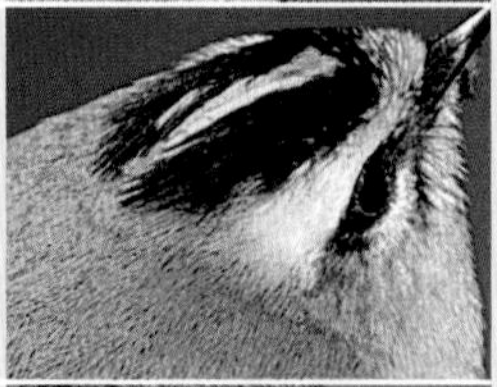

5 What colour is the throat?

6 What colour is the back?

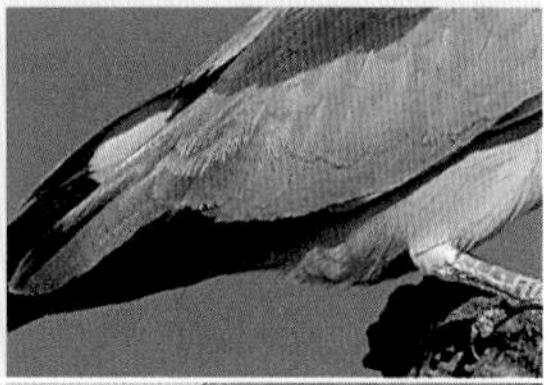

7 Does the bird have wingbars and, if so, what colour are they?

8 What colour is the tail and in particular does it have white outer feathers?

9 What colour is the rump?

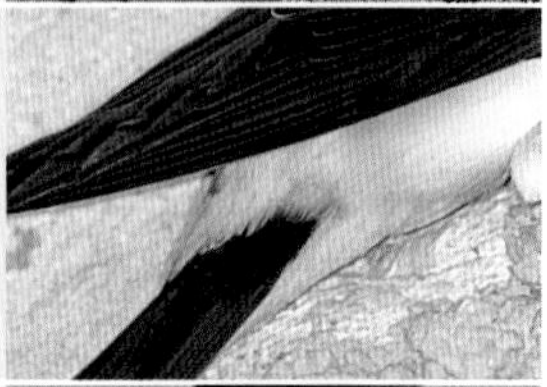

10 What colour is the belly?

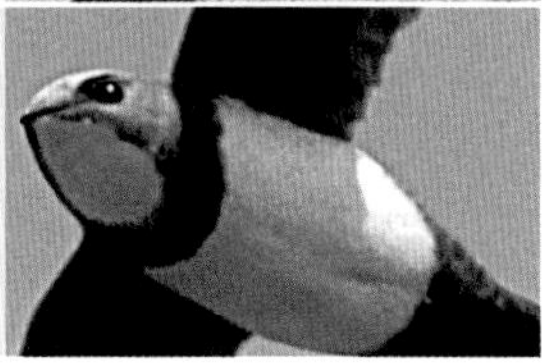

Short cuts

Some novice birdwatchers agonize for hours on end about identification and this can be rather frustrating. To speed things up, you will soon learn that there are a number of short cuts to identifying birds. For a few species, just one distinctive plumage feature in combination with the bird's relative size can be enough to clinch identification, even if you only get a fleeting view. Here are a few examples, but within a few months you are sure to find short cuts of your own.

Classic short cuts

A sparrow-sized and shaped bird with a white rump, seen in a garden or hedgerow, is likely to be a bullfinch.

A sparrow-sized bird with a white rump, seen in an open area of short grassland, and with an upright posture, is likely to be a wheatear.

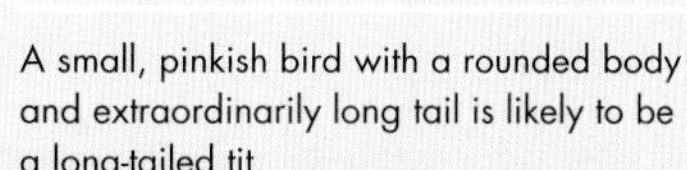

A small, compact bird (smaller than a robin) with a crest, seen in woodland, is likely to be a crested tit.

A starling-sized bird with a crest, seen on garden berries in winter, is likely to be a waxwing.

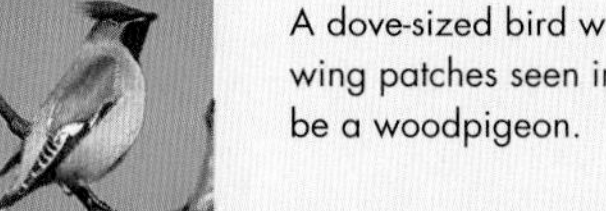

A sparrow-sized bird with yellow wingbars and a pale rump, seen in gardens or scrubby habitat, is likely to be a goldfinch.

A large, all-dark bird with a wedge-shaped tail in flight is likely to be a raven.

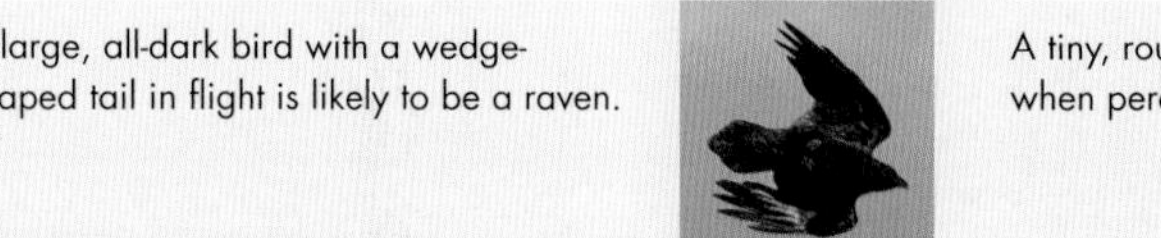

A large, reddish bird with a distinctly forked tail in flight is likely to be a red kite.

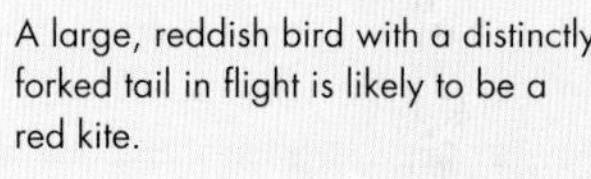

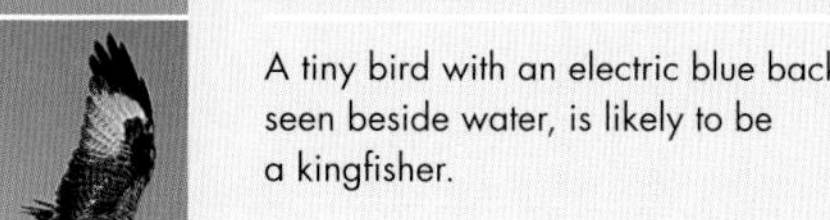

A sparrow-sized bird with a red tail, seen in woodland in summer, is likely to be a redstart.

A sparrow-sized bird with a red tail, seen near the coast in winter, is likely to be a black redstart.

A small, pinkish bird with a rounded body and extraordinarily long tail is likely to be a long-tailed tit.

A dove-sized bird with striking white wing patches seen in flight is likely to be a woodpigeon.

A dove-sized bird with a broad white terminal band on the tail is likely to be a collared dove.

A tiny, rounded bird that cocks its tail up when perched is likely to be a wren.

A tiny bird with an electric blue back, seen beside water, is likely to be a kingfisher.

Bird biology

Birds are an amazingly diverse group. They come in all shapes and sizes and there are reckoned to be about 9,000 species alive in the world today. Of these, 500 or so species occur regularly in Europe and more than 150 of these are found in gardens and neighbouring countryside across the region.

Above All birds spend considerable periods of time preening their feathers to keep them in good order. It ensures that the insulating properties of the plumage are maintained. In the case of water birds, such as this mallard, clean feathers are vital for the water-repellent covering.

The underlying reason for the success of birds, both globally and in our region, stems from their basic biology. Like mammals, they are warm-blooded and can maintain their internal temperature irrespective of the air temperature around them. This means that unlike reptiles (which hibernate), for example, birds that have evolved in temperate and northerly latitudes, and are resident there, are active in the dead of winter.

Feathers

Birds are covered in feathers, which provide insulation and reduce heat loss in cold weather. Those that are found on the wings also provide birds with the means to fly, an ability that is extremely rare among vertebrate animals (only bats are also capable of sustained and powered flight).

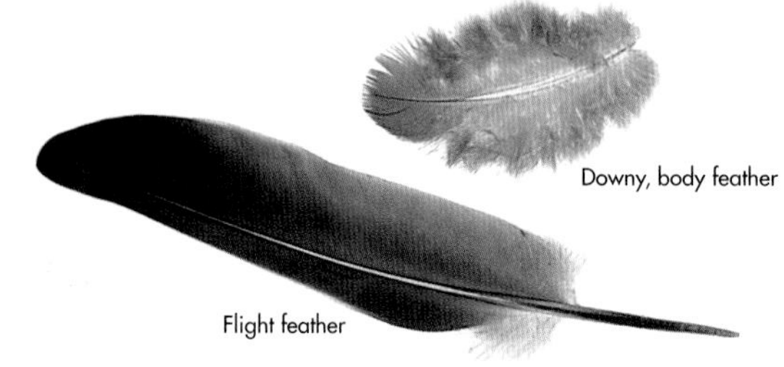

Flight

The ability to fly allows birds to move around and find food more easily than, say, terrestrial mammals. For bird species whose food is only seasonally abundant (insect-eating specialists, for example) being able to fly means they can migrate to better feeding grounds in winter. The ability to fly also means that birds are more able to avoid predators.

Song thrush nest

Chaffinch nest

Above A chaffinch's nest is a deep, cup-shaped structure made from woven grasses, lichens and mosses. A song thrush's nest is made from twigs and lined on the inside with mud.

Nests, eggs and chicks

Do not disturb bird nests during the breeding season, and *never* remove eggs from the nest. If you see a fledgling in the garden, do not approach it. The chances are that its parents are nearby collecting food. It is best to leave them to get on with it. If you have a cat, take it indoors.

Reproduction

Birds reproduce by laying eggs, which are then incubated, the warmth allowing the embryo inside to develop. Nests come in many shapes and sizes and the number of eggs laid varies from species to species. Some chicks, such as those of pheasants and partridges, hatch with feathers, can run from that moment and will find their own food, while in contrast most newly hatched songbird chicks are largely naked, blind and entirely helpless, relying on their parents to feed them. So, the flexible basic biology of birds has allowed them to colonize and exploit almost every habitat on Earth.

Black-headed gull egg (length 57 mm/2 in)

Lapwing egg (length 45 mm/1¾ in)

House sparrow egg (length 21 mm/1 in)

Coal tit egg (length 16 mm/¾ in)

Bills

The bill of a bird (sometimes called a beak) has many uses. It is used for feeding, drinking, preening, nest building, and sometimes as a weapon of either attack or defence. Structurally, the bill is an extension of the jaw and comprises two parts: the upper mandible and the lower mandible. It is covered in a horny, protective layer of skin that, in some cases, is brightly coloured. If you get a good view, you can see the bird's nostrils at the base of the bill. The shape and size of the bill vary according to species and are adapted to suit their lifestyle, particularly the feeding habits. Some of the many varied and extraordinary types of bill are shown below.

Grey heron – large, dagger-like bill

Snipe – long, probing bill

Green woodpecker – robust, chisel-like bill

Chaffinch – stubby, seed-eater's bill

Feet

No species of bird has feet that are quite the same as another, although of course there are usually similarities between closely related species. This diversity reflects the fact that birds use their feet in a variety of ways and for many different purposes. In some species they enable the bird to perch, and are good at gripping branches, while in others they allow the bird to walk on the ground. Many water birds have webbed, or broadly lobed, feet that are used for swimming; although good in water, many water birds find it awkward to walk on land. In birds of prey and owls, the feet are also used for killing prey and hence are powerful and armed with sharp talons.

Mallard – webbed feet for swimming

Kestrel – powerful and armed with sharp talons

Moorhen – long, lobed toes

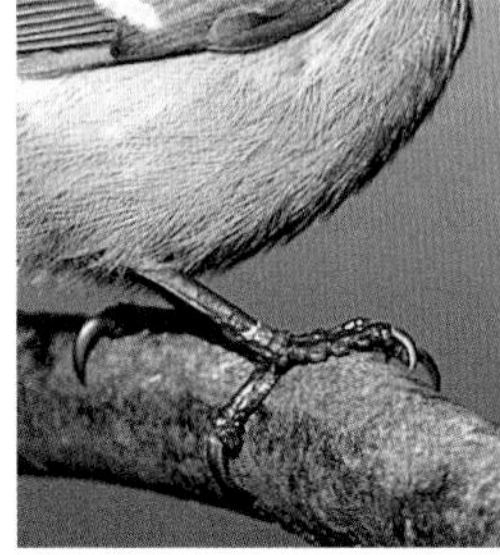

Blue tit – typical perching bird's feet

Wings

Obviously, nearly all birds can fly. Some species fly in order to move from one feeding ground to another, or from a roosting or nesting spot to a feeding area. They take to the air to escape danger and some birds can catch prey while in flight. Unsurprisingly, the shape of a particular species' wings will have evolved to suit the function for which they are intended.

Tails

The primary function of a bird's tail is to fine-tune its balance. In songbirds such as tits and warblers, it is held more or less horizontally when perched. Birds such as woodpeckers and treecreepers use the tail as a support when climbing. Some soaring birds flex their tails to change direction. In a few instances patterns and colours on the tail are important for display.

White stork – huge, broad wings for soaring and gliding

Common buzzard – broad wings for effortless soaring

Pheasant – long, gaudy tail for show

Red kite – forked tail used for aerial manoeuvring

Swift – narrow wings for rapid flight

Brambling – relatively short and rounded wings

Raven – relatively short tail used for balance

House martin – forked tail used for aerial manoeuvring

Lifestyle preferences

One of the joys of birdwatching is the realization that every species is uniquely adapted to life. Even among closely related birds, the fact that they have evolved to have different habitat preferences and to live in totally different regions from season to season can be fascinating.

Habitat preferences

A few species of birds can be found in a wide variety of locations in a broad range of habitats. However, you will soon notice that most are limited to specific habitats, some extremely so, which is why emphasis is placed on their habitat preferences in the text accompanying the species section of this book.

Adaptation to a habitat

If you take a close look at birds with specialist habitat requirements, you will discover precise physical and behavioural adaptations that allow them to survive in their favoured habitat but make them ill equipped to live elsewhere. For example, its behaviour, the shape of its bill and an ability to dive allow the kingfisher to thrive in fish-rich streams and rivers. But, away from water, the species cannot survive because it cannot catch food. Similarly, the shape of its wings, mouth and bill, and its inability to walk on the ground, means that the only way a swift can feed is by hawking for insects on the wing, which is why it must migrate (see page 23).

Habitat and identification

For the birdwatcher, knowing the local habitat has two advantages. First, you can rule out birds that are unlikely to be anywhere near the habitat, and second, when you take your interest further you can target particular habitats as a means of locating species with those precise requirements.

Above Most wild species of European geese migrate south within our region in autumn, typically flying in a 'V' formation.

Above Bramblings migrate south in the autumn to escape the rigours (and lack of food) of winter in northern Europe. They are typically seen in flocks.

Migration and seasonal occurrence

Some birds lead essentially sedentary lives. For example, across much of Europe, during their whole lives most blue tits and green woodpeckers are unlikely to stray more than a few kilometres from where they were hatched. For other species, however, the situation is rather different.

Birds that undertake precise seasonal movements between relatively well defined, and distinctly separate, summer breeding grounds and winter quarters are referred to as migrants. However, they are not the only birds that do not stay in one place all year. Outside the breeding season, some birds are essentially nomadic, forced to keep on the move in search of new sources of dwindling food reserves. Birds such as siskins favour broadly similar types of habitat – woodlands – in summer and winter, simply moving south within Europe in autumn. Others, such as snow buntings, switch habitats altogether, favouring tundra and northern rocky moors in summer, but seashores farther south in winter.

Finding food?

Apart from the weather, the availability (or lack) of food is probably the most significant factor affecting European birds throughout the seasons. It is a particular problem for insect-eating species because their food all but disappears in the dead of winter. They cope with this in three ways.

1 Some, such as treecreepers, eat insects throughout the year and find enough to eat in winter. Their specialized tweezer-like bill helps in this respect.

2 Others, like most members of the tit family – essentially insect-eaters in summer – switch to a diet of seeds and nuts in winter.

3 The extreme approach is to migrate to Africa in autumn and not return to Europe until the following spring. Most warblers, and many other small songbirds, adopt this strategy.

What to expect

The following tables list some of the most commonly seen species in the region. If you live in the north of our region, there is a possibility that some species listed under the 'Winter only' category may occur in their respective habitats in the summer months. However, species that fall under the 'Summer only' heading are extremely unlikely to be found there in winter – most of these species migrate to Africa in the autumn.

Urban parks and gardens

Year round

blue tit • great tit • robin • chaffinch • blackbird • song thrush • starling • house sparrow • greenfinch • collared dove (see above) • feral pigeon

Summer only

swift • house martin • blackcap • black redstart • spotted flycatcher

Winter only

waxwing • siskin • redwing

Farmland and open country

Year round

woodpigeon • jackdaw • rook • corn bunting • kestrel • buzzard • meadow pipit • magpie • pheasant (see above) • yellowhammer

Summer only

swallow • turtle dove

Winter only

fieldfare • redwing

Woodland

Year round

tawny owl • barn owl • great tit • blue tit • robin • jay • nuthatch • treecreeper (see above) • great spotted woodpecker

Summer only

cuckoo • garden warbler • willow warbler • chiffchaff • nightingale • redstart

Wetland habitats

Year round

greylag goose (see above) • mute swan • little grebe • moorhen • snipe • grey heron

Summer only

reed warbler • common sandpiper • common tern • sand martin

Coastal habitats

Year round

herring gull • black-headed gull • little egret • grey heron

Summer only

common tern (see above)

Winter only

twite • snow bunting • wigeon

Mediterranean habitats

Year round

serin • hoopoe (see above) • sardinian warbler • rock sparrow

Summer only

subalpine warbler • turtle dove • bee-eater • roller

Winter only

song thrush • redwing • fieldfare • brambling

Binoculars and telescopes

Some people might argue that all you need to be a birdwatcher is a good pair of eyes. And it is certainly true that many species are large enough and tolerant enough of people for you to get excellent views with the naked eye, but optical aids really help.

While good vision counts for a lot in birdwatching, anybody who is serious about the subject will want to use optical equipment sooner or later. It is not simply a case of magnifying what you are looking at, although this is a benefit in itself, but using a pair of binoculars – the most widely used optical accessories – will also add to your pleasure, allowing you to get to know more about the bird in a way that can never be achieved unaided.

Types of binoculars

Visit any supplier of optical equipment and you will be faced with a bewildering choice of makes and models, not to mention a range of prices that go from the affordable to the cost of a small, secondhand car. So where do you start?

Size

Firstly, all binoculars, regardless of make or model, will be described in terms of a pair of numbers: 8x30, 8x40 or 10x40 are typical sets of numbers. What do these numbers mean?

The first number in the pair denotes the magnification (in these examples either 8x or 10x) while the second figure denotes the diameter in millimetres of the end lens – the larger the diameter, the more light enters the binoculars. Generally speaking, smaller-magnification binoculars are smaller, lighter and easier to hold, but many people prefer to forego these advantages in favour of greater magnification.

Try them out

Really, it all comes down to personal preference. Before you purchase a pair of binoculars, however, do check that they are thoroughly suited to your grip, and in particular that the focusing arrangement suits your fingers.

Telescopes and tripods

A telescope will provide you with even greater magnification and clarity than a pair of binoculars, and most serious birdwatchers own one. Again the choice of available models is bewildering, some coming with fixed-magnification eyepieces, others with a zoom facility. It is really a matter of choosing a model that suits your eye, and how much money you have to spend.

Bear in mind that you will also need a tripod to support the telescope, and a pan-and-tilt type is the best option when it comes to the tripod head. Owning a tripod may seem like a bit of an extravagance but you will soon find that it enhances your birdwatching. And you can always leave it indoors, with the telescope set up and focused on bird feeders in your garden.

Caution

When using binoculars or a telescope, do not look in the direction of the sun because you could accidentally damage your eyes.

10X BINOCULARS

8X BINOCULARS

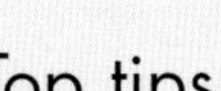

Top tips

- Keep still.
- Always have a pair of binoculars close to hand.
- Keep any pets indoors.
- Keep your distance and use optical aids to their best effect.
- Learn about birds' feeding patterns.
- Look out for key migration routes at certain times of year.

20X TELESCOPE

The bird-friendly garden

Some people are fortunate enough to move into a house with a well-established garden that already attracts plenty of wildlife. However, if you take possession of a new plot, or inherit a garden that is stark and barren, a complete rethink is often required. The accompanying garden plan provides ideas for just such a blank canvas. Those not familiar with the concept may assume that, in order to satisfy the requirements of birds, a wildlife-friendly garden has to be an undisciplined, chaotic affair. However, this is far from the truth. To create a bird-friendly garden you do not need to abandon the land to nature completely – on the contrary, a wildlife garden can be stylish as well as environmentally friendly.

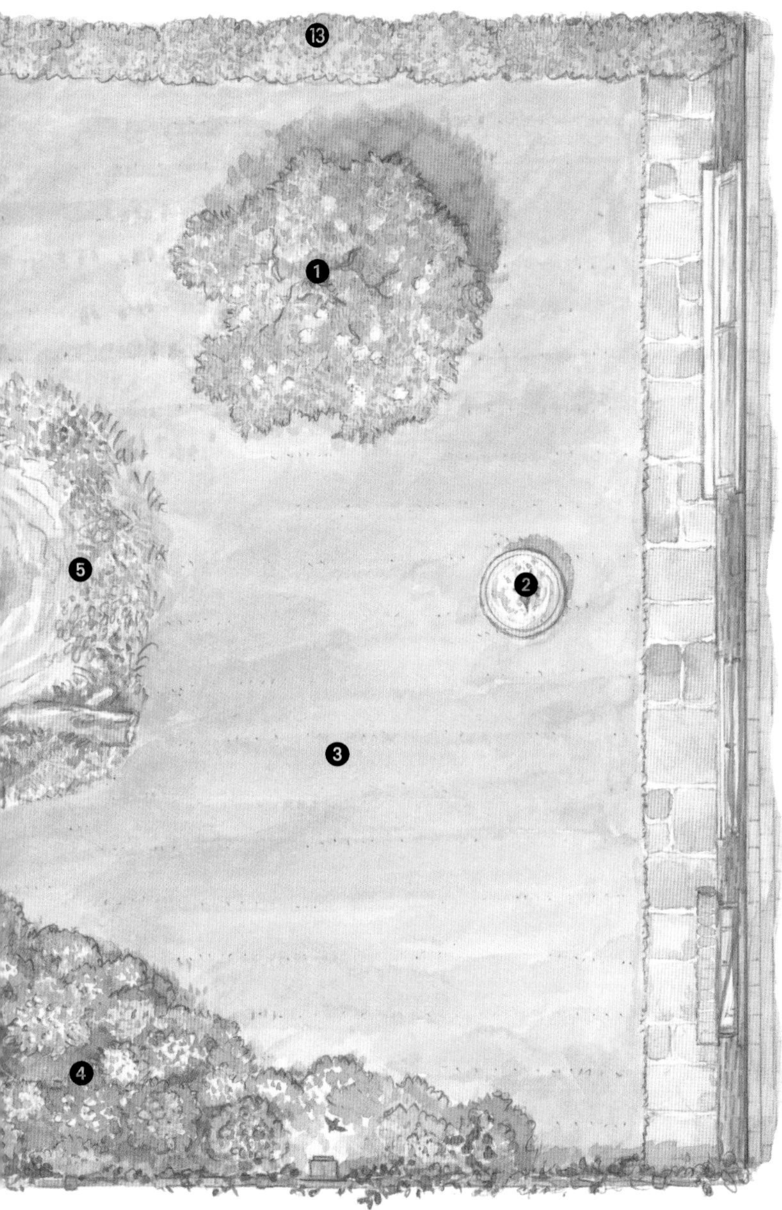

1. Mature berry-bearing tree from which feeders can be hung
2. Bird bath
3. Untreated lawn, full of earthworms that are food for thrushes.
4. Herbaceous border, planted with seed-bearing plants – food for goldfinches
5. Pond, stocked with a variety of native plants
6. Log pile – a refuge for invertebrates and amphibians
7. Wildflower meadow, seeded with native species
8. Nest box
9. Wild corner, containing species such as stinging nettle
10. Seat, for sitting and contemplating nature
11. Vegetable patch
12. Compost bin
13. Dense hedge, comprising native species such as hawthorn and blackthorn

Creating a garden for birds

It is always nice to stamp your mark on a garden and what better way to do it than by designing, planting and managing it at least partly for the benefit of wildlife in general, and birds in particular? If you are fortunate enough to own a large garden, space may not be a major concern. However, most modern European gardens are comparatively small and so more thought must go into their planning. With this in mind, the plan on pages 28–29 provides a possible design for a bird-friendly garden. It has been divided into four blocks, unified by a central pond. You can enlarge or shrink the design to suit your particular garden needs. Alternatively, you can select just one of the four that is of particular interest to you. Here is a brief summary of the contents of, and approaches to managing, each of these garden blocks.

Lawn and recreational area

- Do not use chemicals on the lawn and learn to tolerate – maybe even enjoy – the flowers of daisies, if not creeping buttercups.
- Remove persistent undesirable 'weeds' such as thistles and plantains with a trowel.
- It is an obvious point but the shorter you crop your lawn, the more likely you are to cause patches to die off during dry spells.
- Plant a berry- or fruit-bearing tree (rowan, plum or apple perhaps). This will provide food for birds in the autumn and winter and your bird feeders can be suspended from the branches.
- Be thankful if you have a thriving earthworm population – they aerate the soil and provide food for thrushes.

Vegetable garden

- Divide the area into four blocks, separated by a criss-cross gravel path.
- Grow vegetables in three of the blocks, but remember to alternate your crops each year to help reduce the build-up of soil pests and pathogens.
- In the fourth block, grow cordon fruit trees – ones that have been trained to grow at an angle along a low fence.
- At the back of the plot, grow runner beans and similar plants on climbing frames and site a compost heap here.
- Do not use chemicals in the vegetable garden, partly for your own good but also because of the impact they will have on wildlife.

Above Elder bushes produce heavily scented flowers in spring, and a rich crop of berries in autumn, which birds feast upon.

Above Goldfinches are fond of teasel seeds. Indeed, the size and shape of their bills are perfectly adapted for seed extraction.

Wildflower meadow

- Sow this area with a wildflower seed mixture having first dug and scarified the surface.
- Keep a narrow path (the width of a mower) cut short throughout the season, but do not cut the grass and wildflowers themselves until autumn at the earliest.
- If you leave the cutting until late winter, then birds will be able to find seeds to eat.
- When you do cut the meadow, however, always remember to remove and compost what you cut.

Herbaceous border

- Aim to include a good proportion of seed-producing plants and ones that attract insects, and this way, your herbaceous border will provide the greatest value to wildlife. Teasel (*Dipsacus fullonum*), iceplant (*Sedum spectabile*) and red-hot poker (*Kniphofia* spp.) are all particularly good choices.

Pond

- Dig the centre of the pond to at least 1.5 m (4½ ft) deep and shelve the margins gradually.
- Line the pond with a butyl liner laid over sand.
- Stock the pond with a mixture of non-invasive and relatively slow-growing plants (ideally container-grown) such as water-lilies (*Nymphaea* spp. and *Nuphar* spp.) as well as Canadian pondweed (*Elodea* spp.).
- On one side, create a log pile and log garden, and plant ferns and other damp-loving species in the cracks and crevices. The logs will serve as refuges for frogs and newts in winter, and as the timber decomposes colonies of invertebrates will develop as food for birds.

Above Aphids may dismay the gardener but predators consume great quantities – not only ladybirds but blue tits and warblers too.

Planting the garden with birds in mind

The species of plants that you grow in your garden can have a profound effect upon its suitability for wildlife in general, and how attractive it is to birds in particular. Some plants are far more useful as sources of food for birds than others and, as a general rule, it pays to plant native species as opposed to alien ones if you want to enhance your garden's wildlife appeal.

Hedges

Try to plant native, spiny and dense bushes because these will provide security for the birds. If they produce berries in autumn then so much the better. Species such as blackthorn, hawthorn, hazel, dogwood, elder and holly are ideal.

Berry-bearing bushes

Berries are a staple part of the winter diet of many species, especially members of the thrush family. Species such as hawthorn, rowan, guelder-rose, holly and alder-buckthorn are all good native berry-producers and these are feasted upon by the birds. Ornamental cotoneasters are also laden with berries in winter but the fact that they persist for much longer demonstrates that they are less appealing than their native counterparts.

Fruit trees

In good seasons, fruit trees provide garden owners with a bountiful supply of delicious food, fresh from the tree. In many years, more fruit are produced than can be consumed and there are always plenty of windfalls and slightly damaged specimens that can be left unpicked. These will provide a valuable source of food for birds in the autumn and winter.

Above If you plant berry-bearing bushes, then in autumn and winter you are sure to be visited by flocks of hungry redwings.

Seed and nut producers

All our native shrubs and trees produce seeds in the autumn and where these are protected by hard cases they are referred to as nuts. Although it often requires a specialist feeder to be able to exploit them, these are valuable sources of food for many birds. On a smaller scale, many of the more familiar herbaceous perennials that are grown as border plants in the garden produce copious quantities of seeds in autumn. So delay tidying up your borders until early spring and you will be providing the birds with a natural source of food.

Water

Last but not least, don't forget to provide water for your garden birds, both for drinking and for bathing.

Even remarkably small baths will act like magnets for almost all garden species. As with feeders, you will notice a hierarchy or pecking order among the birds that visit your bird bath. Great tits outrank blue tits, but are driven off by greenfinches. In their turn, they make way for blackbirds and woodpigeons. Make larger ponds as natural-looking as you can to attract a greater variety of birds. If possible, have a shallow margin which allows the birds to approach the water without having to immerse themselves straightaway. A selection of branches placed as perches around the margins will also be appreciated by the visitors.

Above Hazel is a good shrub for a hedge. Its leaves are eaten by insects – food for birds – and jays and nuthatches enjoy the nuts.

Above When winter is at its deepest, open-country species such as the fieldfare often visit gardens in search of windfall apples.

Supplementary food

A well-conceived bird-friendly garden may well provide for the needs of most of its residents and bird visitors, especially during the summer months. However, many people choose to provide additional food for birds in the garden and this supplement is particularly appreciated in winter. Of course the provision of food benefits the birds and this is reason enough to do it. But it also ensures that you get to see many more individual birds than would otherwise be the case, and often a greater variety too. Decades of feeding by garden bird enthusiasts have ensured that there is good understanding of the most popular and nutritious foods for birds.

Peanuts

Peanuts are an energy-rich favourite with a wide range of garden birds, notably blue and great tits, greenfinches and house sparrows. They are widely available and relatively cheap to purchase in bulk. Be careful to buy bird-friendly peanuts from a good stockist, however, because if stored incorrectly they can become contaminated by a chemical called *aflatoxin* that is lethal if consumed.

Sunflower seeds

These seeds are extremely popular with garden birds, notably finches. In autumn, coal tits and nuthatches will remove them from feeders and store them in caches for later retrieval.

Niger seeds

These tiny, black seeds come from a relative of the sunflower. They are extremely popular with bullfinches and goldfinches.

Mixed seeds and grains

The precise mixture and proportions of the component elements vary. Most contain a mixture of seeds from wild plants and sunflowers, and cereal grains. If placed on a table they will attract all the usual garden birds. However, if you scatter them in quantities on

Peanuts

Sunflower seeds

Niger seeds

bare, grassy ground, then species such as yellowhammers and bramblings may also be lured into the garden.

Fat and kitchen scraps

Many suppliers of bird food sell fat balls ready prepared. However, it is easy enough to make your own by melting some suet, adding food such as seed and dry breadcrumbs and letting the mixture cool and solidify in a mould. Try cutting a coconut in half, and then suspend it from a loop of wire through a drilled hole. Once the coconut flesh has been eaten by the birds you can fill the empty shell with fat mixture.

Live food and carrion

Many small birds prefer live food to any alternatives, and so you could try putting out a bowl of mealworms to see if this proves popular. Adventurous owners of large gardens could consider baiting for birds of prey with carrion. Road-kill rabbits make a perfect meal for buzzards, for example.

Above Food for birds with a difference – buzzards can sometimes be tempted by placing road-kill rabbits in a prominent location.

Mixed seeds and grains

Coconut

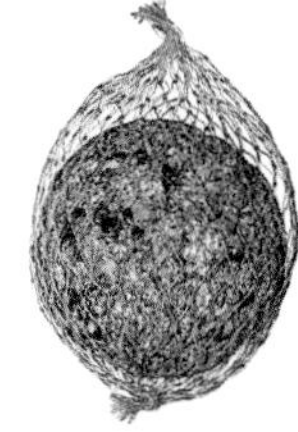

Fat ball

How to feed birds in the garden

At first sight it may seem blindingly obvious how to feed garden birds – just scatter food in the garden and let the birds do the rest. However, although in some instances scattering food on a lawn or on bare ground can be a good idea, by doing so you may run a risk of attracting unwelcome visitors such as rats, while also putting the birds themselves at risk from ground predators such as cats. Consequently, over the last few decades inventive minds have come up with an array of ways of selectively feeding just those species that you might want to attract.

Bird tables

The focal point for many garden feeding stations is the bird table. Most are made of wood, and comprise a table, roughly 40 x 40 cm (16 x 16 in), supported on a post or sometimes suspended by a chain. Most bird tables have a rim around the perimeter to stop food being blown off and a roof to keep the rain off. A range of bird tables can be purchased from a wide variety of outlets but it is not difficult to make your own.

The tables can be stocked with seeds but they also provide an excellent location for scraps of food from the kitchen, including stale bread, dried fruit and grated cheese.

Above A classic bird table has a weatherproof roof, to keep the food fresh, and a rim to stop scraps blowing away.

Hanging feeders

Most people who are enthusiastic about feeding birds in the garden supplement the supplies of the bird table by providing hanging feeders. Broadly speaking, there are two basic forms:

- wire-mesh feeders that allow birds to extract seeds or nuts through the gaps;
- cylindrical plastic feeders with staggered port holes through which the birds get to the food.

Both have advantages and disadvantages: mesh feeders allow access to the food around the entire surface area of the feeder but, being open to the elements, there is a danger of food going mouldy if it gets wet; cylindrical plastic feeders keep the food dry but access is restricted.

If you have problems with grey squirrels in the garden, which will quickly wreck plastic and wire-mesh feeders, buy models where the source of the food is protected by a stout wire frame.

Other ways to provide food

Other options for feeding birds include balls of fat embedded with seeds, which can be hung up in mesh bags. Another way of presenting a fat and seed mixture is to drill a small log with holes, fill these with the food mixture, and hang it from a chain.

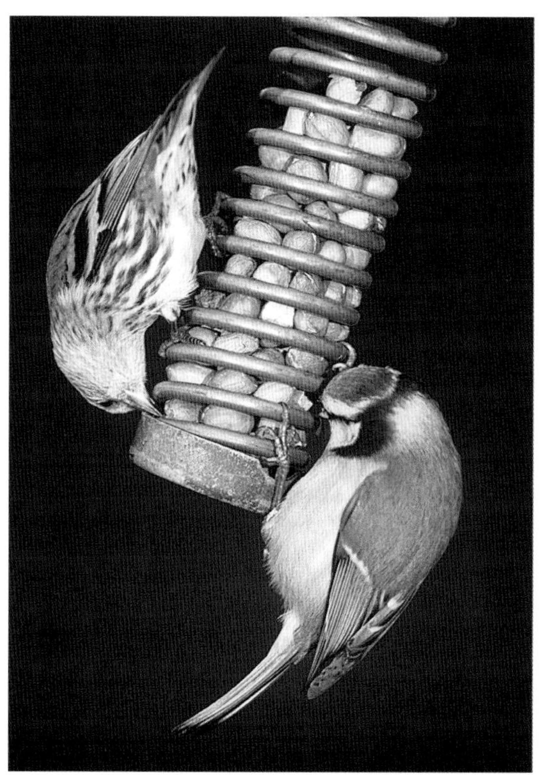

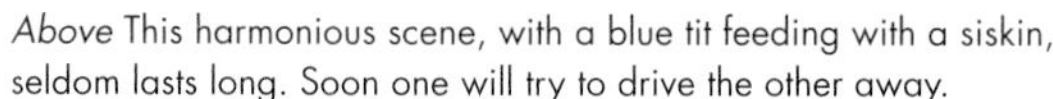

Above This harmonious scene, with a blue tit feeding with a siskin, seldom lasts long. Soon one will try to drive the other away.

Depending on the way that your garden is arranged, it is often best to hang your feeders from the branches of an isolated tree, so that the birds will be able see if a cat or other predator is lurking nearby. Similarly, site the bird table in the middle of the lawn, perhaps in the vicinity of the tree in which the feeders are suspended. You will have to accept the fact that, where feeding birds is concerned, there is a lot of spillage which accumulates underneath the feeders on the lawn. Try to tolerate this because birds such as dunnocks, chaffinches and marsh tits relish these fallen scraps and will clean up over time.

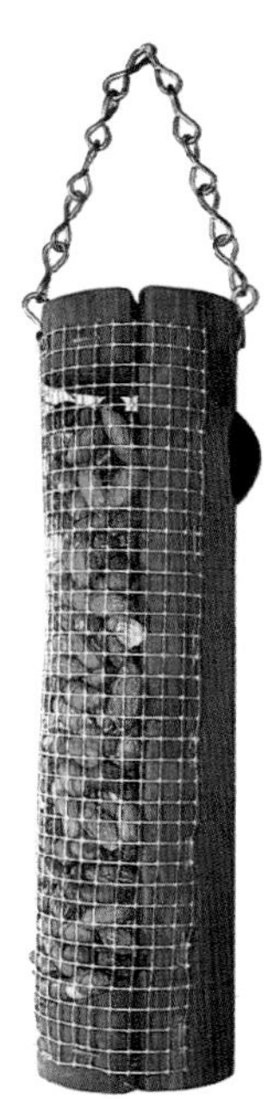

Above left One of the easiest feeders to make uses split logs and chicken wire – available in most garden centres. A hole is drilled through the log in order to replenish the food.

Above right A more sophisticated version of a peanut feeder involves two square wooden blacks that support a wire cage. Nuts are fed through a hole in the top block; this is rubber-bunged at other times to keep the rain out.

Left During the winter months, fat, in which seeds are embedded, is relished by many birds. It is a rather messy product, however, and is best presented by hanging up a log drilled with holes. The fat mixture can be pressed into the holes. The drilled holes are shown here prior to the seed and fat mixture having been added.

Attracting nesting birds

In addition to attracting birds into your garden to feed, you can also provide them with places to nest. Some birds prefer to use natural sites, while others take happily to artificial ones.

Natural and existing nesting and roosting sites

If you are fortunate enough to own a mature and well-stocked garden, then the chances are that you will have plenty of excellent sites in which birds can roost overnight and nest during the spring and summer. Of course the requirements differ from species to species, and so the more nooks, crannies and dense bushes you can provide, the greater the variety of birds you are likely to attract.

Shrubs and bushes

Dense, many-branched and spiny hedgerow shrubs provide ideal roosting sites for birds outside the breeding season, and will also be used for nesting by such species as robin, blackbird, song thrush, chaffinch and dunnock. Ideal native species to plant include hawthorn, blackthorn and holly.

Some people view the presence of ivy and bramble in the garden with dismay, mainly because of their invasive habits. However, when gardening

Above Robins like nesting in forgotten corners of the garden. Take care when tidying up in spring to avoid disturbing a nest.

Above Be thankful if you have a dense ivy patch in your garden – it will be used almost certainly by nesting blackbirds and wrens.

with birds in mind it pays to show a bit of tolerance. Both are invaluable species for wildlife in general, and for birds in particular. The tangled branches and dense foliage of ivy provide nest sites for species such as spotted flycatchers and wrens. And the thorny tangle of a bramble patch is ideal for nesting whitethroats and dunnocks.

Above Hawthorn forms a dense bush, ideal for nesting birds. The flowers yield nectar for insects; the berries are food for thrushes.

Garden nest sites and potential occupants

Conifer hedge
greenfinch • blackbird • goldcrest

Native deciduous hedge
blackbird • chaffinch • blackcap • garden warbler • long-tailed tit

Deciduous tree
mistle thrush • woodpigeon (above) • treecreeper

Garden shed or outbuilding
robin • blackbird • swallow

Wall-climbing shrub
spotted flycatcher

Eaves
house martin

Loft space
swift • starling • house sparrow • collared dove

Bramble patch
dunnock • garden warbler • long-tailed tit

Nest boxes

Under natural conditions, many woodland bird species nest in natural holes and crevices in tree trunks. Although mature gardens often come to resemble woodland margins or glades, suitable nest sites for the associated birds are often in short supply. However, if you put out artifical nest boxes, species such as blue and great tits in particular readily take advantage of them.

The standard bird box

As its name suggests, the standard bird box is basically that – a box with a hole through which the birds gain access, a sloping roof to encourage water to run off and some means of attaching it to a tree or wall. A variety of materials can be used, but treated plywood (marine ply is particularly suitable) and native hardwoods are both popular.

Standard bird boxes are designed to accommodate small songbirds, and the diameter of the hole will influence the identity of the occupant:

2.5 cm (1 in) – blue tits
2.8 cm (1⅛ in) – great tits
3.2 cm (1⅜ in) – house sparrows and nuthatches

Of course some species will enlarge the hole to suit their needs and a nuthatch will typically plaster the hole (and much of the box too) with mud.

Siting the nest box

Site the box in a shady location (not on a south-facing wall or tree trunk, for example) and ensure that it is high enough off the ground to be out of reach of small children as well as cats. Buy (or make) a box with a hinged lid, or one that is constructed using screws, not nails. This will allow you to easily open the box and clean out the contents in winter (this helps reduce the build-up of parasites such as fleas). Check your boxes for signs of wear and tear and repair them if necessary. Actively discourage marauding grey squirrels, which will damage nest boxes.

Left Made from native hardwood – this one is oak – a nest box should last for several decades if repairs are carried out.

Above Ancestral, hole-nesting and hole-roosting habits are exploited by people who keep white doves when they create dovecotes.

Above The prize for any bird box enthusiast is occupancy by a pied flycatcher.

Different types of nest box design

Hole-fronted nest boxes are by far the most popular style and will satisfy the requirements of many garden birds. However, some species are a bit more selective and specialized in their nesting habits. To encourage them to breed in the garden, you need to provide boxes or nesting sites that suit their needs.

Open-fronted nest boxes

Larger garden songbirds, such as blackbirds and song thrushes, will nest under natural conditions in a dense hedge, although they may sometimes be happy with a well-concealed ledge in a shed or outbuilding. To improve the chances of these species nesting, site open-fronted nest boxes in the garden, attached to a shady tree trunk or house wall. The overall design of the box is roughly similar to an open-fronted one but, as the name suggests, the front is open allowing access to relative large birds.

On a much larger, grander scale, the same principle can be used for tawny owl nest boxes. Bear in mind, however, that this species is aggressive near its nest, so any owl nest box should be sited high in a tree and well away from areas where children play.

Communal nesting

Just a few years ago, nobody would have considered the house sparrow worth special treatment in the garden. Today, however, numbers have declined

Above Attached to the branch of a large tree, this sizeable box is occupied by a tawny owl family.

significantly and you can certainly play a part in helping to encourage this species. House sparrows will happily use hole-fronted nest boxes but because they nest communally you will need to site several in close proximity to one another. An alternative is to make or buy a special house sparrow nest box that has separate chambers and entrances for three or four families.

Buildings

Given a bit of encouragement, some bird species will actually use your house as a place to nest. Indeed, swifts seldom nest anywhere other than in the loft spaces of houses. So, if you want to encourage this species, make sure they can gain access to the loft

Above Pied wagtails often positively seek out urban and garden sites – sheds in particular – for nesting.

Dos and don'ts for garden-nesting birds

- If you discover a bird nesting in a bush or shrub in the garden, avoid pruning the plant in question. You run the risk of causing it to desert its eggs or chicks if the disturbance is too great and, if your pruning is too vigorous, you may expose the nest to the prying eyes of predators.
- If a bird takes up residence in one of your nest boxes, avoid spending too much time in the vicinity unless the bird in question is completely accustomed to the presence of people. Typically what happens is the bird will avoid returning to the box while you are nearby, thereby causing the eggs or chicks to chill. Also, its alarm calls may alert predators to the presence of the nest.
- Just occasionally great spotted woodpeckers will discover an occupied nest box and attempt to extract and eat the eggs or chicks by drilling through the side of the box. To thwart its efforts, try shrouding the entire box in a couple of layers of chicken wire, making sure, of course, to leave the entrance hole clear so the resident birds can gain entry. This procedure should only be a last resort and the wire should be affixed as rapidly as possible.
- Keep an eye on your shed, greenhouse and garage in case a robin, blackbird or swallow takes up residence and builds a nest. Because the birds are usually secretive at this stage in their lives, it is all too easy to overlook their presence and inadvertently shut the door or the window through which they gain access, either locking them in or barring their entry.

via the eaves. House martins build mud-cup nests attached to the eaves of houses, so you could encourage them to start colonies by fixing artificial nest boxes (which resemble those made by the birds) to the walls of a house.

Perhaps the grandest example of the encouragement employed to attract a bird to nest on a house is seen with white storks. In parts of southern and eastern Europe where this species occurs, home-owners sometimes install old cart wheels or metal-framed platforms on the roof, on which the birds build their huge twiggy nests.

Above Nowadays, swifts nest almost exclusively in the loft spaces of houses and church towers.

Environmental concerns

We are reminded on an almost daily basis about the threat that modern society poses to the environment. Global warming, pollution and habitat destruction regularly feature in the news. This highlights the fact that many aspects of the way we lead our lives have nothing but a negative impact on wildlife.

In Europe, destruction or degradation of habitats is achieved in a variety of ways. New housing and road developments are obvious candidates and predictably they destroy almost all the wildlife interest of the land on which they are sited. But modern farming has probably had the most tragic impact on wildlife in recent years. The quantities and 'efficiency' of modern herbicides and pesticides do an effective job of eliminating weed seeds and invertebrates and consequently, on areas farmed using modern techniques there is little for birds to eat.

Above If you grow brambles in your garden and can exercise a bit of restraint, leave some of the crop for the birds to eat.

Above Native shrubs provide food for more caterpillar species than alien plants do. In turn, caterpillars are food for birds.

How to help

The last 50 years or so has seen a tragic impact on all forms of wildlife but, being at the top of the food chain and clearly visible, the effect is most keenly felt when it affects our birds. Fortunately, however, a network of official nature reserves across the region does do something to alleviate the problems faced by wildlife, and birds in particular, as we enter the 21st century. But, on a smaller scale, everybody can do something to assist. With a little bit of effort you can set up your own nature reserve in your garden. Cynics may see this as merely a token gesture, but the reality is that by encouraging birds and creating a wildlife haven in the garden you will be making a small but positive step for conservation.

Above A few species of slugs and snails are a menace to seedlings. In their turn, they will be eaten by song thrushes.

Above One of the most beneficial plants you can grow or encourage is ivy. It is a misconception that it is parasitic. The cover it provides harbours nesting and roosting birds, and insects feed on its flowers and hibernate among its leaves.

Top tips for gardening with birds in mind

- Adopt an organic policy in your garden, and use natural alternatives to chemicals and sprays.
- Grow plants that provide food (such as seeds and fruit) for birds.
- Set aside a feeding area for the birds, where feeders can be hung, and a table sited.
- Tolerate (and in many cases enourage) insects and other invertebrates in the garden – they serve as food for many bird species.
- Site nest boxes in the garden.
- Plant dense hedges for birds to nest and roost in.
- Provide a water feature (such as a bath or pond) for birds to bathe in and drink from.
- Try to grow as many native plant species as possible – their leaves are more likely to provide food for insects (which in turn are eaten by birds) than alien plant species.
- Always try to 'Think Green' by composting waste vegetable matter and recycling and reusing as many things from the garden as possible.
- Discourage cats in the garden; if you own one, try to keep it indoors as much as possible.

Blue tit

Parus caeruleus

REGION: Widespread and common resident across most of Europe except the far north • SIZE: 11–12 cm (4½–5 in) • FOOD: Small insects, spiders and other invertebrates, as well as seeds and nuts in season • CALL: Utters a nasal chattering call when agitated • SONG: A series of whistles and trills • SEX DIFFERENCES: Sexes similar both in size and plumage although males are usually slightly more colourful than females • JUVENILE: Similar to an adult but with much duller colours • FLIGHT: Rapid with whirring wingbeats, in short bursts from tree to tree • NEST: Constructed in a tree hole or other natural cavity, the nest is made from mosses and grasses, and lined with feathers. They readily take to nest boxes.

Blue tits are colourful and pugnacious little birds familiar to most people who feed birds in their gardens. They are extremely agile and inquisitive, allowing them to make the best use of available food. Although the bill is short and stubby, this does not appear to stop them when it comes to extracting peanut fragments from feeders.

In good years, blue tits will raise two, sometimes three, broods of youngsters if they have a secure nest box in the garden, and a plentiful supply of food. During the breeding season, insects, rather than seeds, are the most important element in the diet of nestlings. In cold, damp years, when insects are scarce, fewer blue tit broods and fledglings are raised than in warm, dry weather.

Habitat

All sorts of wooded habitats, including mature gardens and parks.

Adult

How to attract this bird to your garden

This is one of the easiest species to attract to the garden and whether or not you make any attempt to do so it is likely to be present. During the winter, blue tits are fond of peanuts and sunflower seeds and will come to feeders almost as soon as they are put out. Put hole-fronted nest boxes for them in secure locations in mature trees and in spring and summer even a modest-sized garden will usually support two or three pairs.

Can be mistaken for

Great tit (see pages 48–49), but note the blue tit's striking black eyestripe.

Above Parent blue tits work tirelessly to feed their offspring on insects. By the time the young fledge, their parents' plumage will be worn and dowdy.

Above If the feeding is good, up to a dozen young may reach the point of fledging.

Great tit

Parus major

REGION: Widespread and generally common resident across most of Europe although less numerous in upland and northern regions •SIZE: 14–15 cm (5½–6 in) • FOOD: Insects (particularly caterpillars), spiders and other invertebrates, plus seeds and nuts in season • CALL: Utters a harsh, chattering *tche-tche-tche* when alarmed • SONG: a strident and nasal *teecha-teecha-teecha* • SEX DIFFERENCES: Both sexes have similarly colourful plumage and a bold head pattern, but a male has an appreciably wider dark line on the breast than a female • JUVENILE: Similar to an adult female but with much duller plumage • FLIGHT: Rapid and level, on whirring wingbeats • NEST: A deep, cup-shaped structure made from woven mosses and grasses, often lined with animal hair. They usually nest in a hole or crevice in a tree but also readily take to nest boxes.

From early spring onwards, male great tits sing their strident and distinctive songs from near potential nest sites, including nest boxes. They raise two or three broods each year, depending on how much food is available, and each brood is likely to contain 6–12 young. Both parents take turns to feed the young, and, unsurprisingly, by the end of the breeding season their plumage will have taken a battering and have become tattered and worn.

Great tits are frequent visitors to bird feeders, especially ones where peanuts and fat are available, and they are often dominant in the pecking order of smaller birds in the garden. It is not unusual to see two or three great tits at a feeder at any given time, with a lot of coming and going. Although it may be tempting to think that the same birds are returning, ringing studies

Above Without the line on the centre of the breast (wider in males than females), it is difficult to determine the sex of a great tit.

have shown that a succession of great tits is likely to be visiting the feeder, each waiting in turn for a feeding bird to leave before venturing to get its fill of peanuts.

Habitat

A wide range of wooded habitats, surprisingly including urban parks and gardens.

How to attract this bird to your garden

If you provide peanut feeders you will attract great tits from all around in the winter. Put up hole-fronted nest boxes in suitable locations and you may find that they are occupied in spring and summer.

Can be mistaken for

Blue tit (see pages 46–47) but the great tit is bigger and has a dark line extending down the centre of the breast.

Coal tit

Parus ater

REGION: Widespread across much of Europe, except the very far north • SIZE: 11–12 cm (4½–5 in) • FOOD: Small invertebrates (especially aphids and caterpillars in the summer) as well as seeds and nuts in season • CALL: A thin, rather sad-sounding note • SONG: A rapid series of thin notes, sounding like *tichu-tichu-tichu*; more rapid and higher-pitched than that of a great tit • SEX DIFFERENCES: The sexes are similar • JUVENILE: Similar to the adults but the markings show less contrast • FLIGHT: Short bursts of rapid wingbeats • NEST: A disproportionately large cup-shaped structure of mosses and shredded grasses, lined with animal hair, and sited in a crevice or hole in a tree.

A combination of white cheeks and wingbars, and a white stripe down the rear part of the crown make the coal tit a distinctive bird. Indeed, the stripe is unique among birds of this size. Although much of the remaining upperparts are grey or white, the underparts (particularly the flanks) are flushed with a subtle shade of pinkish buff, which lends a touch of colour to this otherwise rather black-and-white species.

The coal tit is a delightful little bird whose small size and proportionately thin bill give it something of the proportions of a warbler or a goldcrest. Its energetic yet delicate feeding action adds to this impression. This species regularly visits feeders with peanuts or sunflowers and bird tables where birdseed is scattered. Their visits are brief, however, and they normally arrive when there are no great tits and blue tits about, to avoid confrontations with their larger, more aggressive cousins.

Above The coal tit is the only bird of its size with a striking white stripe on the nape.

Habitat

Coal tits favour wooded habitats, particularly areas where conifers are dominant. However, they can also be found in deciduous woodland, especially in winter, and will visit gardens if food is available. They are absent from particularly hot and arid regions in summer.

How to attract this bird to your garden

Plant a few conifer trees (especially larches and pines) and, after a while, this species should be present all year-round. If you live close to woodland areas then you are likely to attract small numbers of coal tits into your garden in winter by providing peanut feeders for them.

Can be mistaken for

Blue tit (see pages 46–47), but the coal tit is essentially black-and-white in colour. Also the goldcrest (see pages 222–223) which is even smaller and has a beautiful yellowish-green hue to its plumage.

Adult

Marsh tit

Parus palustris

REGION: Widespread across central Europe; absent from the far north and south • SIZE: 12–13 cm (*c.* 5 in) • FOOD: Mainly insects (caterpillars are a favourite in spring and summer), but also seeds and nuts in season • CALL: A strident *pitchoo* • SONG: A loud and repetitive series of *chip-chip-chip* notes • SEX DIFFERENCES: The sexes are similar • JUVENILE: Similar to the adults • FLIGHT: Short bursts of flight on rapid wingbeats, from bush to bush, or branch to branch • NEST: A cup-shaped construction of woven mosses and grasses, lined with animal hair, and sited in a tree hole; these birds occasionally use a nest box.

Freqent visitors to the bird table in woodland areas, marsh tits are plump-bodied and pugnaceous little birds. Their pale cheeks contrast with the dark cap and, when viewed in good light, you can see that the flanks are suffused with a warm pinkish-buff colour. Marsh tits occasionally breed in hole-fronted nest boxes sited in dense shade.

Habitat

Favours deciduous woodland with dense cover. May also be seen in mature gardens, especially in rural areas.

How to attract this bird to your garden

Put out peanut feeders during the winter: they will visit them and forage for fallen fragments on the ground below.

Can be mistaken for

Willow tit (see page 53), but check which habitat you are in and learn the difference between their calls.

Above Seen from the front, a marsh tit reveals a neat black bib and a rather thickset neck.

SIMILAR SPECIES

Willow tit

Parus montanus

LENGTH: 12–13 cm (*c.* 5 in)

Superficially almost identical to a marsh tit. However, the peculiarly nasal call, and their preference for wet woodland habitats, are useful as identification clues. At close range, keen-eyed observers may spot the pale panel on the wings of a willow tit. They can be found in central and northern Europe. They seldom visit bird feeders. They prefer to nest in sites in rotting tree stumps; but they will occasionally occupy nest boxes that are filled with sawdust and wood shavings, whereby the birds will excavate a nest for themselves.

Marsh tit

Blue tit

Willow tit

Adult

Crested tit

Parus cristatus

REGION: A widespread resident with a patchy distribution across central, western and northern mainland Europe and areas of native Scots pine in the Scottish highlands • SIZE: 11–12 cm (4½–5 in) • FOOD: Small insects and other invertebrates, and seeds and nuts in season • CALL: Has a distinctive, high-pitched trill • SONG: Rapid, high-pitched warbling phrases • SEX DIFFERENCES: The sexes are similar • JUVENILE: Similar to the adults but with less contrast in the plumage • FLIGHT: Rapid and direct, on whirring wingbeats • NEST: Made from woven mosses and shredded grass stems, lined with animal hair, and placed in a crevice or hole in a decaying tree stump.

This charming little bird has a particularly striking head, which makes it relatively straightforward to identify accurately. The first feature that most people spot is usually the crest, which the birds can lower or raise at will and which is patterned with striking black-and-white markings. The face is mainly white except for black lines behind the eye and on the throat. At close range, keen-eyed observers should be able to see the beady, red eye, another feature that is very unusual in a European bird of this size.

Adult

Above Crested tits nest in holes excavated in decaying tree stumps – natural equivalents to man-made nest boxes.

Watching crested tits feeding, especially during the summer months, can be a neck-breaking exercise because they love to forage for insects high in the tree canopy. At this time of year, when there are often hungry mouths to feed in the nest, birds often forage in pairs and this can make locating them a bit easier.

During the winter, crested tits will sometimes visit bird feeders. However, the species is rather sedentary and not given to wandering. So you are unlikely to encounter it unless you live within its range and in a garden surrounded by an area of suitable wooded habitat.

Habitat

Usually associated with deciduous woodland in central Europe but restricted to the mature coniferous forest farther north in its range.

How to attract this bird to your garden

Leave decaying birch and conifer stumps *in situ* in the garden and crested tits may decide to nest there. They prefer to excavate a fresh nest chamber in the rooting wood each year.

Can be mistaken for

Almost unmistakable for a bird of this size, because of its crest.

Long-tailed tit

Aegithalos caudatus

REGION: A widespread resident across much of Europe, but absent from, or scarce in, the far north • SIZE: 14 cm (5½ in) • FOOD: Small insects and other invertebrates, and occasionally seeds and nut fragments • CALL: Members of a flock utter rattling contact calls; the alarm call is a high, thin note • SONG: Subdued and seldom heard • SEX DIFFERENCES: The sexes are similar but adults from the far north of the mainland European range have pure white heads • JUVENILE: Has dark sides to the head (pale in adults) and much duller colours on the back and underparts • FLIGHT: Looks like an animated feather duster in flight, with whirring short, rounded wings and a disproportionately long tail • NEST: An intricate spherical structure, made from lichens, mosses and spiders' silk, lined with feathers and animal hair. Typically it is sited in the middle of a thorny bush.

The long-tailed tit has an appearance that is unique among small European garden birds. The head and body can appear almost round, especially when the feathers are fluffed up in cold weather, while the tail is incredibly long for a bird of its size. In poor light, it can appear almost black-and-white but a good view will reveal a subtle pinkish-buff flush to both the back and underparts.

Outside the breeding season, long-tailed tits move around in parties of 10–20 birds that stay in contact with one another using their distinctive calls. They are incredibly active birds, constantly on the move in search of insects, with their actions exaggerated by movements of the tail. Although the bill is almost ridiculously small and stubby, it does not appear to make collecting aphids and small caterpillars difficult. Some individual long-tailed tits have learned to use it to extract unwanted fragments of peanuts from garden bird feeders.

Habitat

Found in a wide variety of wooded habitats, from heaths, hedgerows and mature gardens with trees to deciduous woodland.

Above Despite being a sizeable structure, a long-tailed tit's nest is remarkably unobtrusive thanks to its constituent lichens and mosses.

How to attract this bird to your garden

During the winter, flocks of long-tailed tits will sometimes visit peanut feeders in the garden and it is not unusual to see six or more feeding side by side. Dusk is a favourite time for them to visit feeders. If you encourage thorny shrubs such as hawthorn or gorse, then pairs may nest in your garden in the spring.

Can be mistaken for

Almost unmistakable, on account of the extremely long tail for a bird of this size and the stubby bill.

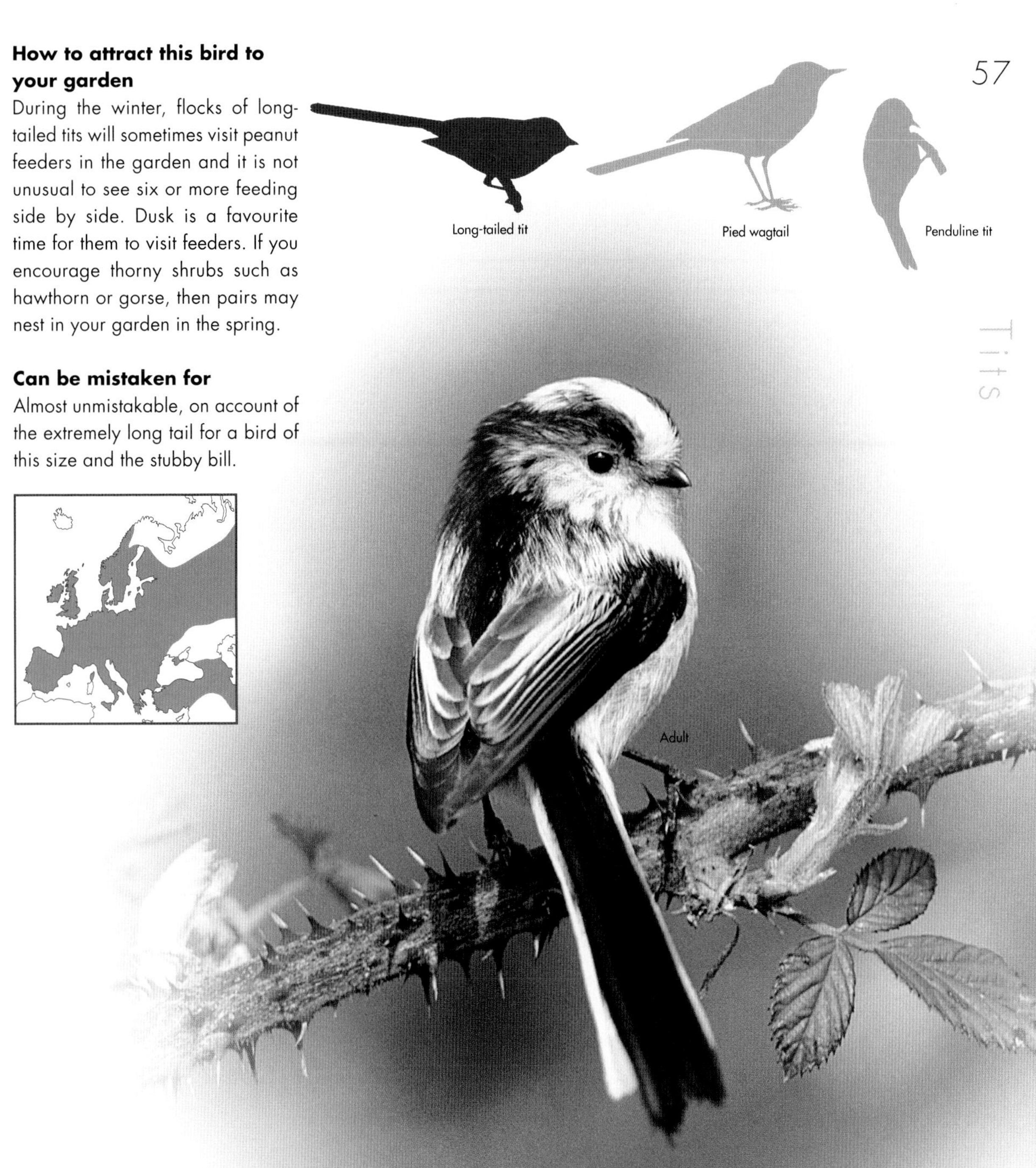

Sombre tit

Parus lugubris

REGION: Restricted to southeastern Europe, mainly Greece and the Balkans • SIZE: 13–14 cm (5–5½ in) • FOOD: Insects, spiders and other invertebrates, as well as seeds and nuts in season • CALL: A harsh, scolding note, not unlike that of a blue tit • SONG: A series of *chip-chip-chip* notes, not unlike that of a marsh tit (see pages 52–53) • SEX DIFFERENCES: The sexes are similar • JUVENILE: Similar to the adults • FLIGHT: Direct and low, on whirring wingbeats • NEST: A woven structure of mosses and feathers, sited in a tree hole or crevice in a stone wall.

Although the sombre tit could hardly be described as colourful, it has particularly striking facial markings: the extensive dark grey-brown cap and bib contrast markedly with its white cheeks. On a dull day, the rest of its body plumage can look rather uniformly grey but in sunshine the back and wings in particular take on a brownish hue.

Sombre tits tend to be rather sedentary and for much of the year they are often seen in pairs. Although they are fairly unobtrusive and spend much of the time foraging for food in cover, they are not particularly wary of people and will sometimes come to investigate, particularly if you make a hissing *psshhh* sound through your clenched teeth.

Habitat

Favours open woodland and scrub, as well as rural gardens and country orchards.

How to attract this bird to your garden

If you live within this species' range then old stone walls or gnarled ancient trees may provide it with nest sites. Sombre tits seldom come to bird feeders.

Can be mistaken for

Marsh tit (see pages 52–53), which is marginally smaller and has warmer plumage colours than this species. The sombre tit has a much larger black bib.

Adult

Penduline tit

Remiz pendulinus

REGION: A summer visitor to eastern Europe, but a local resident in the south. Elsewhere in mainland Europe it is seen as an occasional visitor and on migration • SIZE: 10–12 cm (4–5 in) • FOOD: Small insects and spiders, and seeds • CALL: A thin single note, which is extremely high-pitched • SONG: A series of trills and high-pitched notes • SEX DIFFERENCES: Males have more striking and colourful plumage than females, with a more extensive black 'highwayman's mask' around the eye • JUVENILE: Has much duller plumage colours than the adults, and lacks the black mask around the eye • FLIGHT: Low and direct, in short bursts from one feeding area to another • NEST: One of the most amazing nests of all European birds, it is a pouch (up to 30 cm/12 in long) with an entrance tunnel. The nest is made from the interwoven seed hairs from willows and poplars, held together with spider silk, and is suspended from a thin, pendent willow twig, often directly over water.

An adult male penduline tit is a well-marked bird whose plumage recalls that of a male red-backed shrike. It is associated almost exclusively with wetland areas, nesting in waterside willows and feeding in large reedbeds using its thin and pointed bill to catch insect prey.

In late summer, after the breeding season, family parties sometimes wander away from their nesting territories and occasionally turn up in surprisingly dry habitats. At this time of year, all adults have worn and dowdy-looking plumage and can be rather difficult to identify; they acquire a new set of clean and colourful feathers during their autumn moult.

Habitat

Wetland habitats including reedbeds and river margins.

How to attract this bird to your garden

If you live within this species' range and your garden is on the fringes of a wetland or near a river they may nest in your garden if you have large willow trees. Outside the breeding season, family parties sometimes turn up in hedges and scrub areas, but they are nomadic and seldom stay for long.

Can be mistaken for

Almost unmistakable, taking into account its small size and habitat preferences, but the plumage does bear a passing resemblance to a male red-backed shrike (see pages 174–175).

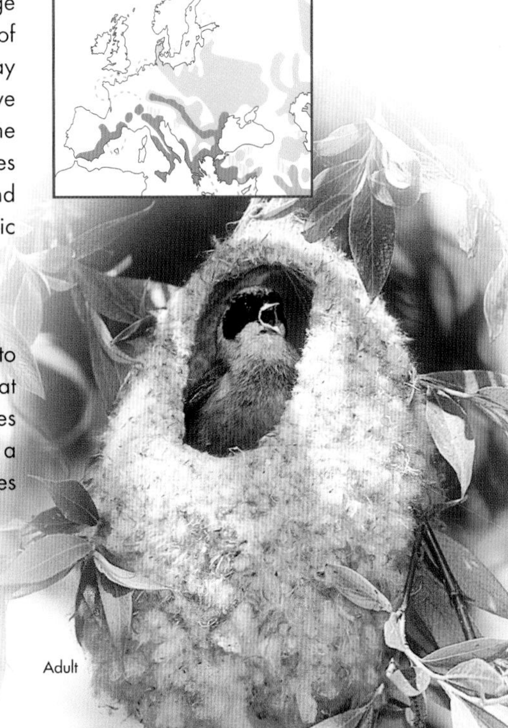

Adult

Nuthatch

Sitta europaea

REGION: Widespread resident across much of mainland Europe, except the far south and north • SIZE: 14 cm (5½ in) • FOOD: Insects and other invertebrates, and seeds and nuts in season • CALL: A loud and repeated piping • SONG: A complex series of whistling notes • SEX DIFFERENCES: The sexes are rather similar although the extent and intensity of the reddish colour on the underparts is more intense in males than females • JUVENILE: Similar to an adult female • FLIGHT: Undulating and rapid, with a distinctive short-bodied silhouette • NEST: Uses a ready-made nest hole (sometimes even a nest box) but typically plasters the entrance with mud to restrict access to other birds, and to disguise the whereabouts of the nest.

The nuthatch is a well-marked and colourful bird and is relatively easy to identify. The jerky way in which it moves when climbing among the branches of a tree also gives a clue to its identity and its habit of climbing down tree trunks, head first, is unique among western European species.

In many ways, the nuthatch behaves like a miniature woodpecker, and it uses its long, dagger-like bill in a similar way to excavate insect larvae from decaying wood. In autumn, it collects acorns; it then wedges the acorn into a crevice in tree bark and hammers open the hard outer casing. Nuthatches sometimes do the same with peanuts from bird feeders, removing a nut whole and then wedging it somewhere so they can peck off fragments.

Habitat

Favours a wide range of woodland habitats where mature deciduous trees dominate, including mature parks and gardens.

Adult

Above The nuthatch is the only garden and woodland bird that routinely walks down tree trunks head first.

Rock nuthatch

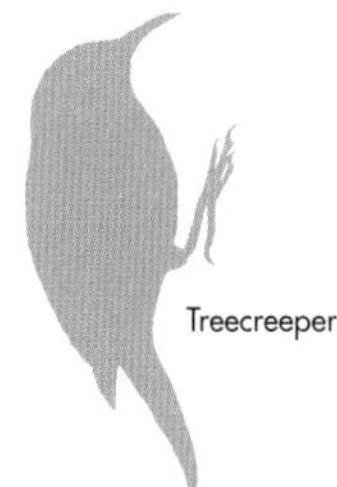

How to attract this bird to your garden

The nuthatch is a regular visitor to garden feeders with peanuts and sunflower seeds. Typically they will try to remove the food intact and fly off with it to feed elsewhere. Nuthatches will sometimes nest in ready-made holes in old, gnarled fruit trees and will occasionally take over a hole-fronted nest box intended for great tits.

Can be mistaken for

Unmistakable in western Europe on account of its body shape and habits, but in the southeast of the region, in rocky habitats, beware of confusing it with the rock nuthatch (see right).

SIMILAR SPECIES

Rock nuthatch

Sitta neumayer

LENGTH: 14–15 cm (5½–6 in)

Appreciably larger than a nuthatch and associated with rocky, not wooded, habitats. The rock nuthatch has blue-grey upperparts, whitish underparts and a thin dark line through the eye. Its bill is proportionately very long. It is restricted to the southeastern parts of Europe (mainly Greece and the Balkans) but it does occur in gardens where the terrain (and that of the surroundings) is rocky, or at least dotted with large boulders.

Treecreeper

Certhia familiaris

REGION: Widespread resident in much of eastern, central and northern Europe but distinctly local in, or absent from, most of the southern and western regions • SIZE: 12–13 cm (*c.* 5 in) • FOOD: Insects and other invertebrates • CALL: A thin, high-pitched note • SONG: A series of high-pitched notes that ends in a trill • SEX DIFFERENCES: The sexes are similar • JUVENILE: Similar to the adults • FLIGHT: Short bursts of flight from one tree trunk to the next • NEST: Made from mosses and animal hair, and sited in a tree crevice or under bark.

Treecreepers are insect-feeders that use their proportionately long and needle-like downcurved bills to probe in and under tree bark. Typically, treecreepers feed by spiralling around and up a tree trunk before dropping down to repeat the process on a neighbouring tree. When climbing, they use their tails as a support.

Treecreepers are rather unobtrusive birds and it is usually easier to see them during the winter months – in deciduous woodland at least – when the leaves will have fallen from the trees.

Habitat

Favours deciduous and mixed woodlands.

How to attract this bird to your garden

You need large, mature trees in order to attract this species to the garden. If you fix a piece of fallen bark tightly to a tree trunk, then a treecreeper might just try to nest beneath it.

Can be mistaken for

Short-toed treecreeper (see opposite); concentrate on the plumage brightness and the call to distinguish between the species, rather than the length of their toes.

Adult

Short-toed treecreeper

Certhia brachydactyla

REGION: A widespread resident across central and southern mainland Europe and the Channel Islands • SIZE: 12–13 cm (*c.* 5 in) • FOOD: Insects and other small invertebrates • CALL: Utters a piercing, high-pitched *zeeht* note • SONG: A series of thin, piercing notes • SEX DIFFERENCES: The sexes are similar • JUVENILE: Similar to the adults • FLIGHT: Low and often gliding flight, from one tree to another • NEST: Sited in a tree crevice or under bark, and made from grasses and mosses.

Like its close cousin (opposite), the short-toed treecreeper uses its long, needle-like bill like a pair of tweezers to extract insects and spiders from among the cracks and crevices in tree bark. At first glance, its movements often give it an almost mouse-like appearance as it creeps quietly up a tree trunk.

The species' streaked brown plumage is dowdier than that of its cousin, the treecreeper, and is a close match for tree bark. This can make it difficult to spot but, when discovered, it is unlikely to fly off as long as it is not disturbed unduly. Short-toed treecreepers are often found in mature broad-leaved or coniferous trees both in town parks and in gardens.

Habitat

Wooded habitats with mature trees.

How to attract this bird to your garden

Encourage mature trees in your garden and it is likely to visit from time to time. If you allow flaky pieces of bark to remain *in situ* then it may even nest.

Can be mistaken for

Treecreeper (see opposite); the short-toed treecreeper's call and more sombre plumage are the best identification features.

Adult

Swift

Apus apus

REGION: Summer visitor to almost the whole of Europe, except the far north. Present in the region from May to September • SIZE: 16–17 cm (6½–7 in); wingspan 40–44 cm (16–17½ in) • FOOD: Flying insects, caught on the wing • CALL: A shrill scream, uttered in flight • SEX DIFFERENCES: The sexes are similar • JUVENILE: Similar to the adults • FLIGHT: Extremely rapid and stiff-winged, with bursts of rapid wingbeats interspersed with long periods of gliding • NEST: A rudimentary arrangement of feathers and saliva, placed in a loft space or roof of a building.

The swift is a superb aeronaut and, apart from when it is on the nest, it spends its entire life in flight, eating, sleeping, feeding and mating on the wing. Its flight silhouette is distinctive, the cigar-shaped body and narrow, swept-back wings creating an anchor-shaped outline. Outside the breeding season, all European swifts fly to Africa for the winter. It has been estimated that, in its lifetime, an individual swift may cover an amazing million miles or more!

You are likely to see several swifts together because they tend to move around in flocks, congregating especially near breeding sites and where the feeding is good. They catch flying insects in their wide gape. A fringe of stiff marginal hairs around the mouth increases their feeding efficiency.

Habitat

Almost all swifts nest in man-made locations and favour lofts and attics in houses, and also church roofs. The sound of screaming parties of swifts, flying low over roofs and along narrow streets, is one of the most characteristic sounds of urban summer, particularly in warmer regions in the south of Europe. In rural areas, you are most likely to see them where flying insects swarm, such as marshes and lake margins where midges and mosquitoes are plentiful.

How to attract this bird to your garden

Allow open access to loft spaces via the eaves, and you stand a good chance of attracting nesting swifts. Be careful, however, not to disturb them.

Can be mistaken for

Almost unmistakable on account of its shape and habits, although it does perhaps bear a passing resemblance to a swallow (see pages 68–69). However, check for the swift's distinctive flight silhouette, and uniformly dark plumage.

Above A swift may alight on the wall of a house, but it is virtually incapable of walking and can do little apart from cling.

SIMILAR SPECIES

Alpine swift

Apus melba

LENGTH: 20–22 cm (8–9 in); WINGSPAN 52–57 cm (21–23 in)

Appreciably larger than a swift, and with a distinctive white belly and throat, separated by a dark collar. A summer visitor to southern Europe, and frequently associated with coastal regions and upland valleys. Often nests in church towers.

Red-rumped swallow

Hirundo daurica

REGION: A summer visitor, mainly to southern Europe; present from April to September • SIZE: 16–18 cm (5½–7 in) • FOOD: Flying insects, caught on the wing • CALL: Utters a sharp *tvick* • SONG: A rapid series of twittering and rattling notes • SEX DIFFERENCES: The sexes are similar, although males are usually more colourful than females • JUVENILE: Has a white (not reddish) rump and noticeably shorter tail streamers than the adult birds • FLIGHT: Low and rapid, with bouts of rapid wingbeats interspersed with long glides • NEST: A cup-shaped structure with an entrance tunnel, made of mud and cemented to the roof of a cave, beneath a bridge or under the eaves of a house.

Above The red-rumped swallow's subtly colourful plumage can be seen at close quarters when birds are observed collecting mud for nest-building.

The red-rumped swallow is an extremely attractive little bird and reasonably easy to identify, even in flight. Look for the buffish-red rump (this feature can appear rather pale and washed out), the reddish nape and the long tail streamers. From below, the bird appears distinctly pale overall, with the exception of the tail and vent, which are contrastingly dark, almost as though the bird has been dipped, tail first, into a pot of black ink.

The species often chooses to nest under the eaves of a house, or in a quiet recess in a barn or garage. If left undisturbed, it can become remarkably indifferent to human observers and, when perched on a wire, for example, it will often allow people to pass within a few metres of it. If you are lucky enough to get such a close encounter, look for the subtle reddish streaking on the breast and flanks.

When feeding, red-rumped swallows often associate with swallows, house martins and sand martins. They congregate wherever insects are abundant, often near water because of the swarms of midges and other insects found there.

Habitat

Rural gardens and upland valleys, usually in the vicinity of a river or marsh where food (aerial insects) is likely to be abundant.

How to attract this bird to your garden

If you create a muddy pond in your garden, red-rumped swallows may use it as a source of building material in spring, and nest under your eaves. Sometimes, a pair of red-rumped swallows will occupy and embellish the abandoned nest of a house martin.

Can be mistaken for

Swallow (see pages 68–69), but easy to tell apart because of this species' reddish nape and rump. Juvenile could be mistaken for a house martin (see pages 70–71), but note this species' white (not buffish) underparts.

Swallow

Hirundo rustica

REGION: Widespread summer visitor to most of Europe, except the far north; present from March to September; some overwinter in southern Europe but most migrate to Africa • SIZE: 19–21 cm (7½–8½ in) • FOOD: Flying insects, caught on the wing • CALL: Utters a sharp *vit* call, often in flight • SONG: A cheerful and rapid series of twittering and rattling notes • SEX DIFFERENCES: The sexes are broadly similar, although males have longer tail streamers and richer colours on the face and throat than females • JUVENILE: Compared to the adults, it has an extremely pale face, and short tail streamers • FLIGHT: Rapid and often low to the ground, with rapid wingbeats interspersed with glides; often twists and turns in flight in pursuit of insects. • NEST: A cup-shaped structure made of mud and grass, cemented to a ledge or ceiling beam in a barn, garage or other outbuilding.

Above Male swallows advertize their territorial presence with a twittering song, often delivered close to their nesting place.

Above The swallow's forked tail and long streamers are an invaluable aid to identification.

For many people the swallow is a harbinger of spring and its arrival from wintering grounds in Africa heralds an improvement in the weather. Swallows are often faithful to the same nest location, year after year, and the young from previous seasons sometimes return to their birthplace to nest as well.

Seen in good light, the species has an attractive bluish sheen to the dark upperparts and this contrasts markedly with the creamy white breast and belly, and reddish face. While courtship is in progress, male and female swallows will sometimes sit side by side on an overhead wire in the garden, twittering at one another. At such times, the male's longer tail streamers can be seen clearly. Newly fledged youngsters will also perch on wires, lining up to be fed with regurgitated balls of insects by their parents.

Habitat

All sorts of open habitats, including meadows, farmland and marshes. It invariably nests in barns, sheds and outbuildings on farms and in rural gardens.

How to attract this bird to your garden

Leave your garage door open in spring and, if you live in a rural area, swallows may decide to take up residence there. Make sure that cats cannot gain access to the nest, however, because incubating swallows, and especially the chicks, are very easy targets for these predators.

Can be mistaken for

Red-rumped swallow (see pages 66–67), which has a reddish rump and nape.

House martin

Delichon urbica

REGION: Widespread summer visitor to the whole of Europe, except the extreme far north; present from April to September • SIZE: 12–13 cm (*c.* 5 in) • FOOD: Flying insects, caught on the wing • CALL: Utters a rattling *prrrt* in flight • SONG: A series of twittering notes, usually sung from an overhead wire in the vicinity of the nest • SEX DIFFERENCES: The sexes are similar • JUVENILE: Similar to the adults but the underparts usually appear rather grubby • FLIGHT: Usually rapid and low, with bursts of rapid wingbeats interspersed with glides. It will sometimes soar and circle to considerable heights if that is where its flying insect prey is concentrated • NEST: A cup-shaped structure made from mud pellets and grass fragments, cemented under the eaves of houses.

In the past, this species would have nested on cliffs and rocky outcrops, but today almost all house martins that visit Europe for the summer nest under the eaves of houses in villages, towns and even the more suburban fringes of cities. They tend to be colonial birds and a minimum of four or five pairs is usually needed to start a colony.

The house martin is a distinctive little bird. In flight, it has a rather triangular wing outline and slightly forked tail. The upperparts are essentially black except for the striking and contrasting white rump. Seen from below, the underparts appear white apart from the tail, which is black.

House martins are fond of sitting on overhead wires and when the young have fledged it is not unusual to see 20 or more perched side by side. As the weeks go by, and the time for migration south approaches, birds from nearby colonies associate more regularly with their neighbours and, by late summer, groups of 100 or more become a common sight. These concentrations herald the species' departure and within a few weeks all will have embarked on their long migration south to Africa.

Above Even when perched, the contrast between a house martin's black tail and white rump and underparts is striking.

Habitat
Associated with towns and villages when nesting, but often feeds over open countryside, or near water.

How to attract this bird to your garden
The species needs little encouragement to nest under the eaves of houses, even in modern ones. However, you can buy (or make) artificial nests to fix to the wall of the house to start them off. The birds need a ready supply of mud in order to build their nests and to repair them so creating a muddy-margined pond in the garden will help them.

Can be mistaken for
Juvenile red-rumped swallow (see pages 66–67), although that particular species has a pale nape.

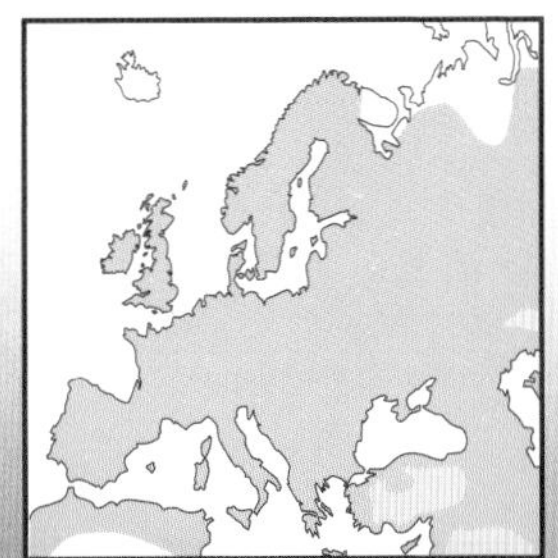

Sand martin

Riparia riparia

REGION: Widespread summer visitor to most of Europe, except the extreme far north • SIZE: 12 cm (5 in) • FOOD: Flying insects, caught on the wing • CALL: A range of rasping twitters • SEX DIFFERENCES: The sexes are similar • JUVENILE: Similar to the adults • FLIGHT: Alternates between bursts of fluttering wingbeats (the wings are often flicked in direct flight) and extended glides; usually seen flying low over water, or near breeding colonies • NEST: Excavates tunnels in sandy banks, often beside water.

The sand martin is often one of the first of our migrant breeding species to arrive back in spring, and it often reaches southern regions as early as March. Newly arrived birds usually congregate near water, catching flying insects and sometimes even picking prey off the surface of the water while in flight.

The species has rather plain plumage, being mainly sandy brown above and whitish below. One feature to look out for is the dark band that runs across the otherwise pale breast.

Habitat

Feeds over rivers, lakes and large ponds but nesting is entirely restricted to sandy banks; for this purpose man-made sand quarries are often favoured.

Can be mistaken for

Crag martin (see right).

Adult

SIMILAR SPECIES

Crag martin

Ptyonoprogne rupestris

LENGTH: 14–15 cm (5½–6 in)

Similar in terms of plumage colour to a sand martin but marginally larger and lacking that species' dark chest band. The underparts are a rather subdued greyish buff and a close view will reveal white spots towards the upper surface of the tip of the tail. The crag martin is resident in southern Europe but an altitudinal migrant, moving to lower regions in winter. It visits muddy ponds in spring to collect mud for its nest.

Meadow pipit

Anthus pratensis

REGION: Resident in northwestern Europe but elsewhere in the region it is a summer visitor to the north, and a winter visitor to the south • SIZE: 14–15 cm (5½–6 in) • FOOD: Insects and small seeds • CALL: A thin *pseet-pseet-pseet* • SONG: A series of descending notes, typically delivered in flight but starting and finishing on the ground • SEX DIFFERENCES: The sexes are similar • JUVENILE: Similar to the adults but usually has a more yellowish hue to the plumage • FLIGHT: Direct, with bouts of rapid wingbeats interspersed with short glides • NEST: A cup-shaped structure, made from woven grasses and sited at the base of a tussock of grass.

At first glance, the meadow pipit is a rather nondescript bird with a streaked brown plumage. The call is distinctive, however, and the proportionately long tail and long, thin bill all give clues to its identity. This species feeds almost exclusively on the ground, searching for insects and seeds in areas of short grass.

During the breeding season, meadow pipits are usually associated with rather wild and remote grassy areas. However, in winter, and especially in harsh weather, they can often be found in more urban settings, including parks and extensive gardens that have a large expanse of lawn.

Habitat

A range of grassy habitats, from meadows to moorland in summer to parks in winter.

How to attract this bird to your garden

It is difficult to tempt this species into your garden with food but open areas of lawn, and rough patches of grass, may do the trick. The chances of seeing this species will be greatest if your garden is located in an area of open farmland or countryside.

Adult

Can be mistaken for

Crested lark (see pages 74–75), which has a noticeable crest and often feeds on disturbed ground rather than grassland.

Crested lark

Galerida cristata

REGION: Widespread resident of lowland, mainland Europe • SIZE: 17–19 cm (7–7.5 in) • FOOD: Insects and seeds • CALL: Whistling call • SONG: Loud and whistling • SEX DIFFERENCES: The sexes are similar • JUVENILE: Similar to the adults • FLIGHT: Direct flight with bouts of rapid wingbeats interspersed with short glides; also capable of hovering • NEST: A woven cup of grasses, usually sited at the base of a clump of grass.

The crested lark feeds almost exclusively on the ground and its streaked and sandy-grey plumage allows it to blend in with its surroundings. It raises its crest when agitated, but lowers it when alarmed, for example, by the presence of a predator.

The species is often remarkably indifferent to people and can be viewed from a distance of just a few metres if you keep still. If alarmed, it prefers to run rather than fly; but, if it does take to the air, look for the distinctive orange patch on the underwing and the reddish outer tail feathers.

Habitat

Although this species can be found in cultivated fields and farmland, it does take to urban settings, so it can often be seen feeding beside roads, and sometimes in the most unpromising of gardens.

How to attract this bird to your garden

If you live in this species' range, you will not have to do much to attract it. In fact, it often seems to favour neglected and disturbed ground, so a well-presented, manicured garden is unlikely to have any appeal for it.

Can be mistaken for

Meadow pipit (see page 73) and the species listed right, which are occasional garden visitors.

Above Crested larks often sing while perched on garden or rough field fences.

SIMILAR SPECIES

Skylark

Alauda arvensis

LENGTH: 18 cm (7 in)

Similar to a crested lark but with a much shorter crest. It favours grassy, open habitats and is seldom, if ever, found in truly urban settings. They breed throughout Europe (except Iceland) and are mostly resident but birds from the far north and east of the species' European range move south and west in autumn. If you live on the fringes of farmland or open country then the chances are that skylarks will be aerial visitors to your garden: they are famed for their trilling and whistling song, which is sung on the wing, often incessantly from dawn to dusk.

Woodlark

Lullula arborea

LENGTH: 15 cm (6 in)

Breeds across southern and central Europe, as far north as southern Scandinavia and southern Britain. Most birds are resident but those from the far north and east move south and west in autumn. Famed for its wonderful, yodelling song, this species favours a mosaic of areas of short and long grass. If you live on the fringes of heathland or cleared wooded areas, it may visit your garden. It has well-marked black and brown upperparts and a striking black-and-white patch on each wing.

Short-toed lark

Calandrella brachydactyla

LENGTH: 14–16 cm (5½–6½ in)

A summer visitor with spring migrants sometimes turning up in gardens in southern Europe; they favour areas of short grassland, so lawns are ideal for attracting them. It has streaked brown upperparts and clean-looking whitish underparts, usually with a dark patch on the sides of the breast.

Skylark

Woodlark

Short-toed lark

White/Pied wagtail

Motacilla alba

REGION: A widespread species in the region, resident in much of western Europe and a summer visitor to much of the north and east; these migrants winter around the Mediterranean. Across most of the region, a subspecies called the white wagtail (*M. a. alba*) is found, but in Britain and Ireland it is represented by a different subspecies called the pied wagtail (*M. a. yarrellii*) • SIZE: 17–19 cm (7–7½ in) • FOOD: Insects and small seeds • CALL: A loud and insistent *chissick* • SEX DIFFERENCES: Males have more contrasting plumage than females of the same subspecies; male white wagtails have a grey back while male pied wagtails have a black back • JUVENILE: Similar to an adult female but with paler plumage overall and less extensive black markings; the underparts are often tinged faintly with yellow • FLIGHT: Bounding and undulating, with bursts of rapid wingbeats interspersed with short glides • NEST: A cup-shaped structure made from grasses, often sited in a crevice or ledge in a man-made structure such as a shed or garage.

Adult male, White wagtail

Above Male pied wagtails have black backs and more extensive dark markings.

Above Immature pied and white wagtails are almost impossible to distinguish.

This species is seldom found far from either habitation or water and it is one of the most familiar of urban birds. It is frequently found in parks and will even feed in city centres and car parks. In the countryside at large, it usually occurs in the vicinity of farm buildings and in places where animals are feeding.

Subtle plumage differences allow pied and white wagtails to be distinguished from one another but, taken as a whole, all birds are easy to identify because of their black, grey and white plumage and the proportionately very long tail, which is pumped up and down as the bird walks. The very loud and distinctive call adds certainty to the identification.

Pied and white wagtails usually feed on the ground but they are agile and aerobatic on the wing and able to catch passing insects in flight. They sometimes breed in bizarre places and one pair is even known to have raised young successfully when the nest was placed under the bonnet of an operational farm tractor.

Habitat

Areas of short grassland, wetland margins and tarmac.

How to attract this bird to your garden

If you have a large area of lawn then this species may be an occasional visitor; paddocks with grazing ponies will be even more attractive.

Can be mistaken for

Almost unmistakable because of its body shape, although beware confusion with its two cousins (see right).

SIMILAR SPECIES

Grey wagtail

Motacilla cinerea

LENGTH: 17–20 cm (7–8 in)

This attractive bird is an occasional visitor to gardens that have a stream running through them, or that are endowed with large ponds. If the stream is large enough and flows year-round then the birds may nest nearby. However, most sightings occur outside the breeding season.

Yellow wagtail

Motacilla flava

LENGTH: 15–16 cm (6–6½ in)

A summer visitor to the whole of mainland Europe and southern Britain. Migrants can be seen throughout the region. This species likes short grass and is particularly fond of feeding near animals.

Grey wagtail

Yellow wagtail

Wren

Troglodytes troglodytes

REGION: Widespread resident across central and southern Europe; populations from the north of the region are summer visitors, migrating south for the winter • SIZE: 9–10 cm (3½–4 in) • FOOD: Insects, spiders and other invertebrates • CALL: Has a loud, rattling alarm call • SONG: Consists of loud, warbling phrases and ends in a trill • SEX DIFFERENCES: The sexes are similar • JUVENILE: Similar to an adult • FLIGHT: Rapid, on whirring wingbeats; seldom seen more than a few metres from the ground • NEST: A neat, spherical structure made from grasses and leaves, lined with feathers, usually sited in a dense bush or patch of ivy.

The wren is one of our smallest birds and at times it can look almost spherical. Although it tends to feed in the cover of dense vegetation, it sometimes emerges and perches prominently, seemingly curious about human visitors to its territory. Characteristically, it usually cocks its tail up almost vertically and utters its distinctive alarm call, which is amazingly loud for such a small bird.

The species is extremely unfussy in its choice of habitat, the common factor being the presence of dense undergrowth where insect food can be caught. For much of the time, wrens are unobtrusive birds and it is perhaps surprising to discover that it is one of the most numerous birds in Europe.

During the winter months, wrens will sometimes use nest boxes in the garden for roosting. Particularly good ones may be used communally, and a dozen or more may occupy the same refuge.

Above Considering the small size of its builder, a wren's nest is surprisingly large. Despite this, however, it blends in well with its surroundings and is difficult to spot.

Habitat

A wide range of habitats, from woodlands and moors to parks and gardens.

How to attract this bird to your garden

If you have dense flower borders, and allow undergrowth to flourish beneath hedgerows, then you are likely to attract wrens to the garden. Dense ivy patches are favoured for nesting, so allow this climbing plant to flourish. They feed on insects so do not use pesticides in any form in the garden.

Can be mistaken for

The wren is almost unmistakable, when taking into account its small size, rounded body shape and rather uniformly brown plumage.

SIMILAR SPECIES

Dipper

Cinclus cinclus

LENGTH: 17–20 cm (7–8 in)

Locally common resident across much of Europe, except Iceland and other parts of the northwest. You only stand a chance of seeing this species in a garden if there is a sizeable stream and the surrounding terrain is rugged. It is never seen away from water and is usually seen perched on a boulder, bobbing up and down in a distinctive manner. The rounded body shape and striking white throat and breast are distinctive.

Waxwing

Bombycilla garrulus

REGION: Best known as a widespread winter visitor to northern and central Europe; occurs as far west as Britain and Ireland in small numbers. Breeds eastwards from northern Scandinavia • SIZE: 18 cm (*c.* 7 in) • FOOD: In winter, almost exclusively berries; some insects during breeding season • CALL: A soft trill • SONG: A mixture of harsh notes and silvery trills • SEX DIFFERENCES: The sexes are similar • JUVENILE: Similar to the adults, but the red 'waxy' tips to inner wing feathers are absent, as are the white margins to the flight feathers • FLIGHT: Rapid and rather starling-like; the wing shape is triangular • NEST: A twiggy structure, high in pine tree.

The numbers of waxwings that occur as winter visitors to the region is rather unpredictable, as is their precise range. In some years (known as 'irruption' years) thousands of birds abandon northern regions because of a combination of overcrowding and food shortages. They tend to be rather nomadic and how far south in the Europe they range depends upon the severity of the weather and the availability of berries.

In winter, when most waxwing sightings occur, the species is seen in flocks, usually containing 10–30 birds, but sometimes numbering hundreds. They feed on berries, particularly those of rowan and hawthorn, and typically a flock will descend *en masse*, the birds gorging themselves before flying to a rooftop or tree in order to digest their meal.

The appearance of waxwings is unique, making them almost unmistakable if seen clearly. The

Above A female waxwing lacks the pale fringe to the male's flight feathers that creates the obvious 'V' markings seen in that sex.

Waxwing

Crested tit

Starling

plumage is a subtle shade of pinkish-buff overall but the face has a striking black bib and eyestripe, and the wings are marked with red, yellow and white. The tail has a bright yellow tip and the head has a prominent crest, which the birds raise when they are agitated.

Habitat

During the winter, they usually favour hedgerows and other berry-rich areas. However, as the season progresses, and food in the countryside at large is depleted, the birds usually move into towns and gardens.

How to attract this bird to your garden

Grow lots of berry-bearing bushes such as rowan and hawthorn (*Sorbus aucuparia* and *Crataegus monogyna* respectively). They will also eat cotoneaster (*Cotoneaster* spp.) berries once everything else has run out.

Can be mistaken for

Almost unmistakable when seen clearly on account of its colours and crest, but in flight could be mistaken for a starling (see pages 116–117); on the wing, their silhouettes are similar.

Dunnock

Prunella modularis

REGION: Widespread and common resident across much of Europe; in the north and east, however, they are migrant summer visitors • SIZE: 13–14 cm (5–5½ in) • FOOD: Insects, spiders and other invertebrates, as well as seeds and fruits in season • CALL: A thin, piping note • SONG: A loud and energetic warble, often delivered from a prominent perch • SEX DIFFERENCES: Sexes are similar, both in terms of size and plumage • JUVENILE: Similar to the adults but with duller colours and more prominent streaking on the underparts • FLIGHT: Reluctant to fly in the open but sometimes seen in short gliding flight from one bush to another • NEST: A neatly woven structure of grasses and twigs, sited deep in the cover of a bush.

Dunnocks are unobtrusive little birds that, except for their subdued yet distinctive call, most people probably would not notice for much of the time. They forage for food mainly on the ground, hopping or creeping along with a crouched posture; with their brownish plumage, they can look almost mouse-like.

Occasionally, dunnocks will feed among the tangled stems of a bramble patch or bush but they seldom venture more than a metre or so from the ground. During harsh winter weather, when food is scarce they will sometimes forage underneath bird tables, searching for fallen scraps of food. However, wherever they feed, they always keep close to cover and dive into the dense undergrowth at the slightest sign of danger. At the start of the breeding season male dunnocks typically lose their wariness. Instead of skulking, they will sit on a prominent perch for minutes on end, singing their rapid, warbler-like song to advertize ownership of a territory. In the past, the dunnock went by the country name of 'hedge sparrow'. Because it is completely unrelated to the true sparrows, this potentially confusing name is no longer used.

Habitat

Found in woodland, hedgerows and scrub, but also in mature gardens with plenty of undergrowth.

Above Seen from the front, a dunnock's lilac-blue underparts provide a subtle contrast to its reddish-brown upperparts.

How to attract this bird to your garden

If you ensure that you have plenty of areas of dark, shady undergrowth and mature hedges, then this species will take up residence in your garden. Being ground-feeders, dunnocks are particularly vulnerable to the depredations of domestic cats, so you are unlikely to have the former if you tolerate the latter.

Can be mistaken for

House sparrow (see pages 122–123); that species has a stubby bill while the dunnock's is thin and warbler-like.

Robin

Erithacus rubecula

REGION: Widespread resident in western and southern Europe; in northeastern Europe and Scandinavia they are migrant summer visitors, moving south for the winter • SIZE: 13–14 cm (5–5½ in) • FOOD: Insects and other invertebrates, plus berries occasionally in winter • CALL: Utters a sharp *tic* alarm call • SONG: Has a rather melancholy song that can be heard in almost any month of the year • SEX DIFFERENCES: The sexes are similar • JUVENILE: Buffish-brown overall, with spots on the breast and streaking on the upperparts • FLIGHT: Low and direct • NEST: A neat, deep cup-shaped structure made of leaves and mosses and lined with animal hair; sited on a ledge in an outbuilding, or in a dense bush.

An adult robin is an extremely attractive bird, the orange-red face and breast making identification a straightforward matter. Although across most of mainland Europe the species can be rather skulking, in parts of its range it becomes tame in the garden and often shows a positive interest in human activity.

Robins are extremely territorial birds. This is particularly evident in parts of their range where they are year-round residents, and territorial owners defend their domains against all comers in all months of the year. This behaviour is sometimes relaxed in severe winter weather, and during the breeding season a pair will share a territory.

As a response to particularly cold conditions in winter, robins fluff themselves up to improve their insulation; at such times, they can look almost spherical. They move with a hopping gait and use their thin bills like a pair of tweezers to pick up insects and worms.

Above A juvenile robin has rather thrush-like spots on the breast.

Habitat

A wide range of wooded habitats, as well as parks and gardens in towns and cities.

How to attract this bird to your garden

If you encourage invertebrates in your garden (by not using pesticides, for instance) then you are likely to attract robins. If you provide mealworms for them, they will respond and will come and investigate for earthworms if you dig the ground over.

Can be mistaken for

Adults are almost unmistakable on account of the red breast, but a juvenile could perhaps be mistaken for a dunnock (see pages 82–83), a juvenile redstart (see pages 92–93) or the species detailed to the right.

SIMILAR SPECIES

Stonechat

Saxicola torquata

LENGTH 12–13 cm (*c.* 5 in)

You are most likely to encounter this species when it is on migration or during the winter months, and it is usually juvenile birds that stray from the species' typical heathland habitat. Stonechats are compact short-tailed birds that sit upright and perch prominently, showing off the juvenile's orange-buff breast, pale throat and darker brown head and back. Its call sounds like two stones being knocked together.

Whinchat

Saxicola rubetra

LENGTH 12–14 cm (*c.* 5–5½ in)

This well-marked species sometimes turns up in open, country gardens on migration and may even nest if you are lucky enough to have a rough, grassy paddock. Males are brighter than females and have a peachy-orange breast and a striking white stripe above the eye.

Stonechat

Wheatear

Oenanthe oenanthe

LENGTH 14–16 cm (5½–6½ in)

This open-country species is likely to visit a garden only when it is migrating (juveniles in autumn especially) and even then only if the landscape is open and there is plenty of short grassland. Juvenile birds have buffish plumage and, like adults, they reveal a striking white rump when they fly.

Whinchat

Wheatear

Bluethroat

Luscinia svecica

REGION: Widespread summer visitor to northeast Europe (mainly April to August) and locally farther south; elsewhere it is seen on migration; locally resident in northern Spain • SIZE: 13–14 cm (*c.* 5–5½ in) • FOOD: Insects and other invertebrates • CALL: Utters a sharp *tchick* in alarm • SONG: Rich and melodious, including mimicry of other species • SEX DIFFERENCES: Only males have the full blue throat, the intensity and extent of which is reduced outside the breeding season. Some females show a hint of blue on the throat (only in summer) but on many this feature is absent • JUVENILE: Similar to winter females • FLIGHT: Rapid and low • NEST: A cup-shaped structure, sited in deep cover, often at the base of a grass tussock.

Adult male summer, red-spotted form

Above In winter, male bluethroats lose much of the blue coloration; some summer females have rather similar plumage.

A male bluethroat in breeding plumage is a truly stunning bird, the colours on the throat appearing almost iridescent in good light. Individuals that breed in northern Europe have a red spot in the centre of the throat while males from many other parts of their range have a white spot.

Regardless of the sex of the individual, or the time of year, all birds have rusty-red sides to the base of the tail. These features are perhaps easiest to see as the bird flies away from you. Agitated individuals sometimes raise and lower their tails in an exaggerated manner.

This perky little bird spends much of its time feeding on the ground. It has a hopping gait and a rather upright posture that can be reminiscent of a robin. The species' natural tendency is to skulk close to cover and to dive into deep vegetation at the slightest sign of danger. However, some individuals can be remarkably bold.

Habitat

Bluethroats favour wetland scrub and boggy forest in the summer; on migration, however, they are more usually associated with wetland margins.

How to attract this bird to your garden

If you have a reasonably large pond in your garden, allow the margins to be colonized by dense vegetation and a bluethroat might stop off on migration for a day or two.

Can be mistaken for

An adult male in summer plumage is unmistakable on account of its colours but a juvenile could perhaps be mistaken for a juvenile robin (see pages 84–85); you can tell them apart by this species' clean white throat and red sides to the tail.

Nightingale

Luscinia megarhynchos

REGION: Widespread summer visitor to central, southern and parts of northwestern Europe • SIZE: 16–17 cm (6½–7 in) • FOOD: Insects and other invertebrates • CALL: A soft whistle, but this is seldom heard • SONG: A loud and musical delivery of fluty and clicking sounds • SEX DIFFERENCES: The sexes are similar • JUVENILE: Similar to the adults • FLIGHT: Low and rapid, keeping close to cover • NEST: A depression in the ground, made of leaves and lined with animal hair and grasses.

Arguably the nightingale has the best-known song of any European bird. This partly because its tone and delivery is so rich, varied and accomplished, but also because it is so loud: on a calm night it can carry 300 metres (330 yards) or more. Territorial males begin singing immediately after their arrival in the region and they can be heard both by day and at night.

In contrast to its song, the nightingale's plumage is unremarkable:

Above On migration, nightingales are generally less skulking than on breeding territory. The fluffed-up feathering of a tired migrant can give the bird a warbler-like appearance.

the subdued reddish-brown coloration blends in well with the woodland floor where it spends most of its time. If you get a good view you will see that the tail, which the bird will often raise and flick, is a richer red colour than the rest of the body.

Nightingales tend to feed on the ground, moving with a hopping gait and often turning over leaves in search of insects. Singing birds invariably perch in dense cover and you will usually get only a partial view through leaves.

Habitat

Wooded habitats which have a dense undergrowth.

How to attract this bird to your garden

Small pockets of scrub, or larger coppices in some areas, are often favoured. So leave a wilderness area in your garden and you might attract this species if you live in a rural district.

Can be mistaken for

The song is so distinctive that singing birds are unmistakable; given a poor view, a feeding bird could be confused with a garden warbler (see page 213), although if you spot the rich brown plumage colours you can be almost certain that it is a thrush nightingale or a rufous bush-robin (see right).

SIMILAR SPECIES

Rufous bush-robin

Cercotrichas galactotes

LENGTH: 15–17 cm (6–7 in)

A summer visitor to southern Spain and warm, arid parts of Greece, the rufous bush-robin favours dense areas of dense, thorny scrub but fortunately singing males often perch conspicuously on bare twigs. The long reddish tail (often raised and fanned) is tipped with striking black-and-white spots.

Black redstart

Phoenicurus ochruros

REGION: Occurs year-round in western and southern mainland Europe; in the east of its range, the species is a migrant summer visitor, present mainly from April to September • SIZE: 14 cm (5½ in) • FOOD: Insects and other invertebrates • CALL: Utters a whistling call • SONG: A mixture of whistles and static-like crackling sounds • SEX DIFFERENCES: Only adult males have the smart black, grey and white body plumage; females are overall grey-brown • JUVENILE: Similar to adult females • FLIGHT: Direct and rapid • NEST: A cup-shaped structure made from grasses, sited in a crevice or on a ledge in a building.

These charming little birds are usually quite tolerant of people, in part at least because they usually breed in villages and towns where they cannot avoid human contact. Birds of both sexes, and at all times of the year, show a distinctive reddish orange tail that is frequently quivered when they perch. The black redstart is the only species with such a striking reddish tail that you are likely to encounter in the region during the winter months.

Although the male black redstart's song is distinctive, with its peculiar mechanical-sounding elements, it is easily drowned out by the noise of traffic, so you need to get up early in the morning to hear it at its best.

You are much more likely to see a black redstart standing on a post, boulder or building than you are to observe one perched in a tree or bush. Look out for the bird's typically upright posture and striking black legs.

Above Female and immature black redstarts have rather nondescript body plumage but all birds reveal the striking red tail.

Habitat
Associated with urban locations (including derelict buildings, railway sidings and building sites) in those areas of mainland Europe where it is resident; elsewhere, it favours this habitat during the breeding season, but is often found on or near coasts in winter.

How to attract this bird to your garden
These birds will sometimes nest in garden sheds, or in holes or cavities in buildings. So don't be too tidy with your outbuildings if you want to attract them.

Can be mistaken for
The adult male is unmistakable on account of its colouring, but it is possible to mistake females or juveniles for female redstarts (see pages 92–93); the body plumage, however, is more uniformly grey-brown in the black redstart.

Black redstart

Robin

Redstart

Adult male, summer

Redstart

Phoenicurus phoenicurus

REGION: Widespread summer visitor to much of Europe, present mainly from April to August • SIZE: 14 cm (5½ in) • FOOD: Insects and other invertebrates • CALL: A soft *huiit* or a sharp ticking sound • SONG: Musical but melancholy • SEX DIFFERENCES: Breeding males have bluish-grey upperparts, orange-red underparts, and black and white on the face; females have buffish-brown upperparts and buffish-orange underparts. All birds show a striking, dark-centred reddish tail • JUVENILE: Similar to an adult female • FLIGHT: Rapid and direct • NEST: Cup-shaped and made of woven grasses, lined with animal hair.

Redstarts have a largely insectivorous diet and catch a fair proportion of their food on the wing. Typically they feed like flycatchers, perching inconspicuously on a dead branch to watch for passing insects, which are then caught in aerial sorties. In flight, the striking reddish tail is usually conspicuous.

The species is easiest to detect in spring, when territorial males advertize their presence by singing. When the breeding season is over, they all become rather secretive and lead unobtrusive lives until they begin their autumn migration, heading south to wintering quarters in Africa.

A breeding male redstart is one of our most striking and colourful birds: the underparts and tail are flushed bright reddish-orange. Although the overall appearance and habits of this species should allow easy distinction from a robin, the black face and throat soon dispel any lingering doubts.

Above A female redstart may lack the male's colourful body plumage but the striking red tail is still an invaluable aid to identification.

Habitat

This bird favours open, deciduous woodland, as well as mature parks and gardens.

How to attract this bird to your garden

Their favourite nest site is a hole in an old, gnarled tree or a cavity in a stone wall or building. If you leave plenty of suitable natural sites, they may be attracted to nest, but they will also use nest boxes.

Can be mistaken for

The breeding male is almost unmistakable because of its colouring, although beginners could mistake one for a robin (see pages 84–85); however, this species' reddish tail and black face and throat should make identification easy if you get a clear glimpse. Females could be confused with female black redstarts (see pages 90–91).

Rock thrush

Monticola saxatilis

REGION: A local summer visitor to warmer regions of southern Europe, present mainly from April to August • SIZE: 17–20 cm (7–8 in) • FOOD: Mainly insects and small lizards • CALL: A clicking *tchack* call • SONG: A series of musical but melancholy phrases, sometimes delivered in flight • SEX DIFFERENCES: Breeding males are extremely colourful (blue-grey, reddish-orange and brown) while females are orange-brown overall with a scaly appearance to the feathers; males seen on migration in autumn often have rather worn plumage, so their colours are more subdued • JUVENILE: Similar to adult females • FLIGHT: Rapid, on powerful wingbeats • NEST: A rudimentary structure of grasses, sited in a rock crevice.

The rock thrush is a rather wary bird and, generally speaking, it is likely to have seen you, and slipped behind a rock, before you are aware of its presence. However, if you sit quietly and don't make any sudden movements it may resume its normal habits. When the female is incubating the eggs, the male spends long periods perched on a prominent rock on the lookout for danger.

Rock thrushes have a rather compact, thrush-like outline but a proportionately short tail. In flight, look for the striking white patch on the lower back of the male, which contrasts with the darker wings and the rich orange-red of the tail. Both immature birds and adult females lack this white element in their plumage.

Habitat

Broken, rocky ground and lower mountain slopes.

How to attract this bird to your garden

You are only likely to see this species in your garden if it is surrounded by suitable rocky terrain; better still if the garden itself is adorned with large boulders and rocks.

Can be mistaken for

Breeding males are unmistakable because of their size, shape and colours. Immature birds and adult females could be mistaken for other thrushes, but note the striking, dark-centred tail.

Adult male

Blue rock thrush

Monticola solitarius

REGION: Resident in warmer, southern parts of Europe • SIZE: 21–23 cm (8½–9 in) • FOOD: Mainly insects and small lizards • CALL: Utters various piping notes • SONG: A series of tuneful but melancholy phrases • SEX DIFFERENCES: Adult males are mainly dull blue with darker wings; females are mainly brown, with scaly-looking underparts • JUVENILE: Similar to adult females • FLIGHT: Powerful and direct, with short glides • NEST: A rudimentary structure of grasses, sited in a rock crevice.

Blue rock thrushes are rather wary birds and the typical view that people get is of the head and shoulders of a male peering over the edge of a rocky outcrop, surveying human intruders into its domain. These views are invariably against the light and at such times it can be almost impossible to see any colour in the plumage – the bird will probably appear all dark. However, the proportionately long bill, and the bird's behaviour, will offer clues to its identity.

This species is usually easiest to detect by listening for its musical, fluty song. Although it is not especially loud, it is usually amplified by the rocky surroundings.

Habitat

Favours rocky habitats, ranging from mountain slopes and gorges to coastal cliffs.

How to attract this bird to your garden

You are only likely to find this species if your garden is in rocky terrain. Just occasionally, the species will nest in a hole or cavity in an old building. Be warned, though, they are easily disturbed.

Can be mistaken for

In dull light they can be mistaken for a female blackbird (see pages 96–97), but the bill is proportionately much longer and the habitat preferences are different.

Adult male

Blackbird

Turdus merula

REGION: Widespread resident across most of the region; northern populations are mainly migrant summer visitors to their range • SIZE: 25–27 cm (10–11 in) • FOOD: Insects and other invertebrates, as well as seeds and berries in season • CALL: Utters a loud and harsh, clucking *tchack* in alarm • SONG: One of Europe's best songbirds, the song comprises tuneful, fluty notes. The whole lasts for about six seconds, and is repeated after a pause of similar length • SEX DIFFERENCES: Adult males are uniformly black with a yellow bill while females are uniformly brown • JUVENILE: Similar to adult females • FLIGHT: Rapid and direct • NEST: A cup-shaped structure, made of mud and mosses and lined with grass; sited on a ledge in shed, or in a dense bush.

The blackbird is one of the region's best-known garden birds and almost all suitable locations are likely to have at least one resident pair. Like some other thrush species, it is fond of earthworms and the sight of birds foraging on the lawn is a familiar one. Typically they move in a series of short hops and then the head is cocked on one side to survey the ground for potential prey.

In the winter, numbers of resident blackbirds across much of central and southern Europe are boosted by influxes of migrants from farther

Blackbird

Song thrush

Mistle thrush

Adult male

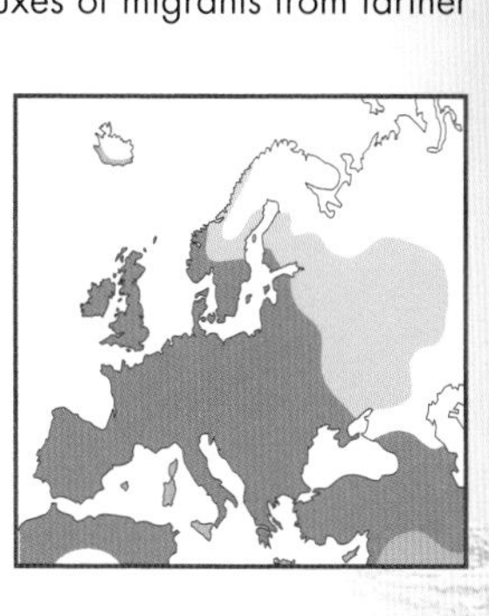

Above The mottled brown plumage of a female blackbird helps it blend in with its surroundings – particularly useful when nesting.

north and east, some originating beyond the region. Seen as a whole, hundreds of thousands, if not millions, of visiting birds are involved and they usually feed and roost alongside residents.

To many people, the blackbird's alarm call is almost as familiar as its song. It is loud and often repeated incessantly if a predator, such as a cat, is located. The call is also uttered as birds go to roost, typically just as darkness is falling.

Habitat

All sorts of habitats ranging from woodland and hedgerows to urban parks and gardens.

How to attract this bird to your garden

So long as you have a decent-sized lawn, which is not sprayed with pesticides, you will have no trouble attracting this bird to the garden. However, being essentially a ground-feeder, it is particularly vulnerable to the depredation of domestic cats.

Can be mistaken for

Adult male is almost unmistakable in an average garden being the only all-dark bird of this size. Female and immature birds could conceivably be mistaken for other thrush species but their uniformly brown underparts (and absence of spots) help with identification.

SIMILAR SPECIES

Ring ouzel

Turdus torquatus

LENGTH: 24–26 cm (9½–10½ in)

Breeds locally in upland districts of northern Europe and, locally, in the mountains of central and southern Europe: it is the upland counterpart of the blackbird, the pale crescent on the breast and scaly-looking underparts allowing you to distinguish them. Migrants can be seen across the region and some individuals winter in southern Europe. Realistically, the only chance of seeing a ring ouzel in the garden is if you live surrounded by rugged, upland terrain. It is distinctly shy and wary.

Fieldfare

Turdus pilaris

REGION: Occurs year-round in much of central Europe; most northern populations are migrant summer visitors, moving south and west for the winter • SIZE: 24–26 cm (9½–10½ in) • FOOD: Insects, earthworms and other invertebrates, as well as fruits and berries in season • CALL: Utters a chattering *chack-chack-chack*, often heard after dark from migrating flocks • SONG: Consists of short bursts of fluty phrases • SEX DIFFERENCES: The sexes are similar • JUVENILE: Similar to adults but the colours are less intense • FLIGHT: Powerful, flapping flight pattern • NEST: Made from grasses and twigs and typically sited in the fork of a tree; usually colonially.

This colourful and well-marked thrush is extremely common in most low-lying areas during the winter months when influxes of birds from farther east boost the numbers. The combination of a chestnut back, blue-grey head and spotted underparts flushed with yellow make identification easy. In flight, the rump is a contrastingly pale grey.

Outside the breeding season, fieldfares are gregarious, forming flocks that are often hundreds, if not thousands, strong. In autumn, when

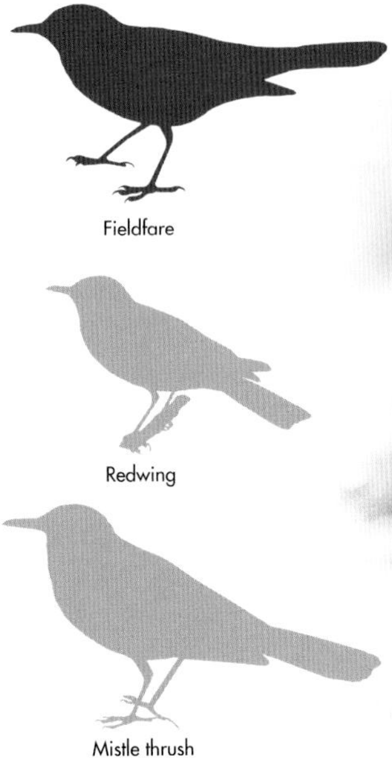

Fieldfare

Redwing

Mistle thrush

Adult

most birds arrive in western and southern Europe, flocks descend upon berry-bearing bushes and strip them within minutes. As the season progresses, and this source of food is depleted, it is more usual to see them feeding in open fields and on short grassland, searching the ground for earthworms.

Winter flocks tend to be nomadic and seldom stay put in the same area for more than a couple of days (sometimes it can be as little as an hour or two) before moving on. They are extremely responsive to local weather conditions and if, for example, the ground freezes in a given area, they will unhesitatingly move on in search of some milder conditions.

Habitat

Outside the breeding season, associated with farmland and open country with hedgerows; in breeding season nests in woodland.

How to attract this bird to your garden

Although fieldfares are primarily birds of open country, you can lure them into the garden in winter by putting out windfall apples; they respond particularly well during severe weather.

Can be mistaken for

Mistle thrush (see page 104–105), although the colourful plumage and pale grey rump are distinctive.

Above Fieldfares breed in northern Europe, and upland regions further south, usually nesting in the fork of a deciduous tree.

Above Fieldfares love berries and even visit cities in search of them in hard winters.

Above The pale breast feathers are flushed with buff and a few dark spots.

Redwing

Turdus iliacus

REGION: Widespread summer visitor to northern Europe; elsewhere it is seen on migration or as a winter visitor • SIZE: 20–22 cm (8–9 in) • FOOD: Insects, earthworms and other invertebrates, as well as berries and fruit in season • CALL: A thin, high-pitched whistle, often heard after dark from migrating flocks • SEX DIFFERENCES: The sexes are similar • JUVENILE: Similar to the adults • FLIGHT: Rapid and direct • NEST: Cup-shaped, made from grasses and twigs, and sited in a bush.

The redwing often associates with its larger cousin, the fieldfare, outside the breeding season and the two species frequently feed alongside one another. Like other thrush species, it spends a lot of time searching for earthworms and other soil invertebrates.

The redwing is one of the most attractive and well-marked of all thrushes. Even if long grass hides the body, it is usually possible to identify them correctly from the striking white stripe that can be seen above the eye, a feature that shows up even at a distance. They also have dark streaking on the breast and a reddish flush on the flanks.

Above A redwing's nest is usually sited in the fork of a tree. Even when incubating, the bird's red flanks and bold white supercilium can be seen clearly.

This latter colour extends to the underwings and is very easy to pick out when birds are in flight.

Habitat

Outside the breeding season, it is associated with farmland and open country with hedgerows; during the breeding season, it is found in woods and mature gardens, within its northerly range.

How to attract this bird to your garden

Wintering birds are attracted to fallen apples and to berry-bearing bushes such as rowan and hawthorn. In their breeding range, you could try putting up an open-fronted nest box to encourage breeding. Redwing pairs will sometimes nest in the roof of a house or on a ledge in a garden shed.

Can be mistaken for

Song thrush (see pages 102–103), although the redwing's bold white stripe above the eye and red flanks are diagnostic.

Redwing

Fieldfare

Song thrush

Adult

Song thrush

Turdus philomelos

REGION: Widespread year-round in much of western Europe although only a winter visitor to the far south; in north and east Europe, it is a migrant summer visitor • SIZE: 23 cm (*c.* 9 in) • FOOD: Insects, earthworms and other invertebrates, plus fruit and berries in season • CALL: A thin *tic*, uttered in flight • SONG: Loud and musical, repeating phrases two or three times • SEX DIFFERENCES: The sexes are similar • JUVENILE: Similar to the adults, but with pale streaking on the back • FLIGHT: Direct, on flapping wingbeats • NEST: A cup-shaped structure, made from twigs and leaves and lined with mud; sited in a dense bush.

Above This newly fledged juvenile song thrush shows pale streaking on the upperparts, characteristic at this age.

Although the song thrush is not especially colourful, the markings and hue of its plumage combine to create a subtly beautiful effect. The pale underparts are adorned with heart-shaped spots and there is an orange-buff flush to both the breast and flanks. This colour extends to the underwings and is apparent in flight.

In central and western Europe, song thrush numbers are highest during the winter months. This is because huge influxes of birds from farther north and east arrive in October and November, in search of milder conditions and more readily available food.

In locations where it is not unduly disturbed or persecuted by domestic cats, the song thrush can become remarkably bold and fearless. It likes to search for earthworms on the lawn but will also forage among low vegetation for snails. If it discovers one, typically the snail will be carried to a favourite stone on which it is smashed repeatedly until the shell shatters. A well-used stone will be surrounded by shell fragments and is known as a thrush's 'anvil'.

Habitat

Deciduous woodland, and mature parks and gardens.

How to attract this bird to your garden

Encourage earthworms and snails (by not using pesticides) and discourage domestic cats which are a major predator of this species in the garden.

Can be mistaken for

Redwing (see pages 100–101), although it lacks that species' striking white stripe above the eye, and red flash on the flanks. The mistle thrush (see pages 104–105) is appreciably larger and has white, not orange-buff, underwings.

Mistle thrush

Turdus viscivorus

REGION: Widespread, year-round, in most of western and southern Europe; numbers are boosted in winter by influxes of birds from the north and east • SIZE: 27 cm (11 in) • FOOD: Insects, earthworms and other invertebrates, plus berries and fruit in season • CALL: A rattling alarm • SONG: Consists of brief, fluty phrases, interspersed with long pauses • SEX DIFFERENCES: The sexes are similar • JUVENILE: Similar to the adults but the upperparts are adorned with pale spots • FLIGHT: Rapid but undulating, on flapping wingbeats • NEST: A cup-shaped structure of twigs and grasses, sited in the fork of a tree.

If you have a large, berry-laden holly bush in your garden then the chances are that a mistle thrush will take up ownership of this valuable source of food during winter, or at least until the berries run out. Typically the owner is extremely possessive and will drive off all comers, expressing its indignation by voicing its distinctive rattling call.

Mistle thrushes have plump bodies for birds of this size, with underparts flushed with orange-buff and marked with rounded dark spots. The upperparts are rather grey-brown in hue (as opposed to the buffish-brown of a song thrush) and white tips to the outer tail feathers are usually distinct in flying birds.

Most songbirds tend to be fair-weather songsters but not so the mistle thrush. Sometimes its distinctive song (which can be recognized as much by the long pauses between phrases as by the song itself) can be heard in the pouring rain, or as darkness approaches.

Habitat
Open woodland, parks and urban gardens.

How to attract this bird to your garden
Encourage earthworms and snails (by not using pesticides) and plant berry-bearing bushes and trees, especially holly.

Can be mistaken for
Song thrush (see pages 102–103) but the mistle thrush is larger, and has white underwings and an overall greyer look to the plumage.

Mistle thrush

Song thrush

Fieldfare

Above This hungry brood of mistle thrushes will take a lot of feeding and will consume thousands of worms and caterpillars before fledging.

Above In winter, the mistle thrush's plump body is emphasized when it fluffs its feathers to improve insulation.

Above Juvenile birds are adorned with pale spots on the upper parts.

Woodpigeon

Columba palumbus

REGION: Widespread resident across the western half of the region; eastern and northern populations are migrant summer visitors to these areas • SIZE: 40–42 cm (16–17 in) • FOOD: Seeds, fruits and the shoots and leaves of low-growing plants, including some crops • CALL: Sings a rather repetitive song comprising five cooing syllables • SEX DIFFERENCES: Sexes are similar, in terms of both size and plumage • JUVENILE: Similar to the adults but without the white on the neck, and with dull (not yellow) eyes • FLIGHT: Direct, with rather shallow, 'clipped' wingbeats • NEST: A bizarrely flimsy construction (for a bird of this size) made of overlaid twigs and sited on the horizontal branch of a bush or tree.

Above In flight, the woodpigeon's white wingbars are distinctive and diagnostic.

This plump-bodied pigeon is a common sight in open country. In flight, striking white patches on the wings allow you to identify them with confidence. Seen close up, the plumage is a subtle blend of lilac-grey on the upperparts and maroon on the breast. The beady eyes are a striking yellow colour.

Woodpigeons are perhaps easiest to see during the winter months when large flocks (sometimes hundreds strong) form and feed on open farmland. The modern farming trend for growing oilseed rape has benefited this species because it provides a valuable source of food in winter (an otherwise lean time of the year). In autumn, birds are fond of feeding on the ivy berries and acorns from oak trees.

On the ground, woodpigeons walk with a rather curious waddling gait, as though their bodies are too large and plump for their legs. When alarmed, they take to the air with a loud clattering of the wings, which serves to alert other members of the flock to potential danger. In the countryside at large, woodpigeons are generally wary of people. However, in urban parks where they are fed, they often overcome their fears and in this environment can become almost ridiculously tame.

Habitat

Associated with mixed farmland areas and open country where woodland and hedgerows provide cover for nesting and roosting, and fields can be used to feed.

How to attract this bird to your garden

Seed sprinkled on the lawn is likely to attract woodpigeons, especially in rural areas. They happily nest in mature bushes and shrubs.

Can be mistaken for

Stock dove (see page 113), but that species has no white on the neck or wings.

Rock dove/Feral pigeon

Columba livia

REGION: The true rock dove is a resident species, restricted to southern Europe and northwest Britain and Ireland; feral pigeons are found in urban settings throughout the region • SIZE: 33 cm (13 in) • FOOD: Seeds, including those of cereals, and buds in season • CALL: A range of cooing sounds • SEX DIFFERENCES: The sexes are similar in the rock dove; there is great variability (but no sex distinction) among feral pigeons • JUVENILE: Essentially indistinguishable from the adults, once fledged • FLIGHT: Rapid and powerful, on pointed, swept-back wings • NEST: A rudimentary structure of twigs, sited on a ledge in a building (caves are often favoured by true rock doves).

Rock doves and feral pigeons are the same species, despite their different habitat preferences, and sometimes appearance. The former is the wild ancestor of its domesticated descendant. Rock doves are relatively scarce and difficult to observe at close quarters, partly because they are nervous, timid birds. The same cannot be said of feral pigeons, which can become extremely tame when fed and allowed to flourish.

All rock doves are rather similar in appearance, having lilac-grey body plumage and two bold black wingbars. The head and neck are darker than the rest of the body and in good light the feathers reveal an almost metallic sheen. In flight, the pale rump is a striking feature. By contrast, feral pigeons come in a wide range of colours, from almost pure white to nearly black. Some individuals, however, are superficially very similar in appearance to their wild ancestors.

Above Unlike its urban cousin, a true rock dove is a wary and alert bird, nervous about coming anywhere near people.

Feral pigeons can occur at such densities in towns and cities that they cause a nuisance, their droppings being a particular cause for concern for some people. However, 'feeding the pigeons' is still a popular pastime for many.

Habitat

Rock doves favour wild and rugged terrain and shun human company while feral pigeons are invariably associated with human habitation and are often tame.

How to attract this bird to your garden

Rock doves are so shy and wary that they are most unlikely to visit your garden. However, with feral pigeons it is a different matter: if you live in a town or city, then by putting out seed on your lawn you are unlikely not to attract a few individuals.

Can be mistaken for

Stock dove (see page 113), but this species favours wooded farmland (not rocky ground or towns) and lacks a pale rump.

Adult, feral pigeon

Collared dove

Streptopelia decaocto

REGION: Widespread resident across much of the region, although absent from much of the Iberian Peninsula • SIZE: 32 cm (*c.* 13 in) • FOOD: Seeds, including cereal grains, and fruits in season • CALL: A nasal coo • SONG: A repetitive (and for some people, irritating) three-syllable coo • SEX DIFFERENCES: The sexes are similar • JUVENILE: Similar to the adults, but without the black half-collar • FLIGHT: Rapid and direct, on flicking wingbeats; glides and dives on stiffly held wings in display flight • NEST: A basic twiggy structure, usually sited in a tree or bush.

Above The broad terminal white band on the tail is distinctive and diagnostic.

Above Young pigeons and doves are fed on the regurgitated contents of their parents' crop – known as 'crop milk'.

The story of the collared dove is a remarkable one. As recently as the start of the twentieth century, it was effectively absent from our region, being restricted to arid regions in the Middle East and Asia. However, during the first decades of the twentieth century its range expanded north and west and by the 1950s it had reached north-western Europe. Since then, it has never looked back and is now widespread and common in many parts.

In comparison with pigeons, the collared dove has a rather slender, elongated body with a proportionately long tail. The plumage is rather uniformly pinkish-buff, darkest on the wings. In flight, arguably the most striking feature is the white-tipped, black-based tail, which is particularly noticeable when fanned in display flight.

Within their European range, collared doves are almost invariably associated with people. In towns and cities they favour gardens and parks. In the countryside at large, they are seldom found far from farm buildings, especially where the farm grows arable crops.

Habitat

Usually found around human habitation, from towns and cities to rural farms.

How to attract this bird to your garden

Most larger urban gardens will have a resident pair of these birds; they can be attracted by scattering seed on the lawn.

Can be mistaken for

Almost unmistakable on account of its plumage colouring and the distinctive neck markings.

Turtle dove

Streptopelia turtur

REGION: Widespread summer visitor to much of Europe (mainly May to August) but absent from parts of the north and west, and declining in many regions • SIZE: 27 cm (11 in) • FOOD: Seeds and leaves. • SONG: A distinctive, continuous purring *coo* • SEX DIFFERENCES: The sexes are similar • JUVENILE: Similar to the adults but the colours are duller and there are no neck markings • FLIGHT: Rapid and direct, on clipped wingbeats • NEST: A twiggy structure, usually sited in a bush.

The turtle dove is an extremely attractive bird and a good view will reveal the well-marked back, the dark-centred orange-brown feathers creating a scaly appearance. The plumage is otherwise lilac-blue or brown, flushed with pink on the breast. Adults have a bright red ring around the eye and a patch of black-and-white stripes on the neck. In flight, the white-tipped, dark tail feathers are a striking feature in birds of all ages.

Turtle doves migrate in flocks, to and from their wintering grounds in Africa. At the end of the breeding season, just before their departure in August or September, they often gather in sizeable groups to feed on seeds in arable fields.

Habitat

Arable fields and open grassland, with scrub and hedgerows for nesting.

How to attract this bird to your garden

If your garden is surrounded by open country then try scattering seeds on your lawn; you are most likely to succeed in the summer months. If you live in warm, southern parts of the region a drinking pool may appeal to the birds.

Can be mistaken for

Collared dove (see pages 110–111), but that species has more uniformly buffish plumage, different habitat preferences and is present all year (turtle doves are seasonal visitors only).

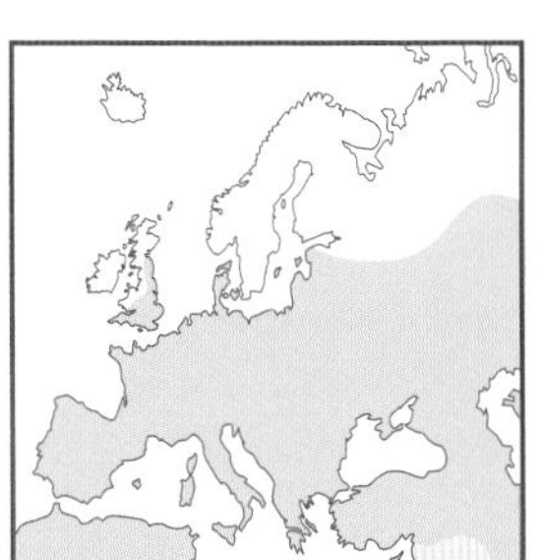

Adult

Stock dove

Columba oenas

REGION: Widespread resident in western Europe; numbers are boosted in winter by influxes of flocks from summer breeding grounds farther east • SIZE: 33 cm (13 in) • FOOD: Seeds, including cereal grains, and shoots and leaves • SONG: A distinctive and much-repeated *oo-u-look* phrase • SEX DIFFERENCES: The sexes are similar • JUVENILE: Similar to the adults, but its wingbars are less striking • FLIGHT: Rapid and direct, with distinctly 'flicked' wingbeats • NEST: A rudimentary twiggy structure, sited in a tree hole or on a ledge in a farm building. The species will sometimes use large, open-fronted nest boxes.

Because it is superficially similar to the woodpigeon, this species is sometimes overlooked and it is often only the distinctive song (heard in spring and summer) that alerts people to its presence in a given area. To confuse matters further, stock doves often feed alongside woodpigeons outside the breeding season.

In poor light, a stock dove can look rather dull and unremarkable. However, in good light, the plumage appears lilac-blue overall, with a strong pinkish flush to the breast. A green metallic sheen adorns the feathers of the nape and there are two short wingbars.

Habitat

Needs open land, in particular arable fields or parkland, for feeding and adjacent hedgerows and woodland for nesting.

How to attract this bird to your garden

You are only likely to attract this species if you live in a rural area, especially one where arable crops predominate. Outside the breeding season, it may be attracted if you scatter seed across open areas of lawn. In spring, it may nest (in a tree hole, for example) in gardens that border open countryside.

Can be mistaken for

Rock dove (see pages 108–109), but note the stock dove's shorter, dark wingbars, the absence of a pale rump and different habitat preference; also woodpigeon (see pages 106–107), but the stock dove has dark wingbars and no white on the neck or wings.

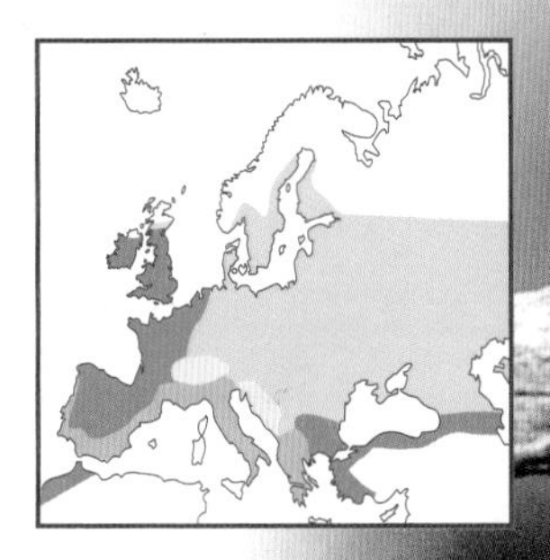

Adult

Rose-coloured starling

Sturnus roseus

REGION: A summer visitor to the east of the region in variable numbers and present from May to August. In so-called invasion years, hundreds of individuals head westwards and some even reach the British Isles. It is also found, in much smaller numbers, among starling flocks in winter • SIZE: 19–22 cm (7½–9 in) • FOOD: Insects and other invertebrates, as well as fruits and berries in season • CALL: Consists of various squawking phrases • SONG: A series of harsh, scratchy and trilling notes • SEX DIFFERENCES: Superficially similar but males typically have much brighter colours than females • JUVENILE: A rather uniform sandy grey-brown colour, darkest on the wings and with a yellow bill • FLIGHT: Rapid wingbeats, interspersed with short glides, on triangular-shaped wings • NEST: An untidy collection of leaves and grasses, tucked away in a crevice or cavity among boulders or in stone walls.

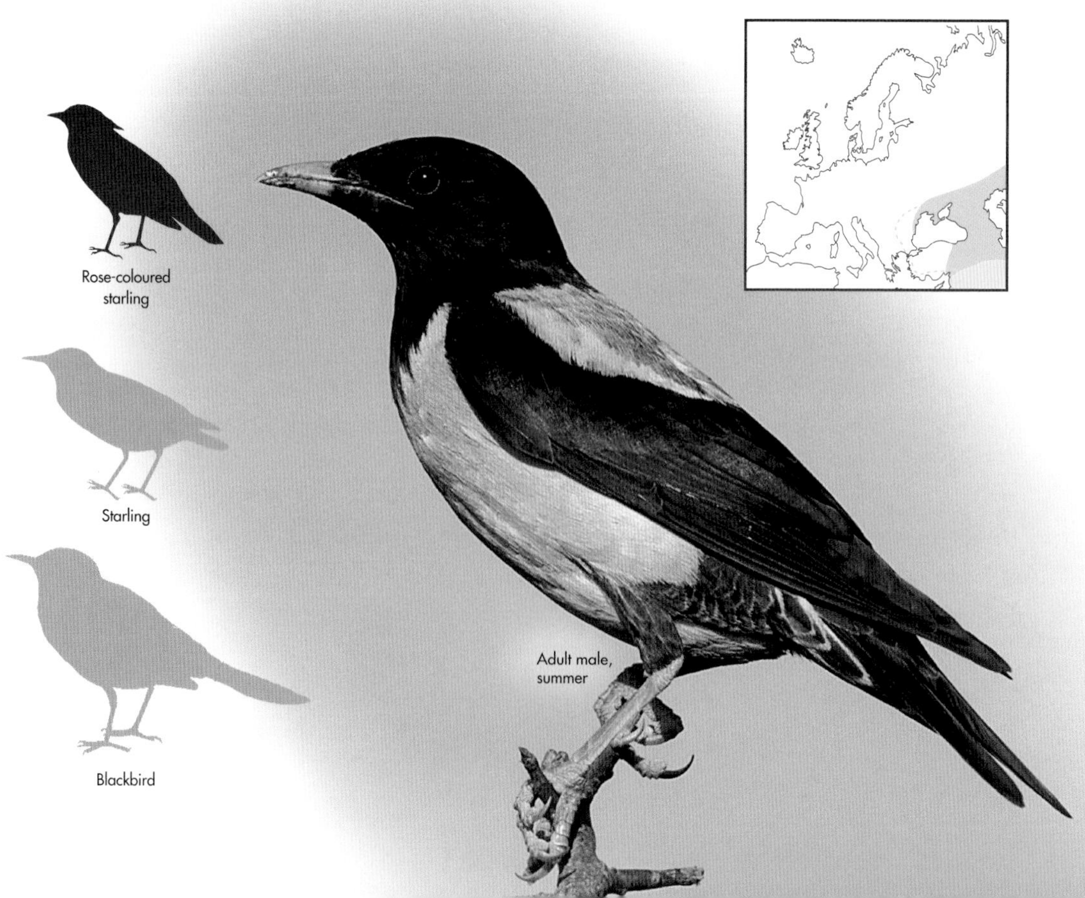

Adult male, summer

A brightly marked male is hard to confuse with any other species although in some individuals the colours can look a bit washed out. During the breeding season, where you see one rose-coloured starling, you are likely to see dozens, if not hundreds, because the species nests colonially. Flocks also go off to feed together and descend on agricultural fields like an army, devouring locusts and other large insects readily.

On the ground, rose-coloured starlings walk with a swaggering gait and often raise their crests if excited or agitated. When feeding in a tree, they can be surprisingly difficult to spot because their pink and blackish plumage blends in very well with dappled foliage.

Habitat

Associated with open farmland during the breeding season, but only in locations where the farming methods are not intensive and hence insects are abundant. It usually nests in nearby stone quarries, even those that are in use.

How to attract this bird to your garden

Newly arrived migrants usually appear (in early May) just as mulberries are beginning to ripen, and they have a real passion for these fruits, so they may investiage if you plant a black mulberry tree (*Morus nigra*). If you attract starling flocks to your garden in winter, try looking for a stray rose-coloured starling among them.

Can be mistaken for

The adults are unmistakable when taking into account their colours, but a juvenile could be confused with a juvenile starling (see pages 116–117); the yellow (not blackish) bill helps distinguish the two.

Above A juvenile rose-coloured starling lacks an adult's bright colours but the striking yellow bill is a useful aid to identification.

Starling

Sturnus vulgaris

REGION: Widespread year-round in much of western and southeast Europe; its numbers are boosted in winter by influxes of birds from farther north and east, where they are summer visitors. Strictly a winter visitor to the Iberian Peninsula (see also spotless starling, page 118) • SIZE: 20–22 cm (8–9 in) • FOOD: A varied diet that includes seeds, fruits and insects • CALL: Various clicks and whistles • SONG: Famed for its ability to mimic not only other bird songs but also such man-made sounds as car alarms and wolf whistles • SEX DIFFERENCES: In summer, females have more white spots on the underparts than males and a pale yellow (not bluish) base to the lower mandible of the bill. In winter, the sexes are similar, both having numerous white spots on the plumage, and brown fringes to the wing feathers • JUVENILE: Rather uniformly buffish-brown with dark bill • FLIGHT: Fast and slightly undulating, the rapid wingbeats interspersed with short glides. Note the triangular wing outline • NEST: A ramshackle affair of twigs and scraps of rubbish, these days usually sited in the roof of a house.

On a dull day, a starling can appear rather uniformly dark. However, seen in good light, a remarkable oily sheen (purplish or greenish, depending on the angle) adorns the feathers. Furthermore, depending on the time of year, the tips of the body feathers are marked with pale spots that add to this species' rather ornate appearance.

Watch a group of starlings feeding on the lawn and you will notice that they have a distinctive gait and walk with a rather leggy swagger. The long, pointed bill is used to probe the ground for earthworms, insect larvae and other invertebrates.

Outside the breeding season, starlings form huge flocks that often comprise thousands (sometimes tens of thousands) of individuals. As dusk approaches, they take to the wing and fly in close formation, diving and veering in unison, as they go to roost. Favoured roosting locations in the countryside are large woodlands but in more urban settings they often spend the night on buildings, bridges and other man-made structures.

Habitat

Often associated with suburban gardens, especially during the breeding season; in winter, the biggest numbers are found on farmland and in open country.

Above A juvenile starling has more subdued and paler plumage colours than an adult, but note the similar body and bill shape.

How to attract this bird to your garden

Little effort is needed to attract this species to the garden and it is a regular visitor to most bird tables, especially in urban locations.

Can be mistaken for

Unmistakable across most of Europe but could be confused with a spotless starling (see page 118), which is more or less restricted to the Iberian Peninsula where the starling is strictly a winter visitor.

Above A flock of songbirds flying over farmland in winter are likely to be starlings.

Spotless starling

Sturnus unicolor

REGION: Resident, restricted to the Iberian Peninsula, Corsica, Sicily and Sardinia • SIZE: 19–22 cm (7½–9 in) • FOOD: A varied diet that includes seeds, fruits and insects • CALL: Various clicks and whistles • SONG: Similar to that of the starling but with less mimicry • SEX DIFFERENCES: The sexes are similar in the summer months; in winter, females are adorned with a few, tiny pale spots • JUVENILE: Similar to winter adult females • FLIGHT: Fast and slightly undulating, with rapid wingbeats interspersed with short glides. Note the triangular wing outline • NEST: An untidy arrangement of twigs (as well as pieces of litter) sited in the roof of old buildings, or in cliff crevices.

This rather uniform species is the southwestern European counterpart of the starling. In most respects, its habits are similar to those of its close relative and it probes the ground for insect grubs, and walks with a characteristic swagger. In good light, note the hint of green or purplish (depending on the angle) sheen to the feathers, and the shaggy crest that is sometimes raised on the nape of the neck.

Spotless starlings are often found around farms. The presence of a drinking pond will act like a magnet for this species in summer.

Habitat

Often found in the vicinity of rural villages and farm buildings or feeding in open countryside.

How to attract this bird to your garden

They may choose to nest in a dilapidated old shed, or in your roof. Food scattered on the ground will attract small flocks, especially outside the breeding season.

Can be mistaken for

Starling (see pages 116–117) during the winter only, because the two species' ranges do not overlap in summer; a good point to look for is the absence (or virtual absence, in the case of winter females) of pale spots on the plumage.

Adult, summer

Golden oriole

Oriolus oriolus

REGION: A widespread summer visitor to much of central and southern Europe • SIZE: 22–24 cm (9–9½ in) • FOOD: Insects and other invertebrates picked off foliage or sometimes taken in mid-air during migration • CALL: Utters strange, almost cat-like alarm calls • SONG: A wonderful series of fluty phrases • SEX DIFFERENCES: Males are much more brightly coloured than females • JUVENILE: Similar to adult females but with more heavily streaked underparts • FLIGHT: Rapid and direct • NEST: Beautifully woven structure, made from grasses and slung in the fork of a branch.

The golden oriole has one of the most beautiful and distinctive songs of any European bird. Indeed the fluty tones often sound distinctly out of place in the context of Europe, and more akin to something you would hear in the tropics.

A male golden oriole's stunning plumage is more than a match for his song. However, although the yellow elements are bright and vivid, the bird itself can be remarkably difficult to spot as it lurks in the dappled shade of tree foliage.

Habitat

Usually associated with deciduous woodland.

How to attract this bird to your garden

If you live in a comparatively treeless area, plant a grove of poplars and after a decade or so the trees may be mature enough to attract nesting birds.

Can be mistaken for

Adults are unmistakable. In flight, a juvenile could perhaps be confused with a green woodpecker (see pages 190–191), although that species' ground-feeding habits and undulating flight allows distinction between the two.

Adult female

Tree sparrow

Passer montanus

REGION: Widespread resident across much of Europe; least numerous where modern farming practices are employed • SIZE: 13–14 cm (*c.* 5½ in) • FOOD: Mainly seeds, but some insects, particularly in summer • CALL: Various sparrow-like chirps, but a distinctive *tik-tik* in flight • SONG: A series of rapid twittering and chirping notes • SEX DIFFERENCES: The sexes are similar • JUVENILE: Similar to the adults but with duller colours • FLIGHT: Flight is rather bouncy • NEST: A large, loose structure of woven grasses and straw, sited in a tree hole; they will also use nest boxes.

As little brown birds go, this is an attractive and well-marked species with a rich, chestnut cap and clean-looking whitish cheeks marked with a dark 'ear' spot. Whitish wingbars add to the effect. Its buffish-brown rump is easiest to see in flight.

Although the tree sparrow is frequently associated with villages and farms, it is generally considered to be the rural counterpart to the house sparrow. Sizeable flocks form outside the breeding season, and often feed on grain spills or forage for fallen seeds in stubble fields that have been harvested but not ploughed. Unsurprisingly, traditional (not to say, untidy) farms provide richer pickings for this species than ones where 21st-century farming methods are favoured.

In many parts of Europe (particularly the northwest) tree sparrow numbers have declined almost catastrophically in the last decade. Changes in agricultural practices,

Above During the winter months, tree sparrows form small flocks and forage, mainly on the ground, for seeds.

notably the lack of winter stubble fields and more 'efficient' harvesting, are thought to have robbed this species (and many other farmland birds) of much of their food.

Tree sparrow

House sparrow

Chaffinch

Habitat

Gardens, allotments and small farms, but only those at the 'untidy' end of the spectrum.

How to attract this bird to your garden

Leave 'wild' patches where weeds can flourish to provide food for this species. Tree sparrows will use hole-fronted nest boxes, but because they tend to nest colonially you will need to site several in close proximity to one another to stand a chance of success.

Can be mistaken for

House sparrow (see pages 122–123), but the chestnut cap and black spot on the 'ear' allow you to be sure of the identity (in addition, the house sparrow's rump is grey rather than buffish-brown); male Spanish sparrows (see page 124) have extensive dark streaking on the body.

Adult

House sparrow

Passer domesticus

REGION: Widespread across most of Europe but its numbers are declining alarmingly in parts of the northwest of the region • SIZE: 14–15 cm (5½–6 in) • FOOD: Mainly seeds, but some insects, particularly in the breeding season • CALL: Various sparrow-like chirps • SONG: A series of call-like chirps • SEX DIFFERENCES: Males are more striking than females, with black on the face, throat and breast, and richer chestnut on the upperparts • JUVENILE: Similar to adult females • FLIGHT: Rapid and bounding • NEST: A large and untidy structure made from grasses and straw, sited in a cavity in a building or sometimes in a thick bush.

Arguably, there is no species that is more closely associated with people than the house sparrow. Invariably it nests in buildings (or close to human habitation) and it is dependent to a large degree on the activities of people for food.

Adult male

Above Female house sparrows are perky little birds, their engaging behaviour making up for their rather drab appearance.

In locations where they are not discouraged, house sparrows can become remarkably tame, and are sometimes even willing to feed from the hand. They are a familiar sight in many cities, often feeding alongside feral pigeons and other urban residents.

Outside the breeding season, the species forms flocks and these are most apparent in farmland areas. Seen in isolation, a female house sparrow looks rather drab and nondescript, almost bunting-like. However, they are invariably seen in the company of males, which makes identification a whole lot easier.

Habitat

Town and city gardens and parks, as well as farms and villages in rural areas.

How to attract this bird to your garden

Scatter seeds on your lawn and you should attract a small flock of this species. They often nest in roof cavities but will also use hole-fronted, communal nest boxes.

Can be mistaken for

Males could be confused with tree sparrows (see pages 120–121), but that species has a chestnut (not grey) cap and a brown (not grey) rump. Females are essentially indistinguishable from female Spanish sparrows (see page 124), but geographical range and the fact that they are always seen in association with males helps identification.

Spanish sparrow

Passer hispaniolensis

REGION: Locally resident in southern Iberia, Sardinia and Sicily; summer visitor to southeastern Europe • SIZE: 14–16 cm (5½–6½ in) • FOOD: Mainly seeds, but some insects, especially in the breeding season • CALL: Various sparrow-like chirps • SONG: A rapid series of call-like chirps • SEX DIFFERENCES: Males are much more strikingly marked than females, with bold black streaking on the back and flanks, and rich chestnut on the crown. Females are drab and essentially indistinguishable from female house sparrows • JUVENILE: Similar to an adult female • FLIGHT: Rapid and bounding • NEST: A large and untidy structure of woven grasses and straw, usually sited in a bush; typically the species nests communally in large colonies.

Where you see one Spanish sparrow you are likely to see tens, if not hundreds, of individuals because throughout their lives they are extremely gregarious. Flocks feed, drink and bathe together and the species even nests communally. Particularly in southeastern Europe, these colonies can be so large (hundreds of pairs) that the noise of the birds is almost deafening.

Like many warm-country birds, the Spanish sparrow is very fond of water and seldom strays far from a reliable site for bathing and drinking.

Habitat

Rural villages and farms, usually in the vicinity of water.

How to attract this bird to your garden

If you live close to water, plant tall, dense shrubs and trees for it to nest in; it seems particularly fond of mature palm trees, when dead leaf fronds are allowed to persist. Also a pool in the garden will be particularly attractive to this species, especially during the hot summer months.

Can be mistaken for

Males are almost unmistakable because of their bold black markings; females are hard to separate from female house sparrows (see pages 122–123), unless you see them with males of the species.

Adult male

Rock sparrow

Petronia petronia

REGION: A widespread but rather local resident in southern Europe • SIZE: 15–17 cm (6–7 in) • FOOD: Insects and seeds • CALL: A rather peculiar nasal note • SONG: Repeated variations of call-like notes • SEX DIFFERENCES: The sexes are similar • JUVENILE: Similar to the adults • FLIGHT: Rapid and direct • NEST: A rudimentary structure of grasses, sited in a cavity in a wall or building, or in a rock crevice.

You are only likely to encounter this species if your garden is bordered by arid, rocky terrain. It can be rather unobtrusive and one of the best ways to detect its presence is to listen for its distinctive call, which is quite unlike the chirp of a house sparrow.

Rock sparrows are often seen perched on a rock, or sometimes on the roof of an old building in a rural location. In good light, you will notice the rather large bill and bold dark and pale stripes on the head. The best feature to look for is the pale yellow spot on the throat. However, you will need a particularly good view to see it because it is often rather indistinct, or partly obscured by other throat feathers.

Habitat

Favours arid, rocky terrain in warmer, southern parts of Europe.

How to attract this bird to your garden

Unrepaired cavities in old buildings may sometimes be used for nesting; the species breeds colonially so several suitable sites must be present in close proximity. A drinking pool in the garden is likely to be popular, particularly during the hot summer months.

Can be mistaken for

Female house sparrow (see pages 122–123), but check for the rock sparrow's striking stripes on the head and the subtle yellow spot on the throat.

Adult

Chaffinch

Fringilla coelebs

REGION: A widespread year-round resident in much of Europe; numbers are boosted during the winter months by influxes of birds from the north and east that migrate back from their summer breeding ranges • SIZE: 15 cm (6 in) • FOOD: Seeds and nuts, but some insects and other invertebrates, particularly during the breeding season • CALL: A sharp *pink-pink* • SONG: A descending series of trilling notes that ends in a flourish • SEX DIFFERENCES: Males are flushed with pink on the face and underparts, and show blue on the head and chestnut on the back. By contrast, females are more uniformly buffish-brown, with a hint of green on the back • JUVENILE: Similar to adult females • FLIGHT: Fast and direct, often with short bursts of rapid wingbeats interspersed with short glides • NEST: A cup-shaped structure, woven from grasses, camouflaged with lichens and sited in a bush.

If you have deciduous trees in your garden then the chances are that small groups of chaffinches will be paying regular visits during the winter, whether or not you put out food for them. At this time of year they often feed on the ground but are not always easy to see because they forage among fallen leaves for seeds.

Above Despite its rather drab, buffish plumage, a female chaffinch shows bold white wingbars and these aid identification.

Male and female chaffinches are both quite striking and distinctive in the air, revealing white patches on the shoulders and wingbars as they take flight. Outside the breeding season, the species tends to form flocks and often associates with other finch species at good feeding locations.

Because of its varied diet and wide choice of habitats, the chaffinch is one of the most numerous birds in the region. Many tens of millions of pairs probably breed in Europe and numbers are swollen in winter when influxes of birds from farther east occur.

Habitat

A wide range of habitats from deciduous woodland and farmland to parks and gardens.

How to attract this bird to your garden

Scatter seeds and nuts on the lawn, or on a bird table, to attract them, particularly in the winter. Encourage dense shrubs, and they may nest in the garden, too.

Can be mistaken for

Brambling in winter plumage (see pages 128–129), but that species has clean, whitish underparts and pale rump.

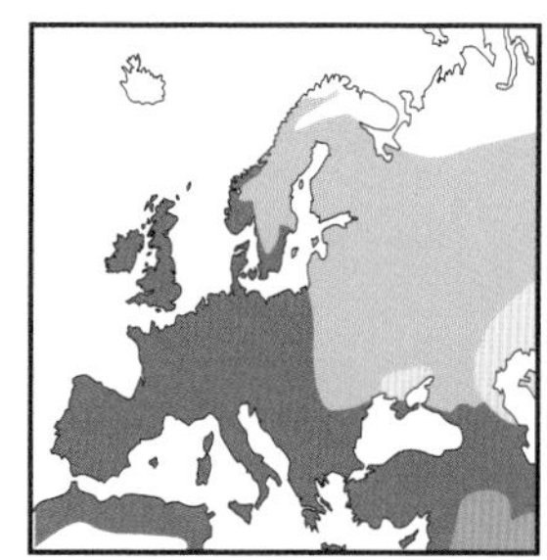

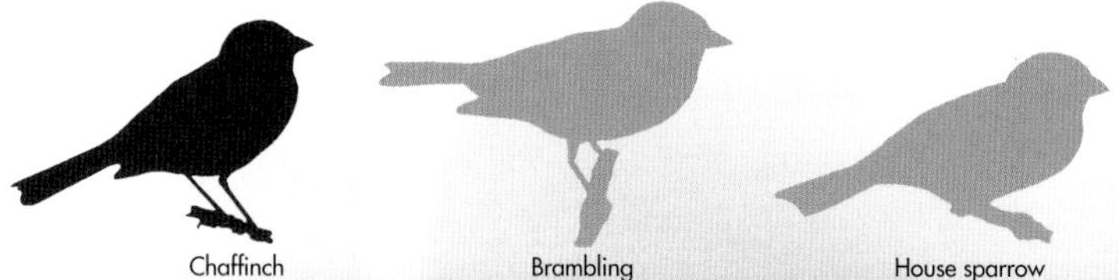

Adult male, summer

Brambling

Fringilla montifringilla

REGION: Widespread summer visitor to northern Europe; strictly a winter visitor to more southerly parts of the region; seen on migration across the region, except Iceland • SIZE: 14–15 cm (5½–6 in) • FOOD: Seeds and nuts, and particularly fond of beech seeds in winter. Also some insects and other invertebrates, particularly during the breeding season • CALL: Utters a harsh *eerrp* • SONG: A distinctive and slowly rendered mixture of rasping, buzzing and whistling notes • SEX DIFFERENCES: Males have more colourful and contrasting plumage than females. In summer the male's head and back are blackish while in winter these areas are much paler due to the presence of pale feather tips • JUVENILE: Similar to an adult female • FLIGHT: Rapid and direct • NEST: A woven structure, made from grasses and camouflaged with lichens, sited in the fork of a tree.

In many ways, the brambling is the northern counterpart to the chaffinch, at least in the context of Europe. Although it is a widespread breeding species in Scandinavia (including in gardens), elsewhere in Europe it is strictly a winter visitor.

Outside the breeding season, bramblings are usually found in flocks that can number hundreds of birds. Although they are sometimes found feeding in stubble fields, their preferred habitat is beech woodland in which the trees are mature enough to produce copious quantities of seed. Lone bramblings are often found among chaffinch flocks. Bramblings are subtly attractive birds that have a very unusual (among birds of this size) orange flush to the breast and on the shoulders. They also have striking pale wingbars that often appear flushed orange during the winter. In flight, the white rump and lower back are striking.

Above Although a female brambling is less striking than a male, the orange flush to the breast and shoulders is easily discerned.

Habitat

Deciduous and mixed woodland during the breeding season; the brambling favours beech woods and farmland in winter.

How to attract this bird to your garden

Put out seeds on the lawn or on a bird table and you may attract this species in winter, especially if you live close to beech woodland.

Can be mistaken for

Chaffinch (see pages 126–127), but a brambling has whiter underparts, pale rump and orange (not pinkish) flush to the breast.

Above In flight, a flock of bramblings keeps in close formation. Note the diagnostic pale rump.

Goldfinch

Carduelis carduelis

REGION: Widespread and occurs year-round in much of Europe; many birds from northern breeding populations move south in winter, or in response to harsh weather • SIZE: 13–14 cm (*c.* 5½ in) • FOOD: Mainly seeds, but some insects, particularly in the breeding season • CALL: Utters a tinkling call • SONG: Rapid and twittering • SEX DIFFERENCES: The sexes are similar • JUVENILE: Has the yellow wingbars of the adults but lacks the striking markings and colours on the face • FLIGHT: Rapid but fluttering and undulating; typically, flocks change direction constantly in flight • NEST: A beautifully woven structure made from moss and animal hair, sited in a bush.

Above Although its body plumage is subdued compared to an adult, a juvenile goldfinch still reveals striking colours on the wings.

During the winter months, small flocks of goldfinches are a familiar sight in places where seed-bearing plants are common. In many situations, the birds are not bothered by the presence of human observers and can be watched from extremely close quarters. If they do take to the wing, they do not usually fly far, and the striking yellow wingbar and hint of a pale rump make them easy to follow.

Goldfinches have relatively long, slender bills that are ideally adapted for extracting seeds from the dead heads of plants such as teasels (*Dipsacus fullonum*) and thistles (for example, *Circium* spp. and *Carduus* spp.). Although they are usually seen feeding a few metres from the ground, flocks are sometimes observed in the tops of alder trees (*Alnus glutinosa*), feeding on their seeds in the company of siskins. Over the last decade or so, goldfinches have become increasingly frequent in gardens. They are adept at hanging on bird feeders and extracting seed fragments with their bills. Once a flock has discovered a source of food, it is likely to remain faithful to the site throughout the winter.

Habitat

Meadows, waste ground, parks and gardens.

How to attract this bird to your garden

Goldfinches are attracted to black sunflower seeds placed in feeders but their favourite food is teasel seeds. So grow this plant in your flower borders and let the dead heads remain *in situ* throughout the winter.

Can be mistaken for

Unmistakable as as adult on account of the colourful plumage; juveniles show more yellow in wings than other small finches and the pale rump also helps in identification.

Linnet

Carduelis cannabina

REGION: Widespread year-round across much of Europe but northern and eastern populations are mainly migrant summer visitors • SIZE: 13–14 cm (*c.* 5½ in) • FOOD: Mainly seeds, but some insects, especially during the breeding season • CALL: A rapid, twittering *teeta-tett*, uttered in flight • SONG: A twittering warble • SEX DIFFERENCES: Males are more colourful than females during the summer months; the sexes are more similar in winter • JUVENILE: Similar to adult females • FLIGHT: Rapid and slightly undulating or bouncing • NEST: A woven structure made from grasses and sited in a bush.

Although female linnets have rather subdued plumage, breeding males are decidedly colourful. The head has a blue-grey colouring but the forehead, as well as the breast, is flushed with rosy pink. To add to the overall effect, the back is a rich chestnut brown.

Linnet

Goldfinch

Siskin

Adult male, summer

Outside the breeding season, the species is seen in flocks, which search on the ground and among the dead heads of meadow flowers for seeds. Linnets are restless birds, however, and seldom stay in the same place for more than a minute or so.

At the start of the breeding season, male linnets are keen songsters and sing their energetic, twittering songs from a prominent perch – often the top of a bush or tree. In good years, pairs may manage to rear two or three broods.

Habitat

Heathland, scrub, waste ground and mature gardens.

How to attract this bird to your garden

If you have herbaceous borders in your garden, delay cutting back the dead flower heads until the early spring and these seed-eaters may visit in autumn and winter.

Can be mistaken for

Twite (see page 134) with which it sometimes associates in winter; however, twites have a more uniformly streaked brown appearance and a yellow bill in winter (this is grey in linnets).

Above A juvenile linnet is superficially similar to an adult female but has a subtly warmer (yellowish) hue.

Above An adult female linnet has pale underparts streaked darker on the breast and flanks.

Twite

Carduelis flavirostris

REGION: Restricted to northwest Europe during the breeding season but its range extends farther south during the winter months • SIZE: 13–14 cm (*c.* 5½ in) • FOOD: Mainly the seeds of low-growing plants • CALL: Utters a sharp little call that sounds a bit like its English name • SEX DIFFERENCES: Male has well-defined streaks and a pinkish rump in summer; winter male resembles a female (throughout the year) with more uniformly buffish-brown plumage and fainter streaks • JUVENILE: Similar to adult females • FLIGHT: Bursts of rapid wingbeats interspersed with short glides • NEST: Sited in a tussock and made of woven grasses and mosses.

A rather nondescript little bird that can confuse the beginner. In many ways, the twite is the northern and upland counterpart of the linnet, at least during the summer months.

During the breeding season, territorial males are often rather bold and will perch conspicuously on fence posts and boulders. In winter, they form flocks that search for seeds in a creeping, almost mouse-like manner. Typically, they are restless birds and seldom stay put for more than a minute or so before taking to the wing as a flock in search of somewhere else to feed.

Habitat

Twites favour moorland habitat during the breeding season but are found on saltmarshes and ploughed coastal fields in winter.

How to attract this bird to your garden

If you live near the coast of northwest Europe, scatter seeds on bare, open ground in the winter and you might be lucky. If you live within the species' breeding range and in suitable habitat, try the same thing in spring and summer.

Can be mistaken for

Linnet (see pages 132–133), which it has been known to associate with during the winter, but look for the unstreaked throat (streaked in linnets); redpoll (see opposite), which has a reddish patch on the forehead, and favours wooded, not open, habitats.

Adult male, summer

Redpoll

Carduelis flammea

REGION: A widespread resident in northern Europe (although some populations in the far north are migrant summer visitors) and upland regions farther south; in lowland central Europe it is a winter visitor • SIZE: 12–14 cm (5–5½ in) • FOOD: Mainly seeds • CALL: Utters a four-note rattling call in flight • SONG: A mixture of rattling and wheezy phrases • SEX DIFFERENCES: Males are flushed with pinkish-red on the breast • JUVENILE: Similar to adult females but it lacks the red forehead • FLIGHT: Bouncy and undulating • NEST: A woven structure of grasses and twigs, sited in a tree or bush.

For all its small size and dumpy appearance, an adult redpoll is an attractive and well-marked little bird. Although it is only the males that are flushed with reddish-pink on the breast, both sexes have striking white wingbars and a unique (for a bird of this size) combination of a red forehead and black chin. Overall, northern birds are paler than those from the south of the species' European range.

Redpolls are easiest to see during the winter, when they form flocks and often mix with siskins (see pages 138–139). Typically the birds feed in the tops of trees, searching for seeds, and alders (*Alnus glutinosa*) are a particular favourite at this time of year (they keep their seed-bearing cones throughout the winter). Redpolls are extremely agile little birds and often hang upside down from slender twigs while feeding.

Habitat

Redpolls favour wooded habitats especially where alder (*Alnus glutinosa*), birches (*Betula sp.*) and larches (*Larix sp.*) predominate.

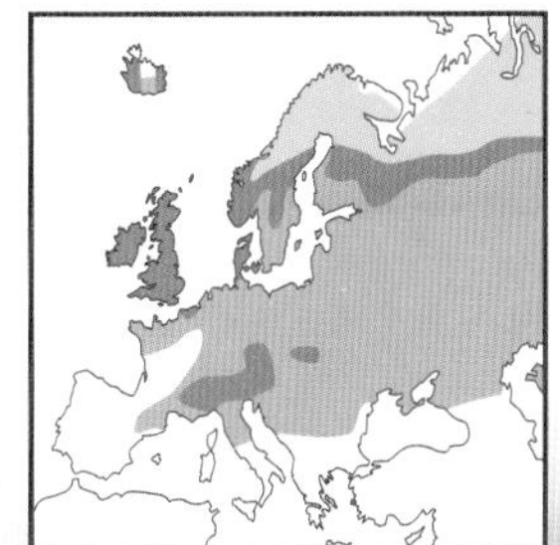

How to attract this bird to your garden

Mature birch and alder trees provide seeds for redpolls in autumn and winter. The species is an increasingly regular visitor to garden feeders, especially where sunflower seeds are provided.

Can be mistaken for

Juvenile could be mistaken for a twite (see opposite) or juvenile linnet (see pages 132–133).

Adult male, winter

Bullfinch

Pyrrhula pyrrhula

REGION: Widespread year-round across much of central and northern Europe; populations from the far north of the species' European range tend to migrate south outside the breeding season and the species is a winter visitor to southern Europe • SIZE: 16–17 cm (6½–7 in) • FOOD: Mainly seeds, berries and buds, but some insects in the breeding season • CALL: A soft piping, with pairs sometimes duetting • SONG: Soft and slow, with subdued piping notes, but seldom heard • SEX DIFFERENCES: Males have a much more intense pinkish-red flush to the underparts than do females • JUVENILE: Similar to adult females but the black cap is absent • FLIGHT: Bouncing and low, typically only over short distances • NEST: A woven structure of thin twigs, sited in a bush.

Although bullfinches are not particularly rare, they lead unobtrusive lives and so are not observed as frequently as some of their cousins. Rather than feed in the open, they prefer to keep to the fringes of bushes and shrubs and will head into the cover these provide at the first sign of danger.

Throughout the year, the species is often found in pairs that stay in contact with one another by means of their piping calls. Although the sound is rather soft, it carries surprisingly far and, once you have learned it you can use it to detect bullfinches in a given area. No other species gives a call that is quite like it.

The colour seen on the breast of an adult male bullfinch is unique among European birds in terms of its precise hue, and is a useful guide to identification. A stubby, black bill and dark cap are

Above A female bullfinch has subdued plumage compared to a male, but the stubby bill and black cap make her recognizable.

common to both sexes and the striking white rump (most obvious in flight) is unique for a bush-dwelling garden bird of this size.

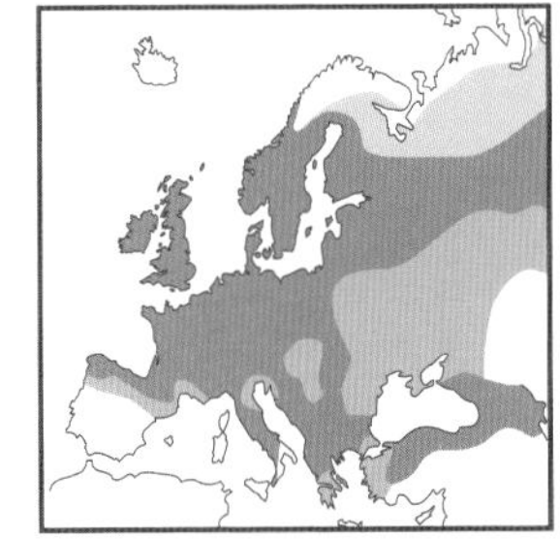

Habitat

Woodland margins, hedgerows and mature parks and gardens.

How to attract this bird to your garden

Bullfinches occasionally learn to visit bird feeders when sunflower seeds are provided. They are extremely fond of the flower buds of fruit trees in early spring, so not all gardeners will be keen to encourage them at this time of year!

Bullfinch Chaffinch Greenfinch

Can be mistaken for

Unmistakable when seen well, on account of the stubby bill, dark cap and white rump.

Adult male

Siskin

Carduelis spinus

REGION: Resident year-round in parts of central Europe; a summer visitor to the north and a winter visitor elsewhere in the region • SIZE: 11–12 cm (4½–5 in) • FOOD: Mainly seeds, but some insects in the breeding season • CALL: Twittering, two-syllable calls • SONG: A series of warbling and twittering notes • SEX DIFFERENCES: Males are more colourful than females, with the face and breast flushed yellow • JUVENILE: Rather uniformly grey-brown and streaked • FLIGHT: Bounding, with rapid wingbeats. In spring, the song is sometimes delivered in flight, which is then achieved on exaggerated, slowly flapping wingbeats • NEST: A woven structure of mosses and twigs, sited high in a conifer.

An adult male siskin is an extremely colourful and distinctive bird, flushed bright yellow across much of the body, and with a black cap and bib. In flight, birds of both sexes are transformed by their yellow wingbars, and by the conspicuous yellow rump and patches at the sides of the tail.

Outside the breeding season, when siskins are most usually encountered in lowland areas, they form flocks and sometimes associate with other finch species, notably redpolls (see page 135). Their thin, pointed bills are ideal for extracting seeds from the cones of alders and the catkins of birch trees. Siskins are regular visitors to garden feeders. Although they are comparatively small birds, they are pugnacious and stand their ground when other, larger, species try to drive them off a particular feeder.

Above A female siskin has pale underparts, streaked on the flanks, and striking yellow wingbars.

Habitat

Favours conifer woodland during the breeding season but usually associated with alder woodland in winter.

How to attract this bird to your garden

The species comes regularly, in small numbers, to bird feeders if peanuts or sunflower seeds are provided. Tall conifers may attract it to nest.

Can be mistaken for

Not unlike a greenfinch (see pages 140–141), especially when adult, but has a more slender bill and streaked flanks, and is smaller.

Siskin

Greenfinch

Goldfinch

Adult male, summer

Greenfinch

Carduelis chloris

REGION: Widespread year-round across much of Europe; numbers are boosted in winter by influxes of birds from farther east • SIZE: 14–15 cm (5½–6 in) • FOOD: Mainly seeds and berries • CALL: Utters a sharp flight call • SONG: A series of well-spaced whistling and wheezing phrases • SEX DIFFERENCES: Males are more colourful than females • JUVENILE: Rather uniformly greyish green, with streaked underparts • FLIGHT: Bounding and rapid. In spring, males sometimes perform a special song flight: the exaggeratedly slow, deep wingbeats give it a passing resemblance to a butterfly • NEST: Made from twigs and mosses and sited in a dense bush (often uses conifer hedges).

Although plumage colour varies throughout the year, and between the sexes, all adult greenfinches are yellowish-green to some degree. They have a diagnostic bright yellow band on the outer wing (striking in flight) and when they take to the wing the yellow sides to the tail are eyecatching.

Greenfinch

Siskin

Goldfinch

Adult male, summer

If you see a greenfinch perched or at a feeder, you will notice that it has a proportionately large head and a rather large, conical pinkish-grey bill. Like all of its finch cousins, it feeds mainly on seeds. The bill size allows the greenfinch to tackle a variety of seeds and berries from garden plants, including rose-hips, and the berries from yew (*Taxus baccata*). Outside the breeding season, greenfinches usually form small flocks. Several of these groups may come together (and form much larger aggregations) towards dusk in order to roost communally.

Above A female greenfinch has more subdued plumage than a male, but the striking yellow wingbar is a good identification point.

Habitat

Gardens, parks and farmland with hedgerows.

How to attract this bird to your garden

If you have a dense conifer hedge, then greenfinches may use this for nesting. The species is a regular visitor to garden feeders and seems particularly fond of sunflower seeds. Delay cutting back the seed-heads of any herbaceous perennial plants in your garden in order to provide the birds with a source of autumn and winter food.

Can be mistaken for

Could be mistaken perhaps for a siskin (see pages 138–139), but it is appreciably larger and has a much more substantial bill.

Above Although similar to an adult female greenfinch, a juvenile can be separated by its streaked and spotted underparts.

Hawfinch

Coccothraustes coccothraustes

REGION: Widespread year-round across much of Europe but generally rather scarce and local • SIZE: 17–18 cm (*c.* 7 in) • FOOD: Mainly seeds, but will eat some insects during the breeding season • CALL: A sharp, robin-like *tic* • SONG: Subdued and seldom heard • SEX DIFFERENCES: The sexes are similar although males are more colourful than females • JUVENILE: Similar to adult females • FLIGHT: Powerful and undulating • NEST: A twiggy structure, often sited in the fork of a tree.

This species is a giant among finches. Compared to its relatives, the body is proportionately large and plump. In addition, the bill is huge and gives the bird a distinctly front-heavy appearance. The bill is used to crack open hard seeds that are beyond the scope of its smaller cousins, such as hornbeam seeds and cherry stones.

The hawfinch is a rather shy bird and easy to miss. Try to learn its call and this will give you a head start when it comes to pinpointing this elusive species. Typically, it forms small flocks outside the breeding season and these can sometimes be discovered feeding unobtrusively among the branches of a tall deciduous tree. These flocks are easiest to locate in the dead of winter, when the leaves have fallen to the ground. In flight, the species is relatively easy to identify, partly on account of its large size (by finch standards) and because the massive head and bill make it look front-heavy. All birds show a considerable amount of white on the wings (more, say, than on a chaffinch) and much of the tail is white, too.

Habitat

Deciduous woodland and mature parks and gardens.

How to attract this bird to your garden

Hawfinches will sometimes visit drinking pools, especially during the summer. In summer, cherry stones are eaten, while in winter they choose hornbeam seeds.

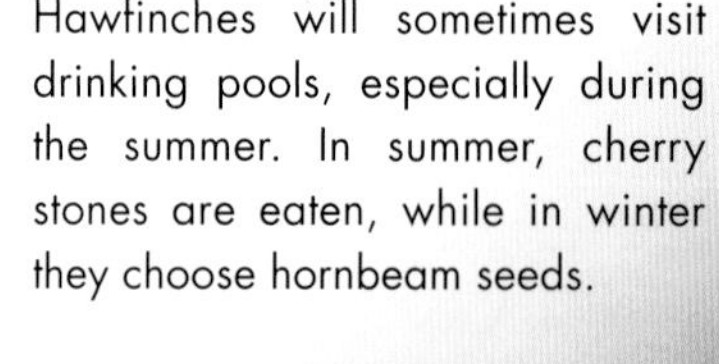

Can be mistaken for

Unmistakable, because of the huge bill size.

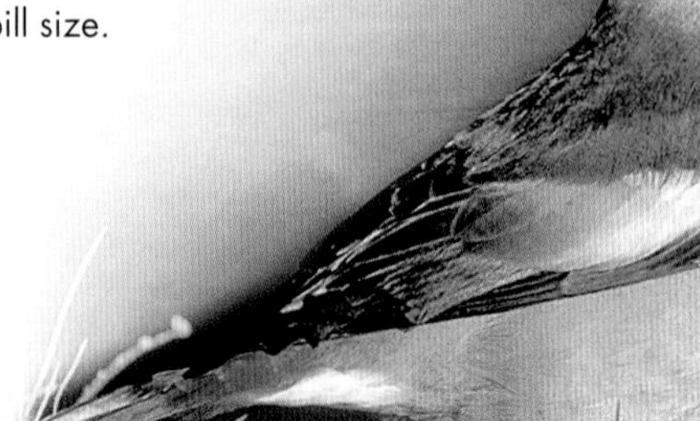

Adult male

Serin

Serinus serinus

REGION: Widespread year-round in southern Europe and a summer visitor in central regions • SIZE: 11–12 cm (4½–5 in) • FOOD: Mainly seeds, but eats some insects during the breeding season • CALL: A buzzing trill • SONG: A fast delivery of rapid, tinkling and jingling phrases • SEX DIFFERENCES: Males, which are flushed with yellow on the face and breast, are much more colourful than females, which are streaked brown overall • JUVENILE: Similar to adult females • FLIGHT: Rapid and undulating; males sometimes deliver song in flight, on exaggeratedly slow wingbeats • NEST: A woven structure of twigs and grasses, sited in a dense tree.

The serin is a welcome visitor to any garden, particularly in the spring when males deliver their wonderfully energetic songs.

Serins tend to feed on the ground, particularly outside the breeding season. At such times, they can be difficult to locate because they often prefer to remain partly hidden in ruts in the ground. Although the bill is stubby and small, it is surprisingly good at manipulating small seeds. If they are startled and take to the wing, the distinctive call is a useful pointer to help you to identify them.

Habitat

Orchards, gardens, parks and open woodland.

How to attract this bird to your garden

Plant a few tall-growing conifers (for nesting purposes) and allow seed-bearing 'weeds' to flourish in a few areas (their seeds are important as food). Serins also like to visit pools, for drinking and bathing, especially in hot weather.

Can be mistaken for

Adult male is almost unmistakable on account of its bright colours, but beware confusion (particularly in the case of females or juveniles) with siskins (see pages 138–139). The serin is extremely small, has a stubby little bill and no yellow on the sides of the tail.

Adult male, summer

Crossbill

Loxia curvirostra

REGION: Widespread but local and patchily distributed across much of Europe. Populations are often nomadic outside the breeding season • SIZE: 15–17 cm (6–7 in) • FOOD: Mainly conifer seeds • CALL: Utters a sharp *kip-kip-kip* in flight • SONG: A series of twitters and trills • SEX DIFFERENCES: Adult males are red while adult females are yellowish-green. Immature birds are patchily coloured • JUVENILE: Buffish-brown with bold, dark streaking • FLIGHT: Rapid and undulating • NEST: A woven, twiggy structure high in a conifer.

The crossbill has a uniquely shaped bill, the upper and lower mandibles of which overlap at the tip. At first glance this adaptation may seem a bit bizarre. However, if you watch a crossbill feeding, the function of the bill will become immediately apparent: it is ideally suited for parting the scales on a pine cone and extracting the seeds within.

The species has such a specialized bill and diet that it is seldom found away from mature conifer forests. However, this dependence of one type of food does have a drawback. Sometimes the harvest of pine cones fails in a particular area and rather than starve any crossbills that live there are forced to abandon the location, and wander far and wide in search of food supplies elsewhere.

Habitat

Conifer woodland.

How to attract this bird to your garden

Crossbills love to visit pools to drink and bathe so if you live in an area of conifer forest a regularly topped-up pond will attract them.

Can be mistaken for

Unmistakable if the bill is seen.

Adult male

Pine grosbeak

Pinicola enucleator

REGION: Restricted as a breeding species to northern Scandinavia; the species spreads southwards in winter, the precise range and extent of the spread depending on the severity of the weather • SIZE: 19–22 cm (7½–9 in) • FOOD: Seeds, buds and shoots of birch and spruce trees; also berries, in season • CALL: Utters a loud, fluty call in flight • SONG: A rapid series of ringing phrases • SEX DIFFERENCES: Males are flushed with red while females are greenish-yellow overall • JUVENILE: Similar to adult females but less colourful • FLIGHT: Fast and undulating • NEST: A twiggy structure, sited close to the trunk of a tree.

Although male and female pine grosbeaks differ in terms of their overall plumage colour, both share the same powerful, rounded bill shape and the striking white wing-bars. Outside the breeding season, the species forms flocks and typically these will descend upon berry-bearing trees in winter to feed. In spring, look for them feeding on the shoots and buds of deciduous trees and spruces.

During the breeding season, pine grosbeaks lead unobtrusive lives and can be extremely difficult to locate. However, during the winter months, feeding birds can be completely indifferent to human watchers and will allow you to approach closely.

Habitat

Conifer woodland.

How to attract this bird to your garden

Grow plenty of berry-bearing bushes and trees, especially rowan (*Sorbus aucuparia*), and a small flock may visit you if you are very lucky.

Can be mistaken for

Crossbill (see opposite page), although these do not have the pine grosbeak's white wingbars and the pine grosbeak's bill does not overlap at the tips.

Adult male

Cirl bunting

Emberiza cirlus

REGION: A widespread resident of southern and western Europe • SIZE: 16–17 cm (6½–7 in) • FOOD: Mainly seeds, but some insects during the breeding season • CALL: A sharp *tzip* • SONG: A rather tuneless rattle • SEX DIFFERENCES: Only males have the dark facial markings; these are at their boldest in spring and early summer. Females are streaked and olive-brown • JUVENILE: Similar to adult females • FLIGHT: Rapid and bounding • NEST: A woven structure of grasses and mosses, sited in a dense bush.

Cirl buntings are rather unobtrusive birds and are seldom especially numerous. Furthermore, they usually form only smallish flocks outside the breeding season and consequently they are easy to miss. The best time to locate them is the spring, when males sing their distinctive rattling songs.

Males are attractive birds: their yellowish faces are adorned with black on the throat and through the eye. An olive-grey breast band, and chestnut patches on the flanks mark the otherwise yellowish underparts; the back is mainly chestnut-brown. Females are more challenging to identify but, fortunately, they are usually seen with males and so you can recognize them by association.

Habitat

Found in the open countryside and farmland areas with small arable fields and plenty of hedgerows and scrub around.

How to attract this bird to your garden

Scatter seed on bare ground and you may be lucky. Provide water for them as they frequently drink from pools, especially during the hot summer months.

Can be mistaken for

Adult males are unmistakable, on account of colours and head markings. Females and juveniles could be confused with yellowhammers of similar sex and age (see pages 148–149), but that species has a chestnut (not olive-brown) rump.

Adult male, summer

Rock bunting

Emberiza cia

REGION: Resident in southern Europe; with birds from higher mountain slopes moving to lower levels in winter • SIZE: 15–17 cm (6–7 in) • FOOD: Mainly seeds, but some insects, especially during the breeding season • CALL: Utters a sharp *tsiip* • SONG: A series of tuneful, rasping phrases • SEX DIFFERENCES: Males are more colourful, and have bolder facial markings, than females • JUVENILE: Similar to adult females • FLIGHT: Rapid and undulating • NEST: A woven structure of grasses and mosses, sited in a dense bush.

Rock buntings are extremely distinctive birds, with blue-grey heads and necks adorned with striking and well-defined black lines; the back is chestnut, while the underparts are flushed with orange-buff. All of these features are seen in both sexes, although males are more boldly marked than females.

Rock buntings are rather unobtrusive and tend to feed on the ground, searching for seeds and insects. Typically pairs remain together throughout the year, even if they move to lower-altitude feeding grounds in winter. They are less likely to be found in flocks than other bunting species.

Above A female rock bunting has more subdued colours than a male.

Habitat

Rocky ground with scattered bushes and grassy areas.

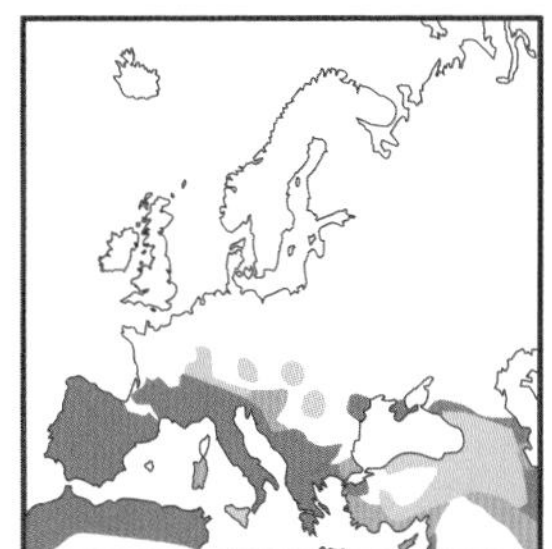

How to attract this bird to your garden

If your house is surrounded by suitable rocky terrain, you may be able to lure birds during summer months by providing a drinking pond.

Can be mistaken for

Almost unmistakable on account of colours and head markings.

Adult male, summer

Yellowhammer

Emberiza citrinella

REGION: Widespread year-round across much of central and northern Europe; a migrant summer visitor to the far north and absent from much of southern Europe, except as an occasional winter visitor • SIZE: 15–17 cm (6–7 in) • FOOD: Mainly seeds, but eats some insects, particularly in the breeding season • CALL: Utters a rasping call • SONG: A series of wheezy, jingling notes • SEX DIFFERENCES: Males are more colourful than females, especially during the breeding season • JUVENILE: Similar to adult females, but with heavy streaking on the head and breast • FLIGHT: Rapid and undulating • NEST: A woven structure of grasses, sited in a dense bush.

In spring, a male yellowhammer is one of our most colourful birds. The head and underparts are bright lemon yellow while the back and rump are a rich chestnut. Females are altogether more subdued in appearance, the head and breast being adorned with dark streaking. In flight, all individuals reveal striking white outer tail feathers when flying away.

Above Although not as colourful as a male, a female yellowhammer is still a strikingly yellow bird.

Yellowhammers are probably easiest to find during the breeding season when males perch prominently on the tops of bushes, singing or simply surveying their territories; at such times, they adopt a rather upright posture. At other times of the year, the species forms small flocks that feed in weedy fields and on ploughed land where they are easy to overlook.

The species does best in areas of lowland Europe where low-intensity arable farming methods are employed and there are plenty of dense, mature hedgerows for nesting and roosting. In winter, small flocks are sometimes found near grain spills, and where livestock are fed.

Habitat

Farmland and open country.

How to attract this bird to your garden

If you live in a rural area, try scattering grain on the ground to attract feeding flocks in winter.

Can be mistaken for

Adult males are unmistakable, but adult females and juveniles could be confused with an immature cirl bunting (see page 146), except for the colour of the rump, which is chestnut in yellowhammers and olive-brown in cirl buntings.

Above The streaked brown plumage of a juvenile yellowhammer is similar to that of other miniature buntings, but it has chestnut on the wings.

Yellowhammer

Reed bunting

Cirl bunting

Adult male,
summer

Reed bunting

Emberiza schoeniclus

REGION: Widespread year-round in much of central Europe, a migrant summer visitor to northern Europe and a winter visitor to the south • SIZE: 14–15 cm (5½–6 in) • FOOD: Mainly seeds in winter but also insects in the breeding season • CALL: Utters a thin call • SONG: A simple series of chinking notes • SEX DIFFERENCES: Both sexes have streaked chestnut upperparts and whitish underparts but only the male (in summer) sports the black cap and throat • JUVENILE: Similar to adult females • FLIGHT: Undulating and rather jerky • NEST: A woven structure of grasses, sited in a dense bush or tussock.

Reed bunting

Ortolan bunting

Yellowhammer

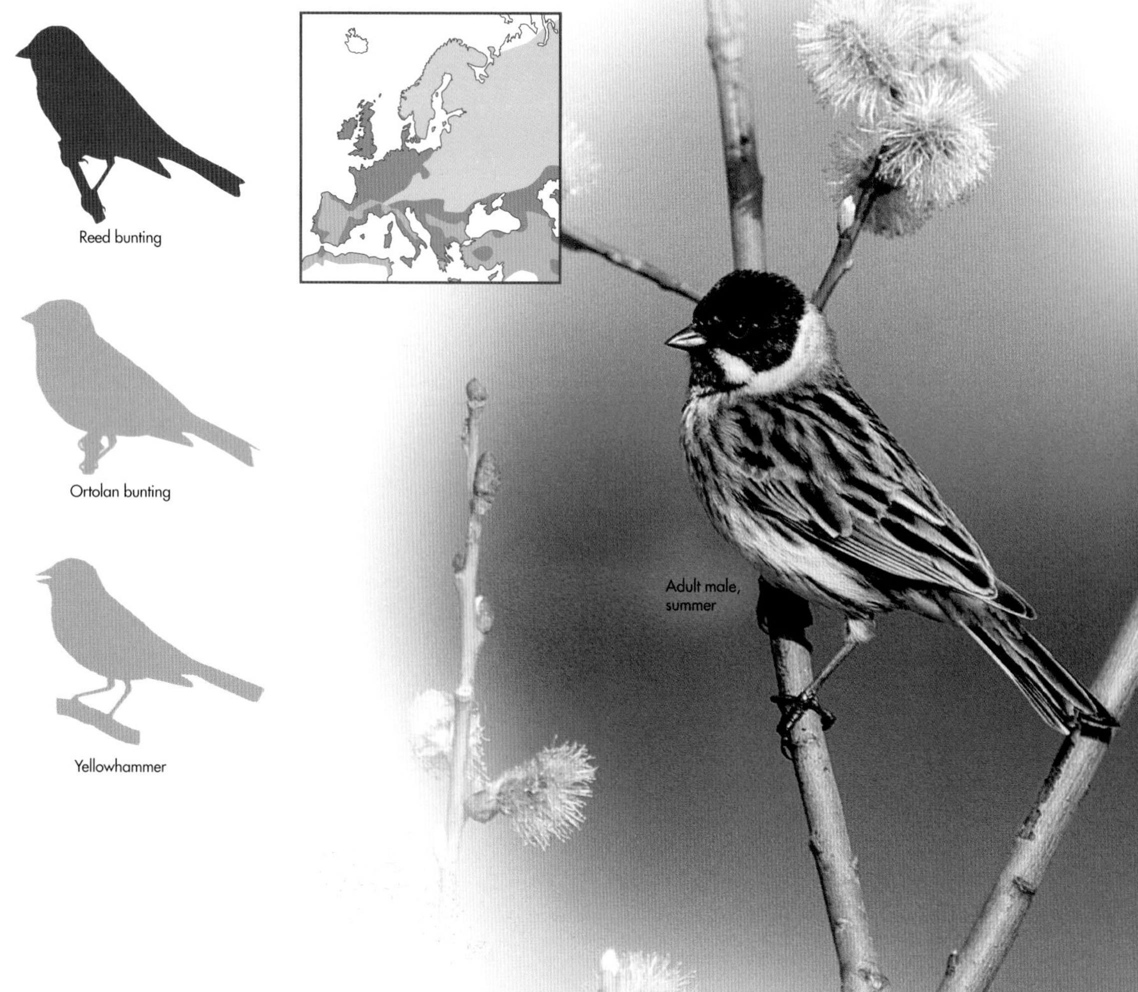

Adult male, summer

Were it not for the striking moustache-like stripes on the side of the face, a reed bunting in winter could look rather sparrow-like. No such doubts exist when it comes to a male in the breeding season, because of the striking pattern on the head: overall it appears black, although the cap and throat are separated by a white moustache-like stripe.

Even if there is just a solitary bush in a male reed bunting's territory, then the chances are he will use this as the focal point. Perched in the topmost branches, he will survey the surroundings for danger and will advertize his presence by singing his rather monotonous song.

In a garden, you are more likely to encounter the reed bunting during the winter months. Roving flocks tend to be rather nomadic at this

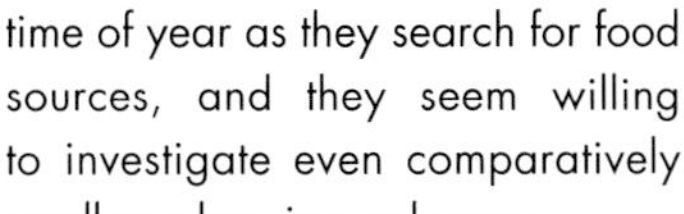

time of year as they search for food sources, and they seem willing to investigate even comparatively small gardens in rural areas.

Habitat

Marshy grassland and farmland.

How to attract this bird to your garden

Scatter seed on the ground during the winter months and you may attract a small feeding flock.

Can be mistaken for

In summer, the adult male is unmistakable given the striking red markings. Female and immature birds could be confused with a juvenile yellowhammer (see pages 148–149), except for the complete absence of even a hint of yellow in the plumage.

Above A female reed bunting lacks the male's dark cap and throat, these areas being brown rather than black.

SIMILAR SPECIES

Little bunting

Emberiza pusilla

LENGTH: 12–14 cm (5–5½ in)

Resembles a diminutive, short-tailed reed bunting but has chestnut cheeks and a crown stripe. The little bunting is found on moors in the far north of Europe during the summer. Although most spend the winter in south Asia, small numbers stay in Europe and usually associate with reed bunting flocks. Typically they are tame.

Ortolan bunting

Emberiza hortulana

REGION: Widespread but local summer visitor to many parts of Europe; seen on migration elsewhere in the region • SIZE: 15–16 cm (6–6½ in) • FOOD: Seeds, insects and other invertebrates • CALL: Utters a thin *tssee* in flight • SONG: A short series of ringing notes • SEX DIFFERENCES: Males are similar to, but more colourful and less streaked than, females • JUVENILE: Similar to adult females • FLIGHT: Bounding and rapid • NEST: A woven structure of grasses, sited in a dense bush.

Ortolan buntings are attractive birds with streaked, reddish-brown on the back and orange-brown on the underparts. The head is greenish-grey overall, with contrasting yellow throat and moustache. Females are duller than males, but all individuals have the yellow eye-ring and pink bill.

They like to feed in areas of short grassland and, prior to autumn migration, they sometimes turn up in ploughed, weedy fields. The species is usually rather shy, often flying off as people approach them. However, close to the nest, males are sometimes bold and seemingly inquisitive about human intruders into their domain.

Habitat

Favours areas of open country with scrub, as well as vegetated mountain slopes.

How to attract this bird to your garden

Provide a permanent drinking pool and birds may visit it during the hot summer months.

Can be mistaken for

Cretzschmar's bunting (see opposite), although that species has a reddish (not yellow) throat and moustache stripe, and is restricted to the far southeast of Europe.

Adult male, summer

Cretzschmar's bunting

Emberiza caesia

REGION: A summer visitor to southeastern Europe, mainly Greece and the Balkans; present mainly May to August • SIZE: 14–15 cm (5½–6 in) • FOOD: Seeds, insects and other invertebrates • CALL: Utters a rasping call • SONG: A short series of ringing notes • SEX DIFFERENCES: Males are more colourful and strikingly marked than females • JUVENILE: Similar to adult females • FLIGHT: Rapid and undulating • NEST: A woven structure of grasses, sited in a dense bush or tussock.

These delightful buntings are often found in areas where the colour of the rocks and soil match those on their back and underparts, while the lichens that coat the rocks are a similar hue to the feathers on their heads. So, although they are colourful, they often blend in surprisingly well with their surroundings. Fortunately, the males often perch on prominent rocks in order to sing and advertize ownership of a territory.

Cretzschmar's buntings favour habitats that are arid and hot during late spring and summer. Although the birds gain much of the water they need by eating insects, they will take advantage of pools of water for bathing and drinking.

Habitat

Rocky slopes with grassland and Mediterranean scrub plants.

How to attract this bird to your garden

If you live in a rural location, provide a drinking pool. You are unlikely to attract it using food.

Can be mistaken for

Ortolan bunting (see opposite), but that species has a yellow (not reddish) throat and moustache stripe. Cretzschmar's bunting has a whitish (not yellow) eyering.

Adult male, summer

Snow bunting

Plectrophenax nivalis

REGION: A summer visitor to northern Scandinavia and Iceland; seen elsewhere in the region in winter or on migration • SIZE: 16–18 cm (6½–7 in) • FOOD: Mainly seeds, but eats some insects and other invertebrates during the breeding season • CALL: A delightful tinkling call is uttered in flight. • SONG: A series of twittering phrases • SEX DIFFERENCES: Males in summer have essentially black-and-white plumage. In females, white elements of males' plumage are grubbier, the cheeks and crown buffish-brown and the back brown; white patches on inner wing; winter males have grubbier plumage and are superficially similar to females • JUVENILE: Similar to adult females but the upperparts are more buffish-brown • FLIGHT: Undulating, with constant changes in direction • NEST: A woven structure of grasses, sited in a dense tussock.

During the winter, small flocks can be found feeding along the tideline of many suitable sandy beaches in northwestern Europe. In the eastern parts of the region, it does occur inland as well, mostly on ploughed arable farmland.

While feeding, snow buntings keep low to the ground and have a rather creeping, almost mouse-like, gait. Consequently, even sizeable flocks can be rather difficult to locate, especially since they usually take advantage of ruts in the ground to shelter from the wind.

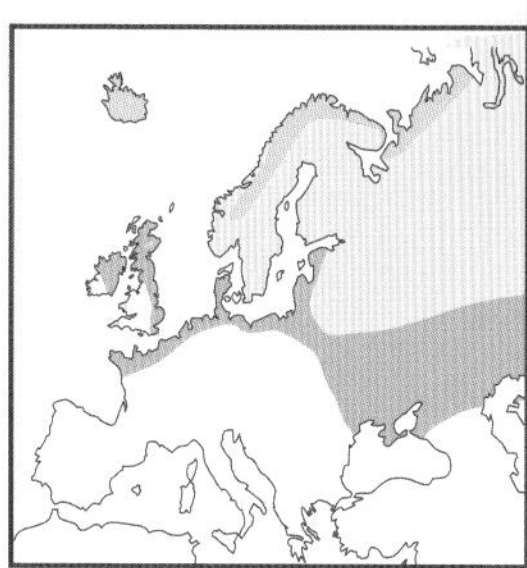

Adult male, summer

However, once a flock takes to the wing this all changes and the extensive patches of white on the wings make them look like animated flurries of snowflakes.

Habitat

Rocky ground and tundra during the breeding season. Mainly favours sandy beaches and coastal grassland in winter but occasionally found on rugged ground near inland mountains; they sometimes congregate in the vicinity of ski-lift centres.

How to attract this bird to your garden

If your garden is surrounded by open, rocky terrain, then this species may be a summer visitor. It sometimes breeds in roof cavities in old buildings and will occasionally use an open-fronted nest box. During the winter, the only realistic chance of seeing this bird in the garden will come if you live near the coast and are surrounded by short grassland. Scatter seeds on the ground and you may improve you chances.

Can be mistaken for

Summer male is unmistakable given its black-and-white plumage and body shape. All individuals are instantly recognizable in flight because of the unprecedented (for a bird of this size) amount of white in the wings.

Above Juveniles are unobtrusive and can be hard to spot, their streaked brown upperparts blending in with their grassy habitat.

Above Snow buntings are fond of bathing, and this helps keep their plumage in good condition.

Black-headed bunting

Emberiza melanocephala

REGION: A summer visitor to southeast Europe, mainly Greece, the Balkans and southeastern Italy • SIZE: 15–17 cm (6–7 in) • FOOD: Seeds and insects • CALL: A sharp *chip* • SONG: A jerky series of raspy, jingling phrases • SEX DIFFERENCES: Only males have the distinctive black cap and bright yellow underparts. In females, these elements (and the plumage generally) are much paler • JUVENILE: Similar to adult females but with streaking on the crown and back • FLIGHT: Rapid and undulating • NEST: A woven structure of grasses, sited in a dense bush.

The black-headed bunting is a comparative latecomer in spring and typically flocks do not arrive from their wintering grounds in southeast Asia until the beginning of May. However, from the moment they appear they make up for lost time and males sing almost continuously in sunny weather, at least until they have acquired a mate and started nesting.

Few birds can rival a male black-headed bunting for the intensity of its colourful plumage. The underparts are a stunningly bright lemon yellow, which contrasts with the chestnut back and jet-black hood.

Habitat

Favours traditionally farmed areas with a mosaic of small arable fields, orchards and patches of scrub.

How to attract this bird to your garden

If you live on the fringes of a rural village, a permanent pond may attract this species, which loves to drink and bathe, in summer.

Can be mistaken for

Adult male is unmistakable. Female and juvenile birds could possibly be confused with their cirl bunting and yellowhammer counterparts (see pages 146 and 148–149). However, black-headed buntings have much cleaner-looking, less streaked plumage.

Adult male, summer

Corn bunting

Miliaria calandra

REGION: A widespread resident in much of central and southern Europe; some eastern populations are migrant summer visitors to their breeding ranges, moving south and west in winter • SIZE: 16–19 cm (6½–7½ in) • FOOD: Seeds and insects • CALL: A buzzing *tsit* • SONG: A unique and distinctive series of raspy, jingling notes that has been likened to the sound of jangling keys • SEX DIFFERENCES: The sexes are similar • JUVENILE: Similar to the adults • FLIGHT: Relatively slow and often rather fluttering. The legs and feet often dangle • NEST: A woven structure of grasses, sited in a dense tussock.

The corn bunting has rather unremarkable streaked brown plumage but can be recognized by its dumpy appearance and large, stubby bill. In the spring, males often perch on fence posts or over-head wires and sing their distinctive songs for hours on end.

Sadly, in many parts of its range, the species has declined in recent years. To blame are modern 'efficient' agricultural pesticides and herbicides, used extensively on modern farms, which do an effective job of virtually eliminating potential food for this species.

Habitat

Open farmland.

How to attract this bird to your garden

If you live in an area of open countryside, where traditional rather than modern farming practices are employed, then you can sometimes lure this species into the garden to drinking pools, or to seed scattered on bare ground.

Can be mistaken for

Superficially a bit sparrow-like (see pages 120–125), but the rather plain plumage and absence of distinctive features are themselves useful pointers to its identity.

Adult

Sparrowhawk

Accipiter nisus

REGION: Widespread and locally common across almost all parts of Europe. Northern populations are migrant, present within their breeding range from April to September and moving south for the winter • SIZE: 30–40 cm (12–16 in); wingspan 60–75 cm (24–30 in) • FOOD: Small to medium-sized birds, which are caught in flight • CALL: Utters a shrill, repeated scream in alarm • SEX DIFFERENCES: Males are roughly 25 per cent smaller than females; their barred underparts are flushed orange-red (these are greyish-white in females) • JUVENILE: Similar to adult females but with heavy dark barring on the underparts and a scaly-looking back • FLIGHT: Hunting flight is low (often only a metre or two above the ground) and speedy, with bursts of rapid wingbeats interspersed with long glides. Displaying males soar over their breeding territories in spring • NEST: Often uses old nests of carrion crows as a starting point but embellishes them with new twigs to create bigger structures.

This is the most frequently encountered bird of prey in gardens. It is often attracted to surprisingly urban settings if garden bird feeders are attracting potential prey, in the form of small songbirds, to a small area. You can recognize the sparrowhawk in flight from its relatively long tail and rather rounded wingtips. When not hunting, birds normally sit, partly concealed, in the cover of a bush or an ivy-covered tree.

On the whole, sparrowhawks are rather secretive birds, preferring to hunt at dawn and dusk. However, keen-eyed observers can sometimes

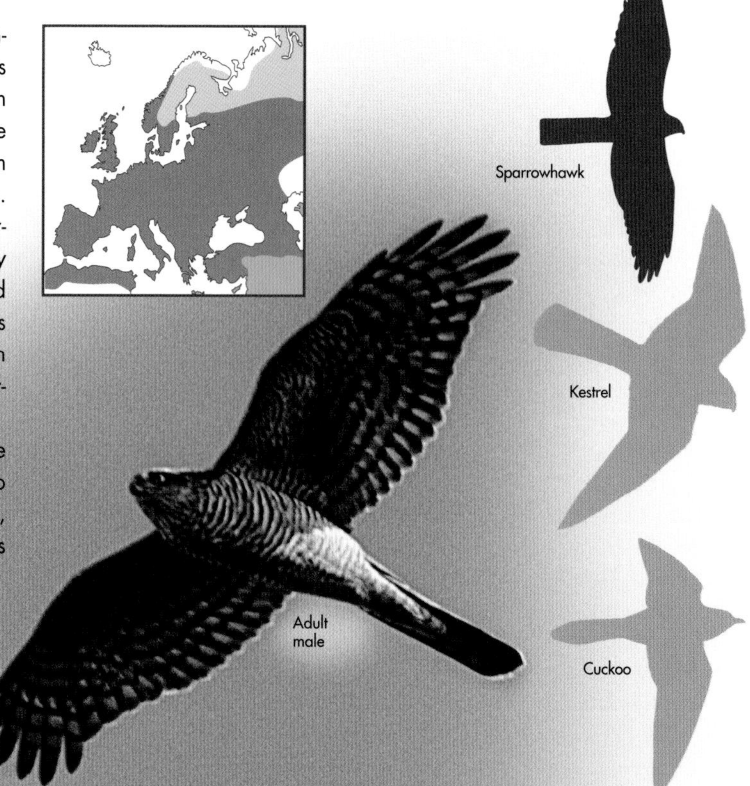

Above An adult female sparrowhawk has rather grey-brown upperparts, with strong dark barring below.

detect their presence by discovering their favoured 'plucking post' – a secluded spot (often an old tree stump) where they take their prey to pluck the feathers before eating it. Male sparrowhawks usually specialize in catching small birds (up to the size of a chaffinch or blackbird, perhaps) while females (the larger of the sexes) routinely capture woodpigeons.

Habitat

Usually associated with partly wooded country (for nesting and roosting) with adjacent areas of open country (for hunting). If the tree cover is sufficient, it can also be found in the leafy suburbs of larger towns and cities.

How to attract this bird to your garden

If you put out feeders for birds such as tits and finches, sooner or later their presence will be noted by your local resident sparrowhawk. Some people may view their depredations with a degree of dismay but those with a more enlightened and informed attitude regard sparrowhawks as part of the natural order of things, and a sign of a healthy environment.

Can be mistaken for

Kestrel (see pages 162–163), although this species diagnostically hovers. In direct, low-level flight it could be confused with a cuckoo (see page 179).

SIMILAR SPECIES

Goshawk

Accipiter gentilis

LENGTH: 50–60 cm (20–24 in); wingspan 95–105 cm (38–42 in)

Superficially similar to a female sparrowhawk but much larger (almost buzzard-sized) and with a proportionately shorter tail, plumper body and broader wings. A good view of a sitting bird will reveal the striking white stripe above the eye. Goshawks feed in a similar manner to sparrowhawks (by surprise attack) and specialize in catching woodpigeons. The species is widespread but locally common only in well-wooded parts of mainland Europe.

Buzzard

Buteo buteo

REGION: Widespread and locally common resident in much of western, central and southern Europe; in northeast of range it is a summer visitor • SIZE: 45–55 cm (18–22 in); wingspan 115–130 cm (46–52 in) • FOOD: Small to medium-sized mammals, reptiles and amphibians, although a large part of its diet comprises earthworms; it will also scavenge carrion • CALL: A loud mew, which is often delivered in flight • SEX DIFFERENCES: Males are smaller than females but the sexes are difficult to tell apart by their plumage as individuals vary greatly • JUVENILE: Usually more streaked on the underparts than the adults.

This large, bulky and broad-winged raptor often attracts attention to itself with its loud, rather cat-like call. Birds are particularly vocal in early spring while displaying, and in late summer when family parties are on the wing. During the breeding season, they become extremely secretive and are difficult to watch. Buzzards are fond of sitting around for long periods on fence posts and dead branches, on the look-out for potential meals.

Habitat

Favours lightly wooded habitats, especially where a mosaic of small woodlands (for nesting and roosting) are found alongside farmland and open country where they can feed.

How to attract this bird to your garden

Because buzzards dislike confined spaces, you are only likely to attract this species if your garden borders open farmland and the birds have

Can be mistaken for

Red kite (see opposite), although note comments about the shape of the tail.

Adult

Red kite

Milvus milvus

REGION: Widespread and fairly common resident across parts of central, southern and northwestern Europe. Elsewhere within its range, it is a summer visitor • SIZE: 60–70 cm (24–28 in); wingspan 145–165 cm (58–66 in) • FOOD: Catches small mammals and birds and also feeds on earthworms. In addition, it scavenges carcases and is attracted to rubbish dumps • CALL: Utters a strange and distinctive call, not unlikely somebody whistling for their dog • SEX DIFFERENCES: The sexes are similar, both in terms of size and shape • JUVENILE: The reddish plumage elements are duller than in adults • FLIGHT: A superb aeronaut, capable of sustained gliding and soaring. The tail is constantly flexed from side to side for directional control • NEST: A large twiggy structure, placed high in a tree and often using a previously abandoned crow's nest as a starting point.

Red kites are superb aeronauts, using their long, broad wings to glide and soar effortlessly while scanning the ground for food. Note the distinctive, reddish, forked tail.

Earthworms are important in the diet but the species is mainly a scavenger. It snatches small scraps of foods in its talons while in flight, and only reluctantly lands on the ground to feed.

Habitat

Favours a mosaic of open farmland and grassland (for feeding) and copses for nesting and roosting.

How to attract this bird to your garden

Ironically, although this species normally shuns human contact, it is one of the easiest raptors to attract to the garden by placing scraps of meat on open lawn.

Can be mistaken for

Buzzard (see opposite), although the red kite's tail is rounded and not forked.

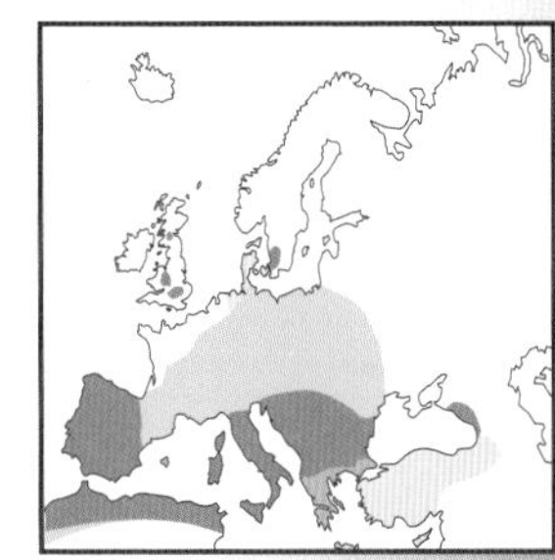

Adult

Kestrel

Falco tinnunculus

REGION: A widespread resident across much of the region; populations from Scandinavia and similar latitudes eastwards are mainly migrant summer visitors to these areas • SIZE: 31–36 cm (12½–14½ in); wingspan 65–80 cm (26–32 in) • FOOD: Mainly small mammals and insects, but some small birds • CALL: Utters a screaming *kee-kee-kee* • SEX DIFFERENCES: Males are colourful and distinctive, with a blue-grey head, a dark-spotted chestnut back and dark-spotted pale underparts; by contrast, females have more uniform brownish, barred upperparts and grubbier underparts • JUVENILE: Similar to adult females but with more extensive dark barring • FLIGHT: Gliding, soaring and rapid direct flight; also hovers • NEST: A rudimentary arrangement, in a tree hole or cavity in a building; sometimes uses an old crow's nest.

The kestrel is probably the region's most familiar bird of prey, at least in lowland areas. This is partly because it is the most numerous of its kind in Europe but also because it has acquired a liking for habitats and locations frequented by people. In particular, it is often seen hovering beside roads, where it feeds on small mammals that usually thrive in the short, road-side grassland.

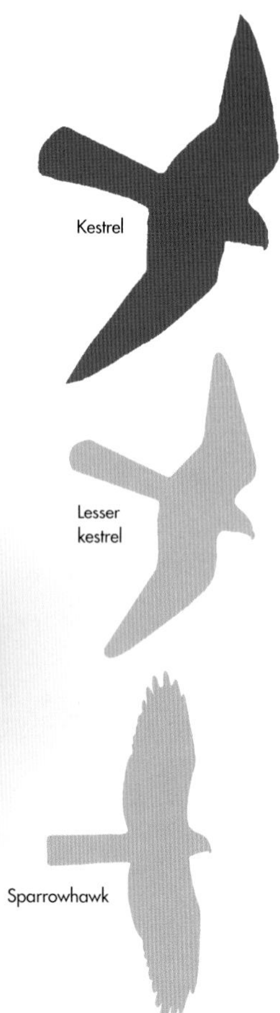

A male kestrel is a particularly attractive bird. The blue-grey colour of the head matches that on the long, dark-tipped tail and contrasts with the rich chestnut-brown back. This latter colour extends onto the inner wing and, in flight, contrasts with the dark wingtips.

Like other birds of prey, the kestrel has extremely keen eyesight, which it uses to locate its prey. Typically a bird will hover (or hang in the wind) 10–15 metres (33–50 ft) or so above a suitable patch of grassland, scanning the ground below for the tell-tale movements of small mammals.

Habitat

Open countryside, coasts and roadside verges.

How to attract this bird to your garden

If your garden is on the fringes of open countryside, try putting up a large, open-fronted nest box to see if a pair of kestrels will inhabit it.

Can be mistaken for

Sparrowhawk (see pages 158–159), although that species has shorter, more rounded wings and a low and direct flight (it never hovers); lesser kestrel (see page 164), although the males of that species have no spots on the chestnut-coloured back.

SIMILAR SPECIES

Peregrine

Falco peregrinus

LENGTH: 40–50 cm (16–20 in) wingspan 90–110 cm (36–44 in)
A powerful falcon with broad-based, pointed wings, blue-grey upperparts and a dark moustache. It is a widespread but scarce resident that specializes in catching flying birds in spectacular diving swoops known as 'stoops'. A widespread but very local resident in northwestern and upland southern Europe, but summer visitor in the north and east.

Merlin

Falco columbarius

LENGTH: 25–30 cm (10–12 in); wingspan 55–70 cm (22–28 in)
Europe's smallest falcon. Males have mainly blue-grey upperparts and barred reddish underparts while females are dark brown above and streaked brown below. The species breeds in northern Europe and winters further south.

Peregrine

Hobby

Falco subbuteo

LENGTH: 30–35 cm (12–14 in); wingspan 70–85 cm (28–34 in)
A summer visitor as far north as southern Scandinavia and Britain, recognized in flight by its anchor-shaped outline. The hobby is fast and agile, capable of catching birds and dragonflies in flight.

Merlin

Hobby

Lesser kestrel

Falco naumanni

REGION: Local summer visitor to southern Europe, present mainly March to September • SIZE: 28–32 cm (11–13 in); wingspan 65–70 cm (26–28 in) • FOOD: Insects, small mammals and some small birds • CALL: Utters a three-note rasping call • SEX DIFFERENCES: Males are much more brightly coloured than females with blue-grey on the head, tail and mid-wing and chestnut on the back • JUVENILE: Similar to adult females with barred brown upperparts and pale, dark-spotted underparts • FLIGHT: Graceful, capable of soaring, gliding and hovering • NEST: A rudimentary affair, usually sited in a crevice in a building.

Although the lesser kestrel has a rather patchy distribution within the region, where it does occur it is often locally common. These birds are usually relatively easy to see, particularly because they typically nest colonially so there are often a dozen or more birds wheeling around at any given time.

Given their association with human dwellings and buildings while nesting, with the birds sometimes squeezing into comparatively tiny spaces to nest, for example between sunken roof tiles, it is not surprising that lesser kestrels often do not mind the presence of humans, so it is easy to watch their comings and goings.

Habitat

Usually associated with abandoned farm buildings or tall buildings (for example, church towers) for nesting; feeds in neighbouring open countryside.

How to attract this bird to your garden

Leave derelict buildings such as old barns or outhouses unrepaired, and lesser kestrels may decide to use them for nesting.

Can be mistaken for

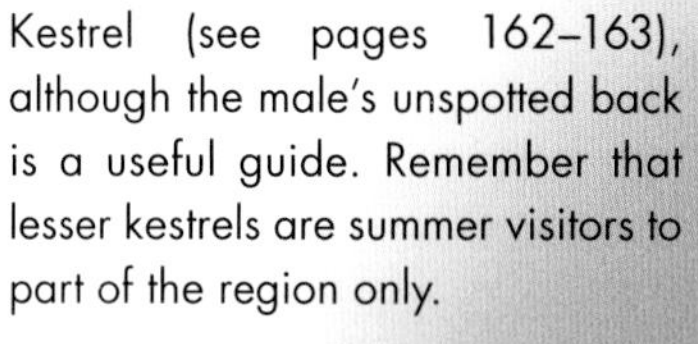

Kestrel (see pages 162–163), although the male's unspotted back is a useful guide. Remember that lesser kestrels are summer visitors to part of the region only.

Immature male

Red-footed falcon

Falco vespertinus

REGION: A summer visitor to the east of the region and widespread on migration in southeastern Europe; present in the region as a whole mainly May–August • SIZE: 30–35 cm (12–14 in); wingspan 65–75 cm (26–30 in) • FOOD: Mainly insects, but some small mammals and birds • CALL: Utters a chattering alarm • SEX DIFFERENCES: Males are mainly uniformly dark blue-grey, with red legs and feet, and red undertail; females are barred blue-grey on the back and orange-buff on the head and underparts, and have a highly visible dark 'highwayman's mask' • JUVENILE: Recalls adult females in terms of overall appearance, but is much less colourful • FLIGHT: A superb aeronaut, capable of gliding, soaring and hovering • NEST: Usually occupies an abandoned rooks' nest.

Red-footed falcons are extremely long-winged and elegant birds in flight. Males are particularly striking, their sooty-grey plumage showing off the red feathering at the base of the tail and the silvery white panels towards the tips of the upper wings. Females are also distinctive, with the dark-barred pale flight and undertail feathers contrasting with orange-buff body and inner wings.

Although these birds will hover occasionally, they prefer to perch for extended periods on overhead wires or fence posts, scanning the ground below for beetles and other prey. They tend to be sociable and typically feed, nest and migrate in parties of ten or more individuals.

Habitat

They nest in copses and clumps of tall trees and feed in neighbouring open farmland and marshes.

How to attract this bird to your garden

If you live near open countryside, you could try putting up several artificial nest platforms in tall trees. The alternative is to plant tall-growing trees, wait for a rookery to become established and then hope that red-footed falcons will oust the rooks.

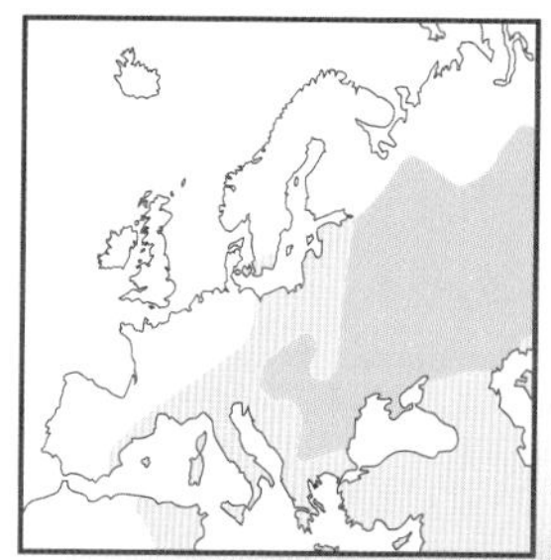

Can be mistaken for

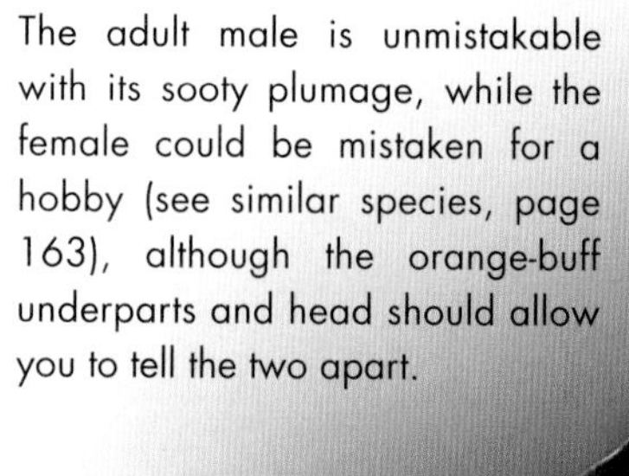

The adult male is unmistakable with its sooty plumage, while the female could be mistaken for a hobby (see similar species, page 163), although the orange-buff underparts and head should allow you to tell the two apart.

Adult male

Barn owl

Tyto alba

REGION: Widespread but patchily distributed resident across the region • SIZE: 35–40 cm (14–16 in); wingspan 80–95 cm (32–38 in) • FOOD: Mainly small mammals • CALL: A blood-curdling scream • SEX DIFFERENCES: The sexes are similar • JUVENILE: Similar to adults • FLIGHT: Slow and graceful, gliding and wheeling on broad wings; capable of hovering momentarily • NEST: A rudimentary affair, on a ledge or in a crevice in a barn or old building or even an old chimney.

Although barn owls hunt mainly at night, they are seen occasionally in the late afternoon, usually in the dead of winter, or when there are young to feed in the summer months. Most individuals are not unduly bothered by the presence of human observers and you can often obtain excellent views.

Adult

Barn owl

Long-eared owl

Tawny owl

Above Barn owls often sit for minutes on end on roadside fence posts, scanning the ground for potential prey.

On the wing, a barn owl looks extremely pale, although birds from central and eastern Europe have darker breasts than those seen elsewhere. The broad, rounded wings are usually held in a 'V' when the bird is gliding, with the legs and talons dangling down. They usually hunt by quartering a field systematically, gliding along and doubling back if something catches their attention. Twitching grass stems or a faint rustle usually indicate the presence of a vole or mouse in the undergrowth and the owls' response is to drop, talons first, to the ground and snatch a victim.

If you think there might be barn owls nesting in a building, check for piles of pellets. These contain the undigested bones and fur from the prey, regurgitated from the crop; don't worry about them, as they are dry and not the least bit smelly.

Habitat

Open farmland and countryside with plenty of rank grassland and abundant small mammals.

How to attract this bird to your garden

Barn owls readily take to nest boxes placed in old barns and derelict (or seldom used) buildings. If you live close to open countryside, try placing a box in a suitable building. Less frequently, they will use a nest box placed in a tree.

Can be mistaken for

Unmistakable when seen well on account of the gleaming white underparts and face, and yellow-brown upperparts.

Tawny owl

Strix aluco

REGION: Widespread resident across much of the region, although absent from the very far northwest and north • SIZE: 38–40 cm (14½–16in); wingspan 85–95 cm (34–38 in) • FOOD: Mainly small mammals, but also some birds and amphibians • CALL: Utters a sharp *kewick* • SONG: Series of moaning, hooting phrases, sometimes given as a duet by members of a pair • SEX DIFFERENCES: The sexes are similar • JUVENILE: Very young birds are whitish and fluffy but after the first moult they are similar to an adult • FLIGHT: Silent and gliding, on broad, rounded wings • NEST: A rudimentary structure usually sited in a tree hole; the species will sometimes use a nest box.

The tawny owl is a strictly nocturnal bird and uses its acute senses of hearing and sight to locate and catch its small mammal prey after darkness. The edges of the flight feathers are specially modified for silent flight.

During the daytime, tawny owls usually roost in the deep shade of an ivy-covered tree; their streaked and marbled brown plumage is excellent camouflage, so they can be difficult to locate during daylight hours. However, if you see or hear small birds noisily mobbing something in a tree, check it out. In the country, tawny owls usually eat voles and mice, but urban individuals often make do with rats and small birds. Typically, the prey is swollen whole and the indigestible remains (bones and fur) are coughed up in the form of pellets. These accumulate beneath regularly used roosting spots.

Above Nesting in a crack in an old tree, this tawny owl family is experiencing cramped conditions.

Habitat

Deciduous woodland, parks and mature gardens.

How to attract this bird to your garden

Try placing a large, open or hole-fronted nest box in a tree and tawny owls may use it.

Can be mistaken for

Unmistakable because of its compact body shape and broad wings.

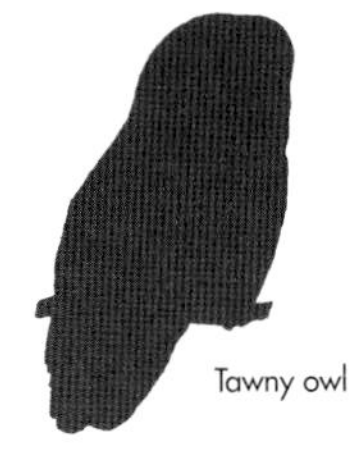

Tawny owl

Barn owl

Long-eared owl

Adult

Long-eared owl

Asio otus

REGION: A widespread resident across much of the region, although birds from northern Europe are mostly migrant summer visitors to that part of the species' range • SIZE: 32–35 cm (13–14 in) • FOOD: Mainly small mammals and birds • CALL: Mainly silent but sometimes utters deep hoots in spring • SEX DIFFERENCES: The sexes are similar • JUVENILE: Similar to the adults • FLIGHT: Slow and graceful, with deep wingbeats and long glides • NEST: Usually uses an old magpie or crow nest.

The long-eared owl is a strictly nocturnal species and, unless disturbed, it is never seen on the wing during the daylight hours. During the day it usually roosts in a dense bush, or close to the trunk of a tree, and its camouflaged plumage ensures that it is easy to miss. During winter, however, long-eared owls are sometimes more obvious, partly because deciduous trees will have dropped their leaves at this time of year but also because the birds sometimes bask in the winter sunshine.

Long-eared owl

Tawny owl

Scops owl

Adult

Above Sitting among a tangle of branches and clumps of fir cones, a long-eared owl can be surprisingly difficult to spot.

Like other owls, this species' true ears are concealed by feathers and located on the margins of the facial disc. The 'ear' tufts for which the long-eared owl is renowned are purely decorative and they are only raised when the bird is agitated.

During the winter months in particular, long-eared owls are occasionally seen at night perched on roadside fence posts, illuminated by car headlights. So long as you do not make any sudden movements or noises, individuals discovered in this way will often sit tight for several minutes, seemingly undisturbed by the presence of humans.

Habitat

Mainly associated with conifer plantations during the breeding season but at other times they can be found in mature hedgerows and areas of scrub adjacent to open, grassy country.

How to attract this bird to your garden

Plant dense stands of conifers and you stand a chance of attracting this species to the garden if you live in a rural area. Look for piles of coughed-up pellets (the undigested remains of prey) that accumulate beneath regular roosting sites.

Can be mistaken for

Tawny owl (see pages 168–169), but long-eared owls are smaller, have a more elongated body and the unmistakeable ear tufts.

Scops owl

Otus scops

REGION: A summer visitor to the southern half of Europe, present from April to September • SIZE: 20 cm (8 in) • FOOD: Nocturnal insects (including moths and beetles) and small reptiles • CALL: A repetitive and extraordinary, sonar-like blip, quite unlike the call of any other European bird, and usually uttered from dusk to dawn • SEX DIFFERENCES: Sexes are similar in size; both occur in both mainly brown or mainly grey forms • JUVENILE: Similar to adults but with less well-defined streaking • FLIGHT: Direct, and often gliding • NEST: In a hole in a mature tree, or occasionally a cavity in a derelict building.

The scops owl's beautifully marked plumage is a near-perfect match for tree bark. It invariably uses this camouflage to good effect by roosting during the daytime close to the trunk of a tree, and so it can be extremely difficult to spot. The easiest way to detect its presence in your garden is to listen for its strange, almost mechanical, call. Unsurprisingly, because they are strictly nocturnal, scops owls are most vocal in the dead of the night. They raise their ear tufts only when they are alert or agitated.

Habitat

Farmland and open country on the fringes of rural villages.

How to attract this bird to your garden

If you live within this species' breeding range then leave mature, gnarled trees (especially olives, *Olea europea,* and other gnarled trees) to provide potential nest holes for this species.

Can be mistaken for

Could possibly be confused with a little owl (see opposite), although the ear tufts, and habit of remaining completely motionless during the day, are good clues to the scops owl's identity.

Adult

Little owl

Athene noctua

REGION: A widespread resident across much of central, southern and northwestern Europe • SIZE: 22 cm (9 in) • FOOD: Mainly insects such as beetles, but also earthworms and, very occasionally, small mammals • CALL: Utters a cat-like mewing sound, particularly at dusk • SEX DIFFERENCES: The sexes are similar • JUVENILE: Similar to the adults, but without the white spots on the crown • FLIGHT: Rapid and undulating, with bursts of rapid wingbeats and short glides • NEST: Sited in a tree hole or a cavity in a wall or building.

The little owl is an attractive and well-marked bird. When relaxed, it adopts a rather rounded, dumpy posture, but if agitated it stretches its body and stands tall on its proportionately long legs. It is hard to miss the staring yellow eyes.

The little owl is one of the easiest owl species to watch since it is at least partly active in daylight (this is when its beetle prey are most in evidence). It is fond of perching on fence posts and dead branches, which also improves the chances of observers finding one.

In flight, the wings are rounded and proportionately long, while the tail is rather short. The bounding flight action can give this species an almost woodpecker-like appearance on the wing.

Habitat

Farmland and open country, with mature hedgerows and gnarled old trees for nesting and roosting. Also found in mature gardens and parks.

How to attract this bird to your garden

The species will use nest boxes so site a large, open-fronted box on the edge of your garden and, if it borders open country, there is a reasonable chance that a pair will take up residence.

Can be mistaken for

Unmistakable because of dumpy, rounded body shape.

Adult

Red-backed shrike

Lanius collurio

REGION: A widespread summer visitor to central and eastern Europe, present mainly May to August. The species' range is contracting in the north and east • SIZE: 16–18 cm (6½–7 in) • FOOD: Mainly insects, but also occasionally lizards and small mammals • CALL: Utters a harsh, grating call • SONG: Subdued, squeaky and seldom heard • SEX DIFFERENCES: Females are much duller than males and have fine and delicate barring on underparts • JUVENILE: Has brown upperparts with pale barring and pale underparts with dark barring. The overall effect is of scaly-looking plumage • FLIGHT: Direct with rapid wingbeats • NEST: A twiggy construction sited in a dense shrub or bush.

The red-backed shrike is an active predator and, despite its small size, it will tackle comparatively large prey items with vigour. Its powerful, hook-tipped bill makes short work of dung beetles and wasps, and if the opportunity arises it will even tackle small rodents and lizards. In times of plenty, the species sometimes creates 'larders', impaling surplus prey on thorns or spines. This action has the added advantage for the shrike that the victim can be dismembered more easily – otherwise it has to be grasped by the feet.

Red-backed shrike

Woodchat shrike

Lesser grey shrike

Adult male

A male red-backed shrike is a stunningly attractive bird, the reddish-brown back contrasting with, and complementing, the blue-grey head and peach-flushed pale underparts. Females and immature birds are much more dowdy.

The species is extremely secretive at the nest but is much easier to see when it is hunting for food. Birds often perch on barbed-wire fences or dead twigs, scanning the ground below for potential prey, which they drop down upon from their look-outs.

Habitat

Heaths and open country with thorny bushes. Sometimes visits mature gardens in rural parts of the south of its range.

How to attract this bird to your garden

Plant plenty of dense, thorny bushes and, if you live in a rural area, you may attract it.

Can be mistaken for

An unmistakable bird when viewed in good light on account of its plumage colours.

Above Markings on the flanks of a female red-backed shrike create a distinctly barred appearance.

Above A juvenile red-backed shrike looks rather scaly, with pale feather margins on the upperparts and dark barring below.

Woodchat shrike

Lanius senator

REGION: Widespread summer visitor to southern and central southern Europe, present mainly May to August • SIZE: 17–19 cm (*c.* 7–7½ in) • FOOD: Mainly insects, but occasionally lizards and small mammals • CALL: Utters a harsh trilling • SONG: Subdued and seldom heard • SEX DIFFERENCES: The sexes are rather similar although, with females, the black and chestnut elements of the plumage are paler than in males • JUVENILE: Mainly greyish-brown, the pale and dark barring creating a 'scaly' appearance • FLIGHT: Direct, with rapid wingbeats • NEST: A twiggy construction, sited in a dense bush or shrub.

The southerly range of the woodchat shrike reflects its prey – abundant insects that flourish in a warm climate.

Like its cousins, the woodchat shrike has a stout, hook-tipped bill that is reminiscent of those seen in birds of prey. It functions in a similar manner, being used to tear and dismember prey before it is eaten. Woodchat shrikes will sometimes impale large victims on barbed wire to help this process.

Above Like other shrike species, woodchats are fond of perching on barbed-wire fences.

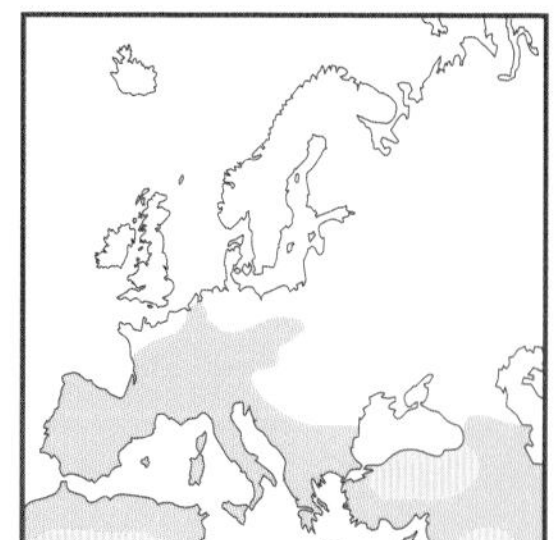

Habitat

Orchards, olive groves and open, natural Mediterranean habitats.

How to attract this bird to your garden

If your garden borders onto open country, this species may visit your garden. If you encourage insect life your chances will improve.

Can be mistaken for

Unmistakable.

Lesser grey shrike

Lanius minor

REGION: Summer visitor, mainly to southeast and eastern Europe, present mainly May to August • SIZE: 19–21 cm (7½–8½ in) • FOOD: Mainly insects and small lizards • CALL: Utters a subdued chattering call in alarm • SONG: A series of harsh and grating screeches • SEX DIFFERENCES: Females have less extensive black on the forehead than males • JUVENILE: Similar plumage pattern to the adults but pale feather margins on the upperparts create a scaly appearance • FLIGHT: Rapid and direct • NEST: A twiggy structure sited deep in a dense bush.

Within the lesser grey shrike's distinctly easterly range, it is seen relatively frequently perched on overhead wires that run beside roads across open farmland. From this elevated vantage point, birds scan the ground below for the telltale movements of potential prey – beetles and large grasshoppers are favourites. The powerful, hook-tipped bill soon dispatches the victim, which is rapidly dismembered and swallowed.

At a distance, or in harsh light, a lesser grey shrike can look rather uniformly grey, black and white. However, if seen well, the salmon-pink flush to the underparts can be appreciated. In flight, the striking, broad white bar on the wings is clearly visible.

Habitat

Orchards, wide open countryside with scattered trees, as well as mature gardens in rural districts.

How to attract this bird to your garden

The species is fond of perching and nesting in tall poplars, so plant some trees if you live on the fringes of open country.

Can be mistaken for

Unmistakable when seen in good light on account of its grey back and pink-flushed underparts.

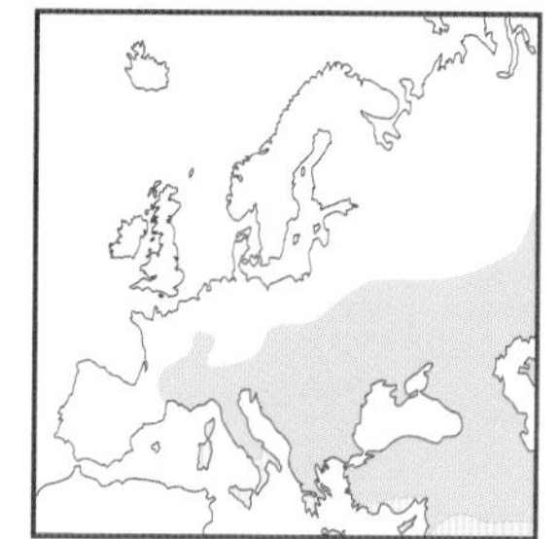

Above An adult female has less contrasting plumage than the male.

Masked shrike

Lanius nubicus

REGION: A summer visitor to southeastern Europe, present mainly from April to August • SIZE: 17–18 cm (*c.* 7 in) • FOOD: Mainly insects and small lizards • CALL: Utters a rattling call when alarmed • SONG: Rather musical and warbler-like • SEX DIFFERENCES: The sexes are similar although the black and orange elements of the plumage are more intense in males than females • JUVENILE: Has mainly pale underparts, and greyish upperparts that are adorned with pale feather edges; these create a scaly appearance • FLIGHT: Rapid and direct • NEST: A neat twiggy construction, adorned with lichens, and usually placed on the upper surface of a broad, flat branch.

Compared to its close relatives, the masked shrike has a rather elongated (not dumpy) body shape and at times it can look almost wagtail-like. The black-and-white markings on the upperparts are extremely well defined and the orange flush on the flanks is of a hue not seen in many other birds.

Unlike its cousins, which often perch prominently, the masked shrike favours more unobtrusive locations for look-outs, often perching on a dead twig in the shade of some overhanging foliage. From this vantage point it watches for prey and keeps a vigilant eye open for potential rivals – it is an extremely territorial species.

Habitat

Olive groves, orchards and open woodland.

How to attract this bird to your garden

If you live in this species' range and in a rural district, then mature trees in your garden may be used for nesting. If you have an orchard, encourage ground-dwelling insects (food for the shrikes) by gardening without using insecticides.

Can be mistaken for

Woodchat shrike (see page 176), although the masked shrike's black (not chestnut) crown and orange flush on the flanks make identification relatively straightforward.

Adult male

Cuckoo

Cuculus canorus

REGION: A widespread summer visitor to much of the region, present mainly April to July • SIZE: 32–36 cm (13–14½ in) • FOOD: Hairy caterpillars • CALL: Female utters a bubbling trill • SONG: A familiar and diagnostic disyllabic *cuck-oo* • SEX DIFFERENCES: The typical grey plumage is seen in both sexes but a few females are reddish-brown with heavy barring • JUVENILE: Has brown, barred upperparts and pale underparts suffused with extensive dark barring • FLIGHT: Rapid, direct and reminiscent of a sparrowhawk • NEST: Does not make a nest. Individual eggs are laid in the nests of host songbirds, which rear the cuckoo chick.

The cuckoo is a nest parasite of small songbirds such as dunnocks, meadow pipits and reed warblers. A female cuckoo watches for the telltale signs of nesting birds. When a suitable candidate is spotted, she waits until the owner leaves and silently flies in, laying her own egg in the nest and sometimes removing one of the host's clutch. Unaware of the deception, the owners of the nest bring up the baby cuckoo, which evicts any remaining companions. By the time it fledges it dwarfs its surrogate parents.

Generally speaking, it is much easier to hear a cuckoo than it is to see one because the species tends to have rather shy and retiring habits. The song is only heard for the first few weeks after the birds' arrival in spring. Thereafter, cuckoos are usually silent.

Habitat

Open river country, particularly reedbeds, farmland and heaths.

How to attract this bird to your garden

If you live in a rural area and encourage songbirds to breed and nest in your garden, once in a while a cuckoo might parasitize one of the nests.

Can be mistaken for

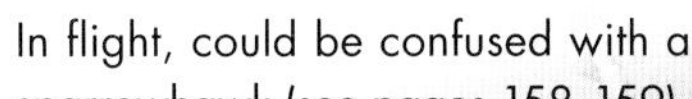

In flight, could be confused with a sparrowhawk (see pages 158–159).

Adult

Bee-eater

Merops apiaster

REGION: Summer visitor to southern and central Europe, present mainly May to August. Occasionally breeds north of typical range • SIZE: 26–29 cm (10½–11½ in) • FOOD: Flying insects, mainly bees, wasps, dragonflies and beetles • CALL: Utters a bubbling trill • SEX DIFFERENCES: The sexes are similar • JUVENILE: Similar to an adult but with duller colours and a shorter projection on the tail • FLIGHT: Graceful and gliding, on narrow, pointed wings • NEST: Excavates a burrow in a sandy bank.

Above In flight, a bee-eater's outline is distinctive and diagnostic even if its wonderful colours cannot be appreciated fully. Note the pointed wings and feather projections from the long tail.

The bee-eater's bubbling call is one of the quintessential sounds of the Mediterranean region and can be heard in warm districts throughout much of lowland southern Europe in summer. The species is extremely aerobatic and is capable of rapid, direct flight when hunting for insects, as well as sustained glides.

The long, slender bill is ideally suited to snatching flying bees and dragonflies. Generally, prey items are carried back to a regularly used perch where they are repeatedly beaten before being swallowed. This action is particularly important in the case of bees and wasps because it helps remove the potentially harmful sting from the tip of the insect's abdomen.

At a glance, a bee-eater's plumage is dominated by blue, chestnut and yellow. However, examine an individual closely and you will find almost every colour of the rainbow making the species one of Europe's most colourful birds. Close up, the beady red eye is obvious.

Habitat

Open countryside and farmland, often in the vicinity of water.

How to attract this bird to your garden

The species will sometimes nest in man-made sandy banks. If you create an artificial site, make sure it is not baked by the sun.

Can be mistaken for

An unmistakable bird because of its shape and amazingly colourful plumage.

SIMILAR SPECIES

Roller

Coracias garrulus

LENGTH: 29–31 cm (11½–12½ in)

A summer visitor to southern parts of the region, present mainly from May to August. The plumage is mainly bright blue, with a rich chestnut hue on the back. They feed on insects and lizards and often perch on overhead wires or on dead branches. Rollers favour open, lightly wooded habitats.

Hoopoe

Upupa epops

REGION: Present year-round in southwestern Europe but elsewhere seen as a summer visitor, present mainly April to September • SIZE: 25–28 cm (10–11 cm) • FOOD: Insects and other invertebrates • CALL: A soft, piping *hoo-poo-poo* • SEX DIFFERENCES: The sexes are similar • JUVENILE: Similar to an adult but with duller colours • FLIGHT: Fluttering and moth-like, on broad, rounded wings • NEST: Sited in a hole in a tree or a stone wall.

Above The relatively slow, flapping flight of a hoopoe, on broad, rounded wings, creates an almost moth-like appearance.

The hoopoe is easily recognized from its distinctive plumage, which is pinkish-buff on the head, neck and back. The complex pattern of black-and-white bars on the wings and tail is really striking, particularly in flight.

If you get a close view of the head, you should see the striking crest, which is buffish-pink with black tips to the feathers. For most of the time, these birds hold the crest down on the crown but can raise them if agitated or excited, or sometimes when they are landing. They probe the ground for grubs and insects with their long, slightly downcurved bills. When feeding, hoopoes are rather unobtrusive birds, partly because their pinkish-buff plumage usually blends in with the soil, but also because they often forage in furrows in the ground rendering them partly hidden from view. Consequently they are surprisingly easy to miss. They are also well camouflaged in trees, particularly when dappled light is passing through foliage, because the pattern on the wings breaks up their outline.

Habitat
Open country, farmland and short grassland.

How to attract this bird to your garden
This species may visit lawns or orchards to feed. Leave gnarled old trees and these may provide it with natural nest holes.

Can be mistaken for
Unmistakable when seen in good light on account of its plumage colours and long bill.

Hoopoe

Bee-eater

Jay

Adult

Kingfisher

Alcedo atthis

REGION: Widespread resident across much of the region, except the north. Farther south, they often disperse in summer and autumn (when smaller rivers often dry up) or in winter (if lakes and rivers freeze) and many birds move to the coast • SIZE: 16–17 cm (6½–7 in) • FOOD: Mainly small fish • CALL: Utters a distinctive, high-pitched call in flight • SEX DIFFERENCES: The sexes are essentially similar although females have a reddish flush to the base of the lower mandible (dark in males) • JUVENILE: Similar to adult males • FLIGHT: Rapid and direct, and usually low over water • NEST: Excavates a burrow in waterside bank.

With its orange-red underparts and blue upperparts, the kingfisher is one of the region's most colourful birds. The iridescent blue feathers on the back are particularly striking in flight and catch the light even if the bird is flying beneath the shade of riverside trees. If you get a close view you will see white on the throat and cheeks, as well as the bright red feet.

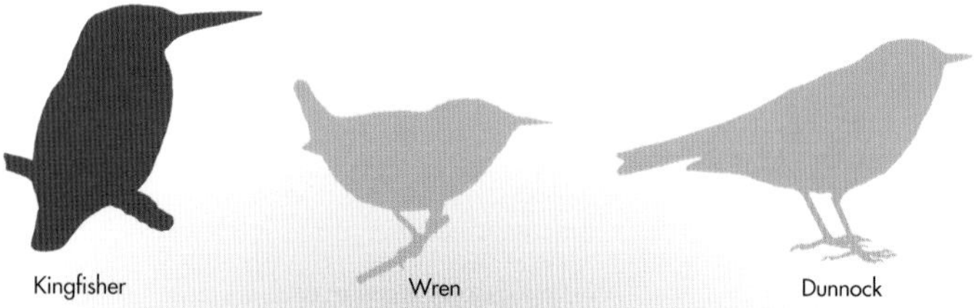

Kingfisher

Wren

Dunnock

Adult male

Kingfishers are seldom seen away from water, because they eat almost nothing but fish. They nest in specially excavated burrows, so they prefer rivers with steep, muddy banks to shallow-sided bodies of water where there is a greater risk of the burrow being flooded.

The kingfisher is a fishing expert. In order to locate their prey, kingfishers will sit motionless on a branch overhanging the water, sometimes for hours on end, watching for telltale ripples at the surface. If no perch is available they will hover briefly. When an opportunity arises they then dive unhesitatingly and catch small fish with their dagger-like bills.

Habitat

Clean, freshwater locations including rivers, streams and lakes; occasionally found on the coast.

How to attract this bird to your garden

Create a wildlife pond and stock it with small fish, and you may succeed in attracting a kingfisher to your garden. Most garden sightings occur in the summer months and relate to wandering, newly fledged juvenile birds, driven away by their parents.

Can be mistaken for

Unmistakable when seen in good light on account of its shape and plumage colours.

Above Perched kingfishers typically adopt an upright pose. This individual's reddish lower mandible shows it is a female.

Above A kingfisher's dive is over in an instant, the bird's whirring wings shaking off any lingering water droplets.

Ring-necked parakeet

Psittacula krameri

REGION: Introduced from Asia, but an established resident in parts of southern Britain • SIZE: 40–42 cm (16–17 in) • FOOD: Mainly fruits, seeds and nuts • CALL: Utters various raucous, squawking calls • SEX DIFFERENCES: The sexes are superficially similar but only the male has the black-and-pink ring around the neck • JUVENILE: Similar to an adult female • FLIGHT: Direct, but often with sudden changes in direction, on rapid wingbeats • NEST: Uses natural tree holes.

The ring-necked parakeet originates from Asia, with its stronghold being the Indian sub-continent. It is popular as a cage bird and, inevitably, some birds escape from captivity or are released. Several colonies have established themselves across Europe. Currently, feral populations in England are the only ones that seem to be thriving and expanding. With its rounded head and powerful, curved bill this species is unmistakably a member of the parrot family. They are adept at opening fruits and seeds, and they sometimes use their feet to hold food.

Few European bird species have such intensely green plumage as ring-necked parakeets. The tail is proportionately very long and, seen in good light, it has a bluish hue above while appearing yellowish beneath.

Habitat

Mature gardens and parks.

How to attract this bird to your garden

Put out fruits and seeds on your bird table and, if you live in an area they have colonized, you may be visited by this species.

Can be mistaken for

Unmistakable on account of its colour and shape.

Adult male

Wryneck

Jynx torquilla

REGION: Widespread summer visitor to central and southern Europe, and more locally across lowland Scandinavia, present mainly May to August. Scarce migrant visitor elsewhere in the region, mainly in spring and autumn • SIZE: 16–17 cm (6½–7 in) • FOOD: Mainly ants • CALL: Territorial birds utter a piping call, reminiscent of a bird of prey • SEX DIFFERENCES: The sexes are similar • JUVENILE: Similar to an adult but the dark crown stripe is less distinct • FLIGHT: Rapid and undulating • NEST: Sited in a tree hole.

The wryneck is an unusual member of the woodpecker family – among other things, it is the only member of the group to migrate. It feeds mainly on the ground and collects ants and other insects with its long, darting tongue. The remarkably intricate plumage markings are an excellent match for tree bark and they can be surprisingly difficult to spot when they are perched off the ground.

Wrynecks have remarkably flexible necks and can turn their heads through almost 360 degrees when they want to survey their surroundings. This flexibility also helps them to search for food, as they can probe at awkward angles under stones and clumps of vegetation.

Habitat

Orchards, mature gardens and parks with short grass and bare ground for feeding, and mature trees with natural holes for nesting.

How to attract this bird to your garden

Leave old, gnarled trees in the garden and they may nest there; occasionally they will use a hole-fronted nest box.

Can be mistaken for

Unmistakable on account of both its shape and its intricate plumage marking.

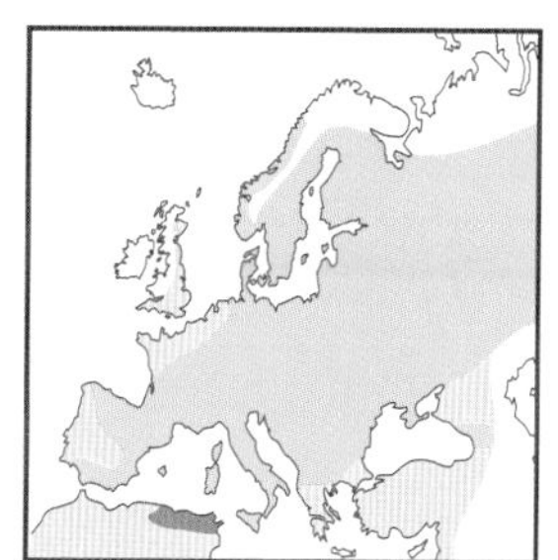

Adult

Black woodpecker

Dryocopus martius

REGION: Widespread in central and northern mainland Europe; local in southeast Europe • SIZE: 40–45 cm (16–18 in) • FOOD: Mainly tree-dwelling ants and other invertebrates • CALL: Utters a rattling alarm call in flight • SONG: A series of loud, yelping calls • SEX DIFFERENCES: The sexes are superficially similar but males have a red crown while in females this colour is limited to the nape • JUVENILE: Similar to adults of the same sex • FLIGHT: Direct, on flapping wingbeats • NEST: Sited in a hole excavated in a mature tree.

The black woodpecker is the largest of its kind in our region and is the size of a carrion crow (see page 202). Indeed, in flight they are not always easy to distinguish although the woodpecker's rather jerky wing-beats are a good clue. Once the bird lands on a tree trunk, however, you will be left in no doubt as to its identity.

In poor light, a black woodpecker's plumage can look uniformly dark but sunlight reveals a brownish tinge to the wing feathers in particular. If you get a good view, the beady whitish eye and the stout, pale bill are striking. The latter is put to good use excavating timber in search of food and, in spring, territorial males announce ownership of their domains by 'drumming' loudly – by repeatedly hammering the bill against the trunk of a tree.

Habitat

Mainly mature conifer and mixed woodland.

How to attract this bird to your garden

Allow large conifers to grow to maturity and you stand an outside chance of luring this species into your garden. You can attract their attention – briefly – by imitating their loud and distinctive call.

Can be mistaken for

Unmistakable if seen clearly on account of its huge size and uniformly dark plumage.

Above A female black woodpecker has less red on its cap than the male.

Adult male

Grey-headed woodpecker

Picus canus

REGION: Widespread resident in central and eastern Europe • SIZE: 28–30 cm (11–12 in) • FOOD: Insects, particularly ants • CALL: Utters a harsh shriek if alarmed • SONG: A series of whistling notes that is easy to imitate • SEX DIFFERENCES: The sexes are superficially similar but only the male has a small patch of red on the forehead • JUVENILE: Similar to adults of the same sex, but duller • FLIGHT: Undulating, pulling in wings between bouts of rapid wingbeats • NEST: Sited in a hole, excavated in a mature tree trunk.

The grey-headed woodpecker is a rather unobtrusive bird and although it is not especially shy it often prefers to shuffle round a tree trunk rather than reveal itself. However, you can sometimes lure males in particular into the open by imitating their whistling song.

The species favours locations where both mature living trees and dead and decaying specimens can be found side by side. This provides the birds with a varied source of food, from tree-dwelling ants to the grubs of wood-boring beetles. Occasionally grey-headed woodpeckers feed on the ground, usually probing soft soil for ants.

Habitat

Open deciduous and mixed woodland and wooded parks.

How to attract this bird to your garden

A combination of mature trees, particularly aspens (*Populus tremulus*), and a short grassy lawn (for feeding) may tempt these birds into your garden especially if you live in a wooded area.

Can be mistaken for

Green woodpecker (see pages 190–191), but that species has a mainly yellowish (not grey) head and more red on the crown.

Above A female has a more uniformly grey head than a male.

Adult male

Green woodpecker

Picus viridis

REGION: Widespread resident across most of Europe; except the far north • SIZE: 32–34 cm (13–13½ in) • FOOD: Mainly ants • CALL: Utters a loud, tri-syllabic laughing shriek in alarm • SONG: A series of ten or more loud, laughing notes • SEX DIFFERENCES: The sexes are superficially similar but in males the centre of the dark 'moustache' stripe is red (it is uniformly black in females) • JUVENILE: Recalls adults but the upperparts are spangled with white spots while the underparts are marked with dark spots; the vent is pinkish-red and the belly grubby white • FLIGHT: Undulating, pulling in wings between bouts of rapid wingbeats • NEST: Sited in a hole excavated in a mature tree trunk.

Seen in good light, green woodpeckers are extremely colourful birds; their backs and wings are mainly green, the crown is scarlet and their rumps are pale yellowish-green. The last of these is particularly striking when a startled bird flies away.

Despite the species' comparatively large size, its diet consists almost exclusively of ants and their larvae and pupae. Consequently, birds spend much of the time foraging on the ground, excavating holes in ant colonies with their chisel-like bills and extracting the insects with their long, sticky-tipped tongues.

Green woodpecker

Great spotted woodpecker

Grey-headed woodpecker

Adult male

During the nesting season, green woodpeckers are extremely secretive and typically are heard far more frequently than they are seen. Birds are extremely good at hiding among tree foliage and have a habit of shuffling round branches and trunks to hide. It is far easier to get good views of a green woodpecker in autumn and winter.

Above A juvenile green woodpecker's plumage is adorned with spots and dark barring.

Habitat

Open deciduous and mixed woodland, parks, commons and mature gardens.

How to attract this bird to your garden

Encourage ant colonies in your lawn, and keep the grass short, and there is a good chance that this species will visit your garden to feed. During the summer months, they will very occasionally visit a garden pond to drink or bathe.

Can be mistaken for

Grey-headed woodpecker (see page 189), but green woodpeckers have an extensive red crown and an otherwise mainly pale yellowish (not grey) head.

Above A green woodpecker's feet and claws are adapted for clinging onto wood but for extra support the tail is useful.

Great spotted woodpecker

Dendrocopus major

REGION: A widespread resident across most of Europe • SIZE: 23–24 cm (9–9½ in) • FOOD: Mainly insects and other invertebrates, but it will visit garden feeders where nuts and fat are provided • CALL: Utters a loud *tchick* alarm • SEX DIFFERENCES: The sexes are superficially similar but males have a red patch on the otherwise black nape (this is uniformly black in females) • JUVENILE: Recalls a grubby-looking adult but has the red crown • FLIGHT: Rapid and undulating, short glides interspersed with bouts of rapid wingbeats • NEST: Sited in a hole excavated in tree trunk.

Because of its habit of visiting garden feeders, this is the easiest European woodpecker species to observe well. Indeed, in some circumstances they can become remarkably tolerant of people. Their plumage is bold and distinctive and particularly striking in flight, when large white panels are visible on the upper wings and the bright red undertail feathers can be seen.

Great spotted woodpecker

Lesser spotted woodpecker

Middle spotted woodpecker

Adult male

In spring, male great spotted woodpeckers announce territorial ownership by 'drumming' loudly – they strike a resonant dead branch repeatedly (up to 15 times in succession) with their chisel-like bills. Females also do this, but to a lesser extent. The bill is the perfect tool for chiselling away timber in search of insects and other invertebrates. It is also ideal for excavating the nest chamber; they choose a new location each year and prefer the dead and decaying stumps of oak and birch trees.

Habitat
Deciduous and mixed woodland, parks and mature gardens.

How to attract this bird to your garden
Stock your garden feeders with nuts and fat and you stand a good chance of being visited by this species, especially in the winter months. This even applies if you live in a town or on the fringes of a city because the species is often found in surprisingly suburban areas.

Can be mistaken for
Lesser spotted woodpecker (see page 194), which is appreciably smaller and barred on the back; middle spotted woodpecker (see page 195), which has a red crown and less extensive dark markings on the face.

Above The true extent of the black-and-white barring on a great spotted woodpecker's wings is only revealed in flight.

Above Juveniles – recognized by their red caps – are adept at climbing and chiselling from the moment they fledge.

Lesser spotted woodpecker

Dendrocopus minor

REGION: A widespread but local resident across much of Europe • SIZE: 14–15 cm (5½–6 in) • FOOD: Insects and other invertebrates • CALL: Utters a faint *kick* in alarm • SONG: Male utters series of shrill piping notes in spring, reminiscent of a bird of prey • SEX DIFFERENCES: The sexes are rather similar but males have a red crown (this is black in females) • JUVENILE: Similar to adults of the same sex • FLIGHT: Rather weak with deep undulations; bouts of wingbeats are interspersed with glides • NEST: Sited in a hole, excavated in a tree trunk or branch.

The lesser spotted woodpecker is a tiny bird compared to its cousins, and is not much larger than a house sparrow. This alone makes it difficult to locate in a woodland habitat and its rather shy and retiring habits only make matters more problematic. The best time to look for the species is in spring when, for a few weeks, males become bolder and announce their presence with a loud and distinctive piping song.

Outside the breeding season, this species often associates with other woodland birds such as tits and forms part of mixed flocks that lead a rather nomadic life at this time of year. With the leaves fallen from the trees, it is sometimes possible to observe the lesser spotted woodpecker's feeding action – the bill taps rapidly against branches and twigs (to locate and extract insects).

Habitat

Deciduous woodland, parks and mature, wooded gardens.

How to attract this bird to your garden

If you have plenty of mature, gnarled old trees in your garden (old fruit trees for example) this species may choose to nest. Unlike the great spotted woodpecker, it seldom visits garden feeders although individuals have been seen to take an interest in black sunflower seeds.

Can be mistaken for

Great spotted woodpecker (see pages 192–193), and middle spotted woodpecker (see opposite) although its small size and barred back make identification simple.

Adult male

Middle spotted woodpecker

Dendrocopus medius

REGION: Widespread resident across central, eastern and parts of western mainland Europe • SIZE: 20–22 cm (8–9 in) • FOOD: Insects and other invertebrates • CALL: A soft *kick* • SONG: A series of thin, piping notes • SEX DIFFERENCES: The sexes are similar although red elements of the plumage are duller in females than males • JUVENILE: Similar to adult females • FLIGHT: Undulating and rather weak • NEST: Sited in a hole excavated in a tree trunk or branch.

The middle spotted woodpecker is a well-proportioned and distinctively marked bird with a rounded head. Compared to those of its cousins, the bill is proportionately rather stubby but nevertheless perfectly adequate when excavating decaying timber in search of wood-boring insects and invertebrates under the bark.

Although these birds are not particularly shy, they are unobtrusive and can be easy to miss. Their calls are quiet and subdued and, unlike the great spotted woodpecker, males do not 'drum' to advertize their territory. They are perhaps easiest to observe in spring when nesting individuals are most active and conspicuous.

Like other woodpeckers, middle spotted woodpeckers excavate nesting holes and chambers, occasionally just a metre or so from the ground, and even old, weathered wooden gateposts are sometimes used for this purpose.

Habitat

Orchards, olive groves and deciduous woodland.

How to attract this bird to your garden

Leave old, gnarled trees and rotting stumps standing and this species may choose to nest.

Can be mistaken for

Great spotted woodpecker (see pages 192–193), especially juveniles, but middle spotted woodpeckers have streaked underparts and more white on the face.

Adult

Jay

Garrulus glandarius

REGION: A widespread resident across much of the region • SIZE: 33–35 (12–14 in) cm • FOOD: Omnivorous; mainly acorns and other seeds and nuts in winter but also insects and the eggs and young of songbirds in spring • CALL: A raucous scream • SONG: a subdued mixture of cackling and mewing notes • SEX DIFFERENCES: The sexes are similar • JUVENILE: Similar to adults but with subdued colours • FLIGHT: Direct but rather slow, on flapping wingbeats • NEST: A twiggy structure sited on the fork of a branch.

Above Most acorns that are consumed by jays in autumn are buried in the ground as a winter food source.

Jays are rather shy and nervous birds, so it is rare to get the opportunity to appreciate the subtly colourful pinkish plumage for any length of time. The most typical view is that of a disturbed bird flying away, when the striking and unmistakable (for a woodland bird of this size) white rump and contrasting black tail are revealed, making it easy to identify.

If you do get a close look at a perched jay, you will see such plumage details as the white crown, streaked with black, the black 'moustache' stripe and the white throat. The beautifully patterned patches of blue, black and white feathers on the wings are particularly striking.

Jays are important in the regeneration and spread of oak woodland. Each autumn, birds gather large quantities of acorns, and bury most of them in the ground. These caches of food are meant as a winter store for the jay in times of hardship but inevitably some are overlooked, germinate and grow into new oak trees.

Habitat

Deciduous woodland, parks and mature gardens.

How to attract this bird to your garden

Jays will sometimes come to garden feeders, especially if whole peanuts are scattered on a bird table. Try collecting acorns in the autumn and putting handfuls out in winter. Most jays find them irresistible.

Can be mistaken for

Unmistakable when seen in good light on account of plumage colours and bold white rump.

Hoopoe

Adult

Magpie

Pica pica

REGION: A widespread resident across much of the region • SIZE: 45–50 (18–20 in) cm • FOOD: Omnivorous. Feeds on seeds, nuts, berries and invertebrates but also eats carrion and, in season, takes the eggs and young of small birds • CALL: A raucous rattling alarm • SONG: Subdued and seldom heard • SEX DIFFERENCES: The sexes are similar • JUVENILE: Similar to the adults • FLIGHT: Direct and fluttering • NEST: A sizeable, almost spherical, twiggy structure sited in a dense tree or bush.

Magpies are distinctive black-and-white birds and are unmistakable both on the ground and in flight with their proportionately long tail and rounded wings, the outer half of which are mainly white. At close range and in good light you can see a metallic bluish sheen on the wing feathers.

Magpies are most frequently seen close to roads where they feed on animal road casualties. The species has something of a bad reputation among some birdwatchers because of its liking for songbird eggs and chicks. Although its habits are undeniable, its impact in the overall scheme of things is trivial and, in any case, its predatory role is an entirely natural part of nature's checks and balances.

Habitat

Open country, woodland, farmland, parks and gardens.

How to attract this bird to your garden

Given this species' feeding habits, you may not want to encourage them into your garden, but it is likely to be part of a magpie's territory anyway.

Can be mistaken for

Unmistakable on account of pied plumage and long tail.

Adult

Azure-winged magpie

Cyanopica cyanus

REGION: A local resident, restricted to the southern Iberian Peninsula • SIZE: 32–35 cm (13–14 in) • FOOD: Omnivorous, feeding mainly on insects and berries • CALL: Utters a grating, rattling call in alarm • SONG: Subdued and seldom heard • SEX DIFFERENCES: The sexes are similar • JUVENILE: Similar to adults but with subdued colours and pale feather tips • FLIGHT: Direct but rather weak • NEST: An untidy, twiggy structure sited high in the tree canopy.

The azure-winged magpie is an amazingly colourful and distinctive bird; its black cap and white throat offset the otherwise azure-blue and pinkish-buff plumage. Although they are generally rather shy, individuals can become surprisingly bold in garden settings where they are not disturbed.

Outside the breeding season, they are often seen in family groups that move from tree to tree in a noisy procession. For birds of this size, they are surprisingly agile and often feed actively in the slender, outermost branches of tall trees.

The azure-winged magpie has a rather bizarre global distribution. Away from the Iberian Peninsula, the nearest location where it occurs is East Asia.

Habitat

Coniferous and mixed woodland, parks and mature gardens.

How to attract this bird to your garden

Create a drinking pool for the best chance of luring this species into the garden. The hot, dry summer months are best.

Can be mistaken for

Unmistakable because of plumage colours and long tail.

Adult

Jackdaw

Corvus monedula

REGION: A widespread resident across much of the region; some northern populations are migrant summer visitors to their range and move south in autumn • SIZE: 31–34 cm (12½–13½ in) • FOOD: Omnivorous • CALL: Utters a sharp *chack* • SEX DIFFERENCES: The sexes are similar • JUVENILE: Similar to adults but the blue-grey colour of the iris in the eye is duller • FLIGHT: Direct, with flapping wingbeats • NEST: An untidy twiggy structure, sited in a natural or man-made crevice (sometimes they use chimneys).

In poor light, a jackdaw can appear uniformly black but if seen clearly the nape is pale grey and contrasts with the darker cap. On the ground, it walks with a characteristic swagger and by nature it is alert and quick to take advantage of any feeding opportunity.

Outside the breeding season, in particular, jackdaws form sizeable flocks that descend on arable fields and grassland to feed. They have also successfully colonized many urban areas, and in parks where they are fed, not persecuted, they can become remarkably tame and bold. Jackdaws will also scavenge at rubbish tips, especially in winter.

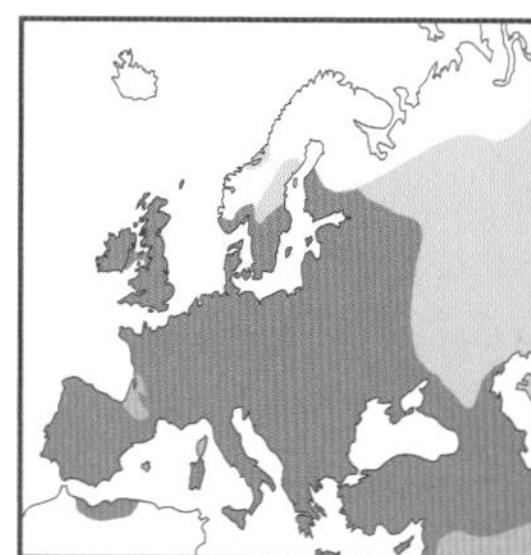

Jackdaw

Rook

Carrion crow

Adult

Above A juvenile jackdaw lacks the sleek, oily sheen to the feathers seen in adult birds.

Jackdaws are skilled aeronauts and often acrobatic and seemingly playful on the wing. Their aerial prowess is most frequently apparent in spring when rival pairs sometimes spar with one another for the right to occupy a particularly choice nest site.

Habitat

Farmland, open country, sea cliffs, parks and towns.

How to attract this bird to your garden

Scatter food on your lawn (for example seed and breadcrumbs) and you may attract jackdaws. However, they seem more inclined to visit gardens in suburban areas than in rural ones.

Can be mistaken for

Carrion crow (see page 202), but appreciably smaller in size; check for the pale eye and grey nape.

Above In flight, a jackdaw's wings reveal long 'fingers' – the primary feathers – which give superb aerial control.

SIMILAR SPECIES

Chough

Pyrrhocorax pyrrhocorax

LENGTH: 38–40 cm (15½–16½ in)

A distinctive member of the crow family with a long, curved, red bill and bright red legs. In flight, note the broad, 'fingered' wingtips. Usually seen in flocks and favours short grassy areas on sea cliffs and inland mountain slopes. A widespread but local resident.

Alpine Chough

Pyrrhocorax graculus

LENGTH: 36–38 cm (14½–15½ in)

Superficially similar to a chough but has a shorter yellow (not red) bill and stays in a strictly upland habitat: they are seldom found away from the snow line in the mountains of southern Europe. The plumage is all dark and the wingtips splay.

Chough

Alpine chough

Carrion crow

Corvus corone corone

REGION: Resident in parts of western and northwestern Europe • SIZE: 45–50 cm (18–20 in) • FOOD: Has an extremely varied diet; scavenges carrion and discarded food, and consumes eggs and nestlings of smaller birds • CALL: A harsh croaking call • SEX DIFFERENCES: Sexes are similar, both in size and plumage • JUVENILE: Similar to adults • FLIGHT: Rapid, on deep wingbeats • NEST: A large, twiggy structure built in a tree.

The carrion crow is uniformly black and you can only see the glossy sheen of the plumage in strong sunlight. Pairs are territorial and nest alone, unlike rooks, which are colonial breeders. They are extremely aggressive to other members of the crow family and will even mob passing birds of prey.

Habitat

Favours a wide variety of habitats from farmland and open country to woodland margins and mature gardens. Also sometimes found in urban parks.

How to attract this bird to your garden

Given this species' predatory skill at finding the nests of songbirds, you may not wish to encourage it into the garden.

Can be mistaken for

Rook (see pages 204–205), which has a white base to its bill; raven (see right), which is a much larger bird with a relatively massive bill.

SIMILAR SPECIES

Raven

Corvus corax

LENGTH: 55–65 cm (22–26 in); wingspan 115–130 cm (46–52 in)
A large buzzard-sized bird with all-black plumage and a huge bill. In flight it 'tumbles'; you can use its wedge-shaped tail and its loud cronking call to help you to identify it. Ravens are widespread in rugged upland areas across the region. They feed mainly by scavenging.

Above The raven is an extremely bulky bird. The highly glossy sheen to its plumage is visible in strong sunlight.

Hooded crow

Corvus corone cornix

REGION: Widespread in eastern and northern Europe, as well as the northwestern fringes; its range overlaps very little with that of its cousin, the carrion crow. Across most of its range it is resident but northeastern populations are summer migrants • SIZE: 45–50 cm (18–20 in) • FOOD: An opportunistic feeder that will scavenge anything from carrion to discarded human food; in season, it also takes the eggs and nestlings of smaller birds • CALL: A harsh croaking • SEX DIFFERENCES: Sexes are similar, in size and plumage • JUVENILE: Similar to the adults but the plumage shows less contrast between the dark and pale elements • FLIGHT: Rapid, with deep, flapping wingbeats • NEST: A large, tangled structure of twigs and branches in a tree.

In many parts of its range, the hooded crow is distinctly wary of people. However, if you venture near the nest in the spring, you are certain to get mobbed by angry adult birds. The same response is shown towards other potential predators and hooded crows will unhesitatingly attack birds of prey that intrude on their territories. Outside the breeding season, the species is usually encountered singly or in pairs.

Habitat

Found in a wide range of open habitats, from moorland and farmland to wetlands and the seashore.

How to attract this bird to your garden

Not everyone will want to attract this species to the garden, especially in spring and summer when it will take its toll of the eggs and young of nesting songbirds. If you do wish to encourage it, however, scraps of almost any sort of food, placed on the bird table, will normally do the trick.

Can be mistaken for

Jackdaw (see pages 200–201), although the size difference between the two species should make them relatively easy to tell apart.

Adult

Rook

Corvus frugilegus

REGION: Widespread resident across much of central and northwestern Europe; populations from northeastern Europe are mainly migrant summer visitors to the region and in the south they are winter visitors • SIZE: 45–48 cm (18–19 in) • FOOD: Omnivorous, favouring insects, earthworms, seeds and fruits • CALL: Utters a grating *kraah-kraah-kraah* • SEX DIFFERENCES: Sexes similar • JUVENILE: Similar to the adults but the skin at the base of the bill is dark and feathered, not bare and whitish • FLIGHT: Powerful and direct, on broad wings with 'fingered' wingtips • NEST: A sizeable twiggy structure, located high in a tall tree.

On a dull day, a rook's plumage can look uniformly black. However, in bright sunlight, you should spot a purplish sheen and, if you see one against the light, the feathers will look almost silvery. The skin at the base of the long bill is bare, which is probably a useful adaptation for a bird that probes muddy ground in search of food. Rooks walk with a stately and sedate swagger. The long 'thigh' feathers give the species a rather 'baggy trousered' appearance.

Rooks breed colonially and it is not uncommon to find 20 or more nests in close proximity to one another in a small farmland copse. Rook colonies are noisy and, from February onwards, there is a lot of activity with birds repairing their

Above An adult rook has a proportionately large head and a rather peaked cap. In good light an oily sheen to the feathers can be discerned.

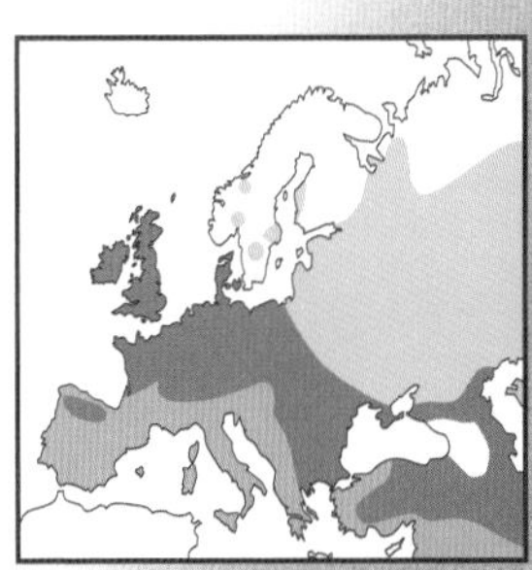

Adult

nests with new twigs and branches; sometimes they resort to stealing these items from their neighbours.

Rooks are social birds throughout the year and typically even feed as a flock. Particularly during the winter months, these aggregations can comprise hundreds, if not thousands, of individuals. They are particularly impressive as they gather together and fly *en masse* to their woodland roosts.

Habitat
Open farmland and grassland for feeding, with nearby woodland for nesting and roosting.

How to attract this bird to your garden
Scattering food (bread, nuts and fruit) on the lawn may attract them.

Can be mistaken for
Juveniles could be mistaken for carrion crows (see page 202), but they have a marginally longer bill and longer wings, and will usually be seen with adult rooks.

Reed warbler

Acrocephalus scirpaceus

REGION: A widespread but only locally common summer visitor to Europe. Present mainly May to August • SIZE: 13–14 cm (c. 5½ in) • FOOD: Insects and other invertebrates • CALL: Utters a sharp *tche* alarm call • SONG: A series of grating and chattering notes • SEX DIFFERENCES: The sexes are similar • JUVENILE: Similar to the adults • FLIGHT: Direct and low • NEST: A grassy cup, woven among the stems of reeds.

The reed warbler can be a difficult bird to observe well among the swaying stems of its favoured reedbed habitat, especially since its rather uniform brown plumage blends in well with its surroundings. Being waterlogged or inundated, reedbeds are not the easiest of places to explore, but the song is distinctive enough for you to be able to identify the species even if you can't see the singer itself. They can be easier to see when they forage for insects among bushes on the drier margins of wetlands.

Habitat

Reedbeds.

How to attract this bird to your garden

Unless you live close to the margins of a large wetland with extensive reedbeds you are unlikely to see this species during the breeding season. If you have a sizeable pond with a well-vegetated margin, however, then it may turn up on migration in spring and autumn, especially if yours is the only pond in the vicinity.

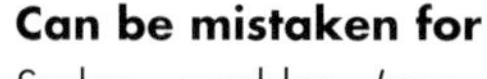

Can be mistaken for

Sedge warbler (see opposite), although it lacks that species' striking eyestripe and dark cap.

Adult

Sedge warbler

Acrocephalus schoenobaenus

REGION: A widespread but only locally common summer visitor to central and northern Europe; present mainly May to August. In much of southern Europe it is seen only on migration • SIZE: 12–13 cm (c. 5 in) • FOOD: Insects and other invertebrates • CALL: Utters a sharp *check* alarm • SONG: Grating and rasping phrases interspersed with whistles • SEX DIFFERENCES: The sexes are similar • JUVENILE: Similar to the adults • FLIGHT: Direct and low, with jerky wingbeats • NEST: A cup of woven grasses, sited deep in a bush or bramble patch.

Compared to some other warbler species, this is a relatively easy bird to observe. Singing males in particular are fond of perching on prominent bramble stems, or on the tops of small bushes.

The well-marked plumage, notably the white stripe above each eye and the dark crown, makes identification rather straightforward. When they fly between one low bush and another, they often fan their tails out and, if you get a good view, you should be able to see the orange-brown rump and lower back.

Habitat

Wetland habitats, including well-vegetated ditches and pond margins, but also drier areas such as arable fields.

How to attract this bird to your garden

If you encourage a dense growth of vegetation and scrub close to a garden pond, this species may turn up on migration, and it may even nest there.

Can be mistaken for

Reed warbler (see opposite page), although that species has much more uniformly brown plumage.

Adult

Melodious warbler

Hippolais polyglotta

REGION: A summer visitor to western and southwestern Europe, present mainly May to August • SIZE: 12–13 cm (*c.* 5 in) • FOOD: Insects and other invertebrates • CALL: Utters various clicking calls in alarm • SONG: Musical and bubbling • SEX DIFFERENCES: The sexes are similar • JUVENILE: Similar to the adults but with duller colours • FLIGHT: Rapid and direct • NEST: A woven structure of grasses, sited in a dense bush and suspended from a forked branch.

The melodious warbler is unobtrusive and spends much of its time searching for insects among the foliage of trees and bushes. Once in a while it will pop out of cover and when it does the rounded and comparatively large head and broad-based bill (by warbler standards) are apparent. All individuals have a yellowish flush to the face, breast and underparts although the colour is more intense in adults than juvenile birds.

Habitat

Damp woodland and gardens that are well vegetated.

How to attract this bird to your garden

Encourage patches of dense scrub and bushes and it may visit your garden.

Can be mistaken for

Juvenile willow warbler (see page 219), but that species is quite appreciably smaller and it has a proportionately smaller bill.

Adult

Olivaceous warbler

Hippolais pallida

REGION: Summer visitor to southwestern and southeastern Europe, present mainly May to August • SIZE: 12–14 cm (*c.* 5–5½ in) • FOOD: Insects and other invertebrates • CALL: Utters a clicking call in alarm • SONG: Is musical and bubbling • SEX DIFFERENCES: The sexes are similar • JUVENILE: Similar to the adults • FLIGHT: Rapid and direct; usually only seen flying short distances between bushes • NEST: A woven structure of grasses, sited in a dense bush.

The olivaceous warbler is an extremely active bird, constantly on the move in its favoured bushes and shrubs in search of insects. Agitated individuals will often flick their tails up and down. Newly arrived migrants are quick to establish breeding territories and males can often be seen singing from exposed twigs and branches.

If you get a good view, the overall impression is of a rather pale, olive-brown bird with a proportionately rather long, thin bill, which is ideal for picking off small prey items.

Habitat

Water margins, in gardens and orchards.

How to attract this bird to your garden

Encourage a few dense bushes and trees and this species may visit your garden and even nest.

Can be mistaken for

Chiffchaff (see pages 220–221), but that species is smaller in size and has a more compact, almost rounded, appearance.

Adult

Lesser whitethroat

Sylvia curruca

REGION: A widespread summer visitor to central, eastern and parts of northwestern Europe. Present mainly May to August • SIZE: 12–13 cm (*c.* 5 in) • FOOD: Mainly insects and other invertebrates; occasionally berries • CALL: Utters a harsh *chek* in alarm • SONG: A rather tuneless rattle, preceded by a brief warbling phrase • SEX DIFFERENCES: The sexes are similar • JUVENILE: Similar to the adults, but with slightly browner plumage overall • FLIGHT: Direct and low • NEST: A woven grassy structure, sited in a dense bush or shrub.

The lesser whitethroat is a rather unobtrusive little bird that spends much of its time foraging for insects among the foliage of dense bushes. Fortunately, however, the male sings a distinctive rattling song in spring so that you can identify them, even if you can't see them. If you do get a good view, look for the blue-grey cap, dark 'mask' through the eyes, and contrasting clean white throat.

In late summer and early autumn, juvenile birds in particular may visit your garden to feed. Typically they search for insects and berries in bushes and shrubs and, compared to the adults, they are not so wary about feeding in the open.

Habitat

Hedgerows, scrub and mature parks and gardens.

How to attract this bird to your garden

Encourage dense hedges of native, broad-leaved shrubs and this species may nest in your garden.

Can be mistaken for

Whitethroat (see pages 214–215), but that species has reddish-brown rather than grey-brown wings, and lacks the dark 'mask' through the eyes and the dark legs.

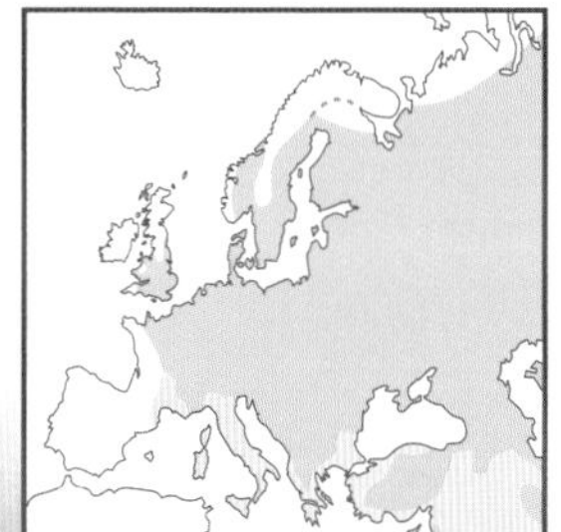

Adult

Subalpine warbler

Sylvia cantillans

REGION: A summer visitor to warm regions of southern Europe, present mainly April to August • SIZE: 12–13 cm (*c.* 5 in) • FOOD: Insects and other invertebrates • CALL: Utters a clicking *chett* in alarm • SONG: A rapid series of high-pitched, squeaky warbling phrases • SEX DIFFERENCES: Males are much more colourful and brightly marked than females • JUVENILE: Similar to adult females but with much browner plumage overall • FLIGHT: Direct and low • NEST: A neat, cup-shaped structure of woven grasses in a dense bush.

Male subalpine warblers are extremely colourful birds with blue-grey upperparts and red underparts, although arguably the most striking feature is the white 'moustache'. Even female and juvenile birds, which are much duller overall, always show a hint of this feature.

The easiest way to check whether this species is present is to listen for the male's warbling song, which is often delivered from a prominent perch. They can be more difficult to find when they are not singing because they spend much of their time foraging for insects among dense foliage.

Habitat

Dense Mediterranean habitats and heathlands with scrub.

How to attract this bird to your garden

Encourage shrubby vegetation and, in rural areas, the species may nest in your garden. It often visits ponds and pools to drink and bathe during the dry, summer months.

Can be mistaken for

The adult male is unmistakable. Female and juvenile birds could perhaps be mistaken for a whitethroat (see pages 214–215), but that species is larger and has the obvious white throat.

Adult male

Sardinian warbler

Sylvia melanocephala

REGION: Resident in warmer, lowland regions of southern Europe • SIZE: 13–14 cm (*c.* 5–5½ in) • FOOD: Mainly insects and other invertebrates • CALL: Utters a loud *tssek* in alarm • SONG: A rapid series of warbling, whistling and chattering phrases • SEX DIFFERENCES: With their black hoods, males are more distinctive and better marked than females, which are mainly grey and brown • JUVENILE: Similar to adult females • FLIGHT: Direct and low • NEST: A cup-shaped structure of woven grasses, sited in a dense bush.

A male Sardinian warbler is an extremely smart bird with a well-defined black hood that contrasts with its clean, white throat and off-sets the bright red ring around the eye. The back and wings are a soft grey colour while the underparts are whitish. By contrast, females are duller and browner overall, with grey, not black, hoods.

The Sardinian warbler is one of the few of its kind to remain in the region throughout the year – most of its cousins migrate to Africa for the winter months. Although it often searches for insects in deep cover, it is not particularly shy and will emerge from the bush in which it is feeding and perch conspicuously from time to time. The species can sometimes be lured out of cover if you make a tongue-smacking imitation of its alarm call.

Habitat

Open woodland, scrub and mature, rural gardens.

How to attract this bird to your garden

Encourage dense, native shrubs and trees to grow in your garden.

Can be mistaken for

Blackcap (see pages 216–217), but check for the extent of the hood, the red eyering and the white throat.

Adult male

Garden warbler

Sylvia borin

REGION: Widespread summer visitor to much of Europe, present mainly April to August • SIZE: 14–15 cm (5½–6 in) • FOOD: Mainly insects and other invertebrates • CALL: Utters a sharp *chek-chek* in alarm • SONG: A rich and musical warble • SEX DIFFERENCES: The sexes are similar • JUVENILE: Similar to the adults • FLIGHT: Direct and low • NEST: A woven, cup-shaped structure, sited among low vegetation.

Although the garden warbler has very nondescript plumage, ironically it is the virtual absence of striking features that provides the best clue to the bird's identity. Few other species of its size have uniformly brown upperparts, buffish-brown underparts and such a stout bill. At close range, the keen-eyed may notice the rather indistinct, but diagnostic, patch of grey on the side of the neck.

What the garden warbler lacks in plumage, it more than makes up for with its song, which could perhaps be confused with that of a blackcap (see pages 216–217). It is loud and even more musical than its cousin's song, some phrases having a thrush-like tone; for many people, the garden warbler almost rivals the nightingale as a songster.

Habitat

Deciduous woodland, well-wooded parks and mature gardens.

How to attract this bird to your garden

Provide dense shrubs and hedges as a nesting habitat and pools and ponds for drinking and bathing.

Can be mistaken for

A juvenile barred warbler (see page 218), although that species has pale wingbars and 'scaly' flanks. The song could be confused with that of a blackcap (see pages 216–217).

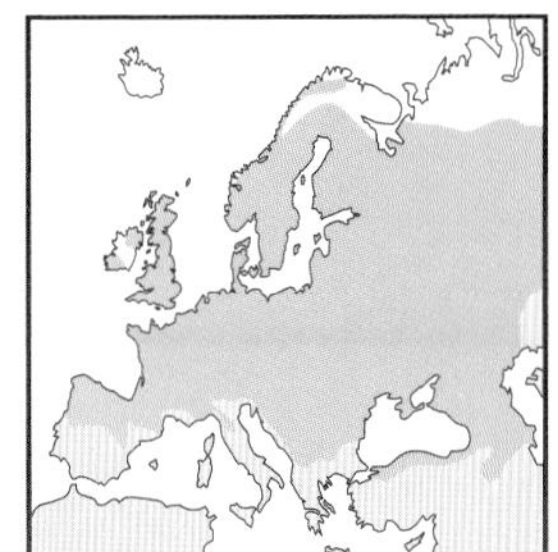

Above The nest is usually tucked away unobtrusively in low vegetation.

Whitethroat

Sylvia communis

REGION: A widespread summer visitor to much of the region, present mainly from April to September • SIZE: 13–15 cm (5–6 in) • FOOD: Mainly insects and other invertebrates • CALL: Utters a harsh *chekk* in alarm • SONG: A rapid series of scratchy, warbling phrases • SEX DIFFERENCES: Males are more brightly marked than females, particularly on the head • JUVENILE: Similar to adult females • FLIGHT: Direct and low • NEST: A cup-shaped structure of woven grasses, sited in a bush or bramble patch.

Whitethroat

Garden warbler

Blackcap

Above Chestnut on the wings and white on the throat are useful pointers for the indentification of this juvenile whitethroat.

The whitethroat is an energetic and pugnacious little bird. Territorial males are frequently seen perched on the top of bramble patches singing their cheerful, warbling songs. Once in a while a particularly exuberant individual will perform a short, undulating song flight.

A male whitethroat has a smart grey cap that contrasts markedly with his clean white throat and offsets the pale eyering. By contrast, the head pattern on a female is much duller but both sexes have chestnut-brown edges to the wing feathers.

Whitethroats eat mainly insects, such as caterpillars and bush-crickets, as well as spiders, all of which are common in their favoured habitats. In summer, however, they will also take berries as they begin to form on bushes and shrubs.

Habitat

Scrub-covered slopes, bramble patches and heathlands.

How to attract this bird to your garden

Encourage dense shrubs and tolerate bramble patches and, if your garden is surrounded by open country, this species may visit.

Can be mistaken for

Could be confused with a lesser whitethroat (see page 210), but this has a dark mask, is smaller and has an entirely different song.

SIMILAR SPECIES

Dartford warbler

Sylvia undata

LENGTH: 13–14 cm (*c.* 5–5½ in)

A resident species in western and southwest Europe, favouring heaths and scrub-covered slopes. The body is rounded and they often hold their proportionately long tail cocked. The upperparts are mainly blue-grey while the underparts are reddish; the males are more colourful than the females.

Blackcap

Sylvia atricapilla

REGION: A widespread summer visitor to much of the region, present mainly April to September; populations from western and southwestern Europe are partly resident in those areas • SIZE: 14–15 cm (5½–6 in) • FOOD: Mainly insects and other invertebrates but also berries, in season • CALL: Utters a sharp *tchek* in alarm • SONG: A rich and musical warble, not unlike that of a garden warbler (see page 213) • SEX DIFFERENCES: Males have black caps while females have reddish-brown caps • JUVENILE: Similar to adult females • FLIGHT: Direct and low • NEST: A woven, cup-shaped structure, sited in a dense bush.

The song of the blackcap is a familiar sound in the spring countryside and, if you live in a rural area, you may well hear it in your garden too. Territorial birds are not especially shy and they will often sing in full view, from a bare and exposed branch.

Caterpillars are a particularly important source of food in spring and early summer, both for adult birds and for their hungry broods. However, as the seasons progress, they will greedily consume ripe blackberries. Some individuals even become stained around the mouth by red juice from these succulent berries.

The majority of European blackcaps migrate and spend the winter months in Africa. However, an increasing number are found in western and southwestern Europe throughout the year; some may be genuine residents while a proportion are short-distance migrants that have come from areas farther north and east in Europe.

Above A female blackcap's reddish-brown cap is extremely unusual among European birds.

Habitat

Deciduous woodlands, hedgerows, wooded parkland and mature gardens.

How to attract this bird to your garden

Dense shrubs and hedges may attract this bird to your garden in spring and summer. Wintering birds in western Europe sometimes pay regular visits to garden feeders and are particularly fond of currants and fat.

Can be mistaken for

Males could perhaps be mistaken for a marsh tit (see pages 52–53), although their larger size and greyish (not buffish) back will help you to identify them correctly; female and juvenile birds are unmistakable because of their reddish-brown caps.

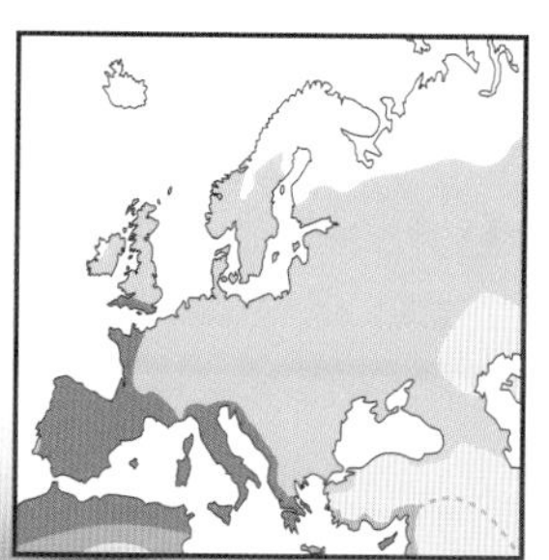

Blackcap

Garden warbler

Whitethroat

Adult male

Barred warbler

Sylvia nisoria

REGION: A summer visitor to eastern Europe, present mainly May to August • SIZE: 15–16 cm (6–6½ in) • FOOD: Mainly insects and other invertebrates, but also berries in season • CALL: Utters a chattering alarm call • SONG: A series of fluty, warbling phrases and rasping notes • SEX DIFFERENCES: The sexes are similar but males have brighter eyes and stronger barring on the underparts • JUVENILE: Has mainly brown upperparts and buffish-brown underparts with a pale throat; note the pale wingbars and 'scaly' feathering on the flanks • FLIGHT: Direct and low • NEST: A woven, cup-shaped structure, sited in a dense bush.

The barred warbler is rather secretive and were it not for its loud, tuneful song it would be easy to overlook. It is often found in the same sort of habitat as the red-backed shrike (see pages 174–175) and the two species sometimes nest surprisingly close to one another.

Juvenile barred warblers are often seen on autumn migration in western Europe, well away from the species' breeding range. Although they still have retiring habits, they are more inclined to feed in the open than adult birds. Berries feature in their diet as well as insects.

Habitat

Open woodland, scrub and mature gardens.

How to attract this bird to your garden

Encourage plenty of cover and dense hedges in your garden and, if you live in a wooded area, it may decide to visit.

Can be mistaken for

The adults are unmistakable, but juveniles could be confused with garden warblers (see page 213); look for the pale wingbars and 'scaly' feathering on the flanks.

Above Adults, recognized by their beady yellow eyes and barred underparts, occasionally visit gardens in spring.

Willow warbler

Phylloscopus trochilus

REGION: A widespread summer visitor to central and northern Europe and seen on migration elsewhere; present mainly April to September • SIZE: 11 cm (4½ in) • FOOD: Insects and other invertebrates • CALL: Utters a soft *hueet* • SONG: A tinkling, descending phrase that ends in a flourish • SEX DIFFERENCES: The sexes are similar • JUVENILE: Strikingly yellowish when compared to an adult • FLIGHT: Direct and low • NEST: A domed structure of woven grass, sited on the ground.

Willow warblers are true harbingers of spring. Typically they arrive back in the region and begin singing just as the buds of leaves and flowers are beginning to burst on trees and bushes.

They are active birds, constantly foraging for insects and spiders among the foliage. Once in a while, a bird will hover momentarily in order to catch an otherwise inaccessible item of food.

In late summer, juvenile birds often visit mature gardens where there are plenty of insects. Juveniles (pictured here) are easier to identify than adults at this time of year, because the yellowish colour to the plumage is particularly bright on the underparts.

Habitat

Deciduous woodland, scrub and mature gardens.

How to attract this bird to your garden

Encourage plenty of dense bushes and shrubs in the garden and this species may visit, if only to feed, or on migration. Willow warblers need a woodland floor covered with undisturbed leaf litter for nesting purposes.

Can be mistaken for

Chiffchaff (see pages 220–221). Listen for the different songs and look at the leg colour to tell them apart (this species has pale reddish legs while those of a chiffchaff are dark).

Above Adults have rather drab plumage compared with juveniles.

Juvenile

Chiffchaff

Phylloscopus collybita

REGION: A widespread summer visitor to central and northern Europe, present mainly March to September. The species is found year-round in parts of southern and western Europe (most northern European chiffchaffs overwinter around the Mediterranean). In the southern Iberian Peninsula it is a winter visitor only • SIZE: 11 cm (4½ in) • FOOD: Insects and other invertebrates • CALL: A soft *hueet* call, similar to that of a willow warbler (see page 219) • SONG: A continually repeated *tsip-tsap* or *chiff-chaff* • SEX DIFFERENCES: The sexes are similar • JUVENILE: Similar to the adults • FLIGHT: Direct and low • NEST: A woven dome-shaped structure of grasses, sited on the ground.

The chiffchaff has one of the most distinctive and easily recognizable songs of any European warbler. From late March onwards, it is a familiar sound to anyone who lives, or spends time, in the countryside. Songsters often perch conspicuously but at other times these birds can be difficult to spot as they forage for insects among dappled foliage.

Adult

The chiffchaff is a small, rather compact warbler and both adults and juveniles share the same olive-brown upperparts and whitish underparts. In many respects this species is similar to an adult willow warbler and its dark (often blackish) legs are the most reliable identification feature if the bird in question is not singing.

On migration, and in winter, chiffchaffs often feed in low bushes and sometimes forage for insects on the ground itself. The needle-like bill is ideally suited to picking up small prey items.

Habitat
Deciduous woodland, scrub and mature gardens.

How to attract this bird to your garden
If you encourage dense shrubs and hedges to grow within your garden, particularly in the vicinity of a pond, this species may make a visit during spring or summer.

Can be mistaken for
Willow warbler (see page 219), but note the different songs of the two species and the willow warbler's reddish (not dark) legs.

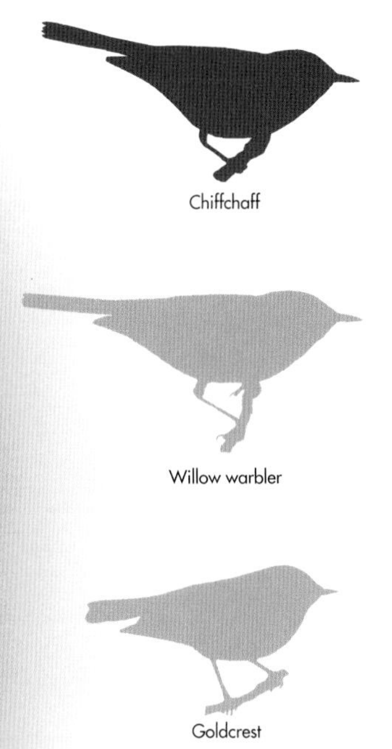

Above Chiffchaffs nest on the ground; their unobtrusive behaviour and rather drab plumage mean predators find them hard to spot.

Goldcrest

Regulus regulus

REGION: A widespread resident across much of central Europe; populations from northern Europe are mainly summer visitors while in much of southern Europe they are winter visitors only • SIZE: 9 cm (3½ in) • FOOD: Mainly insects and other invertebrates • CALL: Utters a thin, high-pitched *tsee-tsee-tsee* • SONG: A series of high-pitched phrases, ending in a flourish • SEX DIFFERENCES: The sexes are superficially similar but the crown colour of males is orange, while in females it is yellow • JUVENILE: Lacks the adults' crown stripe • FLIGHT: Direct and rapid, but is also capable of hovering • NEST: A cup-shaped structure of woven mosses and spider silk, suspended from a twig.

The goldcrest is the smallest bird in the region, with a compact, almost rounded body and a rather short tail. With something so tiny, it is hard to imagine that some individuals migrate hundreds, sometimes thousands, of kilometres each spring and autumn. The eye is proportionately large and beady, emphasized by the otherwise mainly pale face, and the bill is thin and needle-like.

It is easiest to detect the presence of this species in a wood or garden by listening for the extremely high-pitched calls. They are extremely active birds, on the go for most of the hours of daylight, searching foliage for caterpillars, aphids, spiders and other invertebrates.

Outside the breeding season, goldcrests often associate with mixed flocks of other woodland songbirds, notably tits. They probably gain a degree of security from safety in numbers.

Above Goldcrests will often nest in even an isolated conifer in the garden.

Habitat

Conifer and mixed woodland, and mature parks and gardens that include conifers.

How to attract this bird to your garden

Plant conifers in your garden and once they have grown to stately proportions then this species will probably visit, or even nest.

Can be mistaken for

Firecrest (see page 224), but that species has a white stripe above the eye and a dark stripe through.

Firecrest

Regulus ignicapillus

REGION: A summer visitor to central and eastern Europe; elsewhere it may be either a winter visitor or a year-round resident, according to the precise location • SIZE: 9–10 cm (3½–4 in) • FOOD: Insects and other invertebrates • CALL: Utters a thin, high-pitched *tsuu-tsee-tsee* • SONG: A series of thin, high-pitched notes, ending with a short trill • SEX DIFFERENCES: The sexes are similar although the centre of the crown is orange in males but yellow in females • JUVENILE: Similar to the adults but the crown stripe is absent • FLIGHT: Direct and low, but capable of hovering briefly • NEST: A woven, cup-shaped structure of mosses and spider silk, suspended from a twig.

As small birds go, the firecrest is a well-marked and distinctive species. The dark stripe through the eyes and the broad, white stripe above them are often the most striking features, and the greenish-yellow back and golden-yellow flush contrast with the rather clean-looking whitish underparts. The colourful central stripe on the crown can be rather difficult to spot at first and is easiest to observe if the bird is facing you, head on.

Resident and breeding firecrests can be extremely difficult to spot because they feed at the very tops of tall conifers. However, when on migration and in the dead of winter these birds often feed within a few metres of the ground. Just don't expect to get prolonged views.

Habitat

Conifer woodlands, and parklands and gardens with large, mature conifers.

How to attract this bird to your garden

Plant conifers; once they are tall enough this species may visit.

Can be mistaken for

Goldcrest (see pages 222–223), but this species has a dark stripe through the eye and a white stripe above it.

Adult female

Collared flycatcher

Ficedula albicollis

REGION: A summer visitor to eastern Europe, present mainly May to August; widespread in southeastern Europe on migration, mainly in spring • SIZE: 12–13 cm (*c.* 5 in) • FOOD: Insects and other invertebrates • CALL: Utters a thin, whistling alarm call • SONG: A series of whistling notes • SEX DIFFERENCES: In females, many of the black elements of the male's plumage are replaced by grey-brown • JUVENILE: Similar to adult females • FLIGHT: Direct and fast, but capable of hovering momentarily • NEST: Sited in a tree hole.

With its essentially black-and-white plumage, a male collared flycatcher is a striking bird. The black hood is defined by the broad, white collar on the neck. The white on the rump and lower back is particularly easy to spot when the bird hovers.

Collared flycatchers are easiest to observe soon after their arrival from Africa in the spring. Males in particular often perch prominently and sing, advertizing their territories. Once nesting has started, both male and female birds become extremely secretive and hard to locate.

Habitat

Deciduous woodland and well-wooded parks and gardens.

How to attract this bird to your garden

The species will occasionally use a hole-fronted nest box, so install a few of these in your garden and you may be lucky in rural areas. If you have a wooded garden and live near the coast in southeast Europe, you may see spring migrants as they stop off for a few days, especially in late April.

Can be mistaken for

Pied flycatcher (see pages 226–227), but check for the male's white collar and rump. Females are more problematic and it is best to look for the greater amount of white on the wings; they are usually seen in association with male collared flycatchers.

Adult male

Pied flycatcher

Ficedula hypoleuca

REGION: A widespread summer visitor to central and northern Europe; more local in the west; present mainly May to July • SIZE: 12–13 cm (*c.* 5 in) • FOOD: Insects and other invertebrates • CALL: Utters a sharp *tik* • SONG: A series of sweet and ringing notes • SEX DIFFERENCES: Males are essentially black and white; in females many of the black elements of the male's plumage are replaced by brown • JUVENILE: Similar to adult females • FLIGHT: Direct, but also capable of hovering momentarily • NEST: Sited in a tree hole.

In terms of geographical range in Europe, the pied flycatcher is the western and northern counterpart of the collared flycatcher (see page 225). Males are well marked and distinctive, with mainly black upperparts, white on the innerwing and forehead, and clean, white underparts. Females have more subdued plumage that is mainly brown above and white below.

Pied flycatchers will forage for caterpillars and spiders among tree foliage but will also spend time perched on a branch from which they make aerial sorties to catch flying insects. Perched birds often flick their tails and wings.

Pied flycatchers are relatively easy to find during the first few weeks after their arrival in the region. Once nesting has begun, they become rather secretive and when the young fledge they are extremely difficult to locate because they spend most of the time feeding high in tree-top foliage.

Above The female's plumage lacks the contrast of the male, but the extent of white, and the flycatching action, make it easy to identify.

Habitat

Open, deciduous woodland and wooded parks and gardens.

How to attract this bird to your garden

If you live in a wooded area, put up hole-fronted nest boxes on trees in your garden and you may attract a pair.

Can be mistaken for

Collared flycatcher (see page 225), but lacks the broad white collar and white rump of the males of that species.

Spotted flycatcher

Muscicapa striata

REGION: A widespread summer visitor to much of Europe, present mainly May to August • SIZE: 14 cm (5½ in) • FOOD: Insects and other invertebrates • CALL: Utters a soft *tsee* • SONG: A series of subdued, thin notes • SEX DIFFERENCES: The sexes are similar • JUVENILE: Similar to the adults but with pale spots on the back • FLIGHT: Direct, but capable of hovering and frequently makes aerial sorties from a regular perch • NEST: A rather rudimentary nest of grass and mosses, often sited on a ledge, in an abandoned larger nest or in a crevice in a wall.

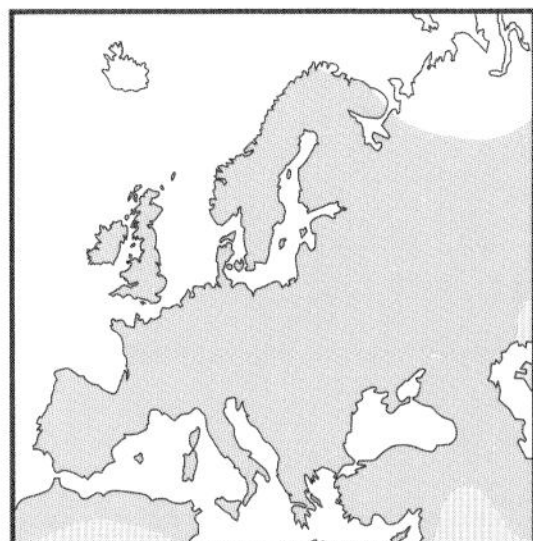

The spotted flycatcher is one of the few small birds that can be identified with a reasonable degree of confidence just from its habits. Within its territory it will have a number of regularly used perches from which it makes circular sorties to catch flying insects, returning to the same perch with its prey. Perched birds usually adopt a distinctive upright posture, which also helps to identify them.

Although their feeding habits frequently catch the eye, in other respects they are much less showy. Even though their plumage is subtly attractive, it is nevertheless decidedly subdued in terms of colour. Until you have learnt to recognize the call, these birds are easy to miss and you will rarely hear their quiet song.

Although they do breed in the countryside at large, they regularly nest in gardens (sometimes on house walls) and usually tolerate people's comings and goings.

Above A juvenile spotted flycatcher has more extensive streaking on the breast than an adult, and pale spots on the back.

Habitat

Glades in open woodlands, and parks and gardens.

How to attract this bird to your garden

Encourage plenty of insects and other invertebrates in the garden (by not using pesticides) and this species may take up summer residence. Although they will sometimes use an open-fronted nest box, they frequently ignore them in favour of something as seemingly inappropriate as a window ledge or the fork in a climbing plant that has been trained up a wall.

Can be mistaken for

Unmistakable, partly because of its flycatching habits and upright posture when perched.

Grey heron

Ardea cinerea

REGION: Present year-round in northwestern Europe; in eastern Europe it is mainly a summer visitor, while in the south it is much more widespread and common during the winter months • SIZE: 85–100 cm (34–40 in) • FOOD: Mainly fish and amphibians, but occasionally small mammals too • CALL: Utters a harsh *franck* in alarm • SEX DIFFERENCES: The sexes are similar • JUVENILE: Resembles the adults but has less distinct dark markings on the head • FLIGHT: Direct, on slow, flapping wingbeats • NEST: A sizeable structure of twigs and branches, sited in a tree; usually nests colonially.

Grey herons are renowned for their patience and one will sometimes stand completely motionless around the margins of a pond, waiting for a fish to swim within striking range of its dagger-like bill. Birds also spend long periods of time standing and preening on dry land and, on sunny days, they sometimes spread drooping wings in order to catch as much heat from the sun's rays as possible.

Adult grey herons are elegant birds, with blue-grey on the back and upperwings, and a pinkish-lilac flush to the pale underparts. There is a striking black patch behind each eye and this colour extends to the long plumes on the nape.

Grey herons are easy to recognize when they are wading in water. In flight, the broad wings give the heron a passing resemblance to a large bird of prey; check for the long, trailing legs, and the way the neck is held 'kinked' in an S-shape, creating a rather front-heavy appearance.

Above With its large, broad wings and long legs, a flying grey heron is an impressive, easily recognized species.

Above Grey herons will often stand motionless for long periods of time, watching for prey. This individual's lack of dark head markings identify it as a juvenile.

Habitat

Mainly lakes and large wetlands, but it will visit surprisingly small garden ponds if there are plenty of fish.

How to attract this bird to your garden

Stock your pond with fish and you may be visited by this species, whether or not you like it! If you are particularly attached to your fish you may need to cover the pond with netting to prevent them being eaten.

Can be mistaken for

Unmistakable when seen in good light on account of size, shape and colour. In silhouette could perhaps be confused with white stork (see page 232) or little egret (see right).

SIMILAR SPECIES

Little egret

Egretta garzetta

LENGTH: 55–65 cm (22–26 in)

A pure white, heron-like bird with a dark, dagger-like bill and dark legs with bright yellow feet. Found in freshwater habitats and on coasts. Feeds actively in pursuit of fish.

Cormorant

Phalacrocorax carbo

LENGTH: 80–100 cm (32–40 in)

A distinctive bird with mainly dark plumage and a hook-tipped bill. Swims well and dives for fish. Often seen perched on waterside trees, drying its wings. A widespread resident across much of Europe.

Little egret

Cormorant

White stork

Ciconia ciconia

REGION: A local summer visitor to mainland Europe, commonest in the Iberian Peninsula and southeast Europe. Present mainly April to September • SIZE: 100–115 cm (40–46 in) • FOOD: Amphibians, reptiles, insects and small birds • CALL: Mainly silent, but noisy bill-clapping displays are performed at nests • SEX DIFFERENCES: The sexes are similar • JUVENILE: Similar to the adult but with duller bill and leg colours • FLIGHT: Seemingly rather effortless, and capable of extended gliding and soaring on long, broad wings • NEST: A massive structure of twigs and branches, often sited on the roof of a building.

Adult

White stork

Little egret

Grey heron

In most parts of this species' European breeding range, the white stork is a symbol of good luck and many people try their best to encourage them to nest on their roof. Because the birds are usually not disturbed or persecuted by people, they are often tolerant of close observation. Even at a distance, it is hard to mistake this species for any other, thanks to its outline, the striking black-and-white plumage and the bright red legs and bill.

White storks are extremely fond of frogs and spend long periods walking in a sedate manner through damp fields, and around the margins of wetlands. In flight, the head and neck, as well as the legs, are held outstretched. Together with the striking black-and-white plumage, this makes it straightforward for the birdwatcher to tell them apart from the similarly sized grey heron.

Given this species' large size it is not surprising that it is, to a degree, reliant on thermals generated by the heat of the sun to assist its flight. Once airborne, however, it is a superb aeronaut and can soar and glide effortlessly, often spiralling upwards to a considerable height.

Above Given the size of the young birds, a large nest is a necessity for a family of white storks.

Habitat

Villages and farms that are close to wetland areas.

How to attract this bird to your garden

If you live in a suitable rural area, you can encourage it to nest on your roof by placing a platform such as an old cartwheel or similar there. Then tie on a few branches for good measure and white storks may choose to nest.

Can be mistaken for

Unmistakable when seen in good light on account of size, plumage colours and red bill.

Greylag goose

Anser anser

REGION: Locallly resident in central Europe; present year-round in northwestern Europe with numbers boosted in winter by migrant visitors. The situation throughout the region is confused by the presence of feral populations (previously domesticated birds that have returned to the wild) • SIZE: 75–90 cm (30–36 in) • FOOD: Plant shoots and leaves • CALL: Utters loud, honking calls • SEX DIFFERENCES: The sexes are similar • JUVENILE: Similar to the adults but with duller colours • FLIGHT: Direct, on powerful and deep wingbeats. Flocks often fly in 'V' formation • NEST: A hollow on the ground, lined with downy feathers.

Greylag geese are the ancestors of the 'farmyard' goose. Although domesticated geese often have white plumage, the close relationship between the two can be discerned by looking at the size, shape and behaviour of the two forms, and by paying attention to their calls.

Greylag geese usually nest beside water. Although genuinely wild birds favour remote locations and are generally wary of people, feral birds are often much more tame. They may even breed beside ornamental ponds and lakes, or on islands in flooded gravel pits. Family groups make an endearing sight, the goslings staying in close proximity to their vigilant parents.

Outside the breeding season, greylag geese often form sizeable flocks and can be seen feeding on grassland and arable fields. Typically, as dusk approaches they will fly off as a flock, and roost on water, which provides them with a degree of protection from terrestrial predators, such as foxes and people.

Above Like other geese species, greylags often feed on grassland or arable crops in fields.

Habitat

Marshes, lakes and arable farmland.

How to attract this bird to your garden

If you have the space to create a large pond, then feral individuals may visit from time to time. If you include a small, well-vegetated island, a pair might even nest there.

Can be mistaken for

The other 'grey' geese species that occur in Europe (mainly in winter), all are wary, favour wild locations and shun human habitation so will not be seen near gardens.

SIMILAR SPECIES

Mute swan

Cygnus olor

LENGTH: 150–160 cm (60–64 in)

A huge and unmistakable resident wetland bird. Adults have pure white plumage while juveniles look grubby. The orange-red bill has a black base. In flight, the neck is held outstretched and the wings produce a throbbing, whining sound.

Canada goose

Branta canadensis

LENGTH: 95–105 cm (38–42 in)

Introduced to the region from North America but now a firmly established resident in northwestern Europe. The black-and-white markings on the head and neck are distinctive and the plumage is otherwise buffish-brown above and whitish below. Associated with wetland habitats, but they do also occur in urban parks. Birds from northern populations move south, or towards the coast in winter, but these movements are weather dependent, not true migration.

Mute swan

Shelduck

Tadorna tadorna

LENGTH: 55–65 cm (22–26 in)

A striking, goose-sized duck with black, white and chestnut plumage. The adults have bright red bills. Locally common resident around the coasts of northwestern Europe and, very occasionally, on inland water. Scandinavian birds tend to move south and west in winter, boosting the numbers of residents in their winter quarters. In southern Europe they are scarce winter visitors and breed only occasionally.

Canada goose

Shelduck

Mallard

Anas platyrhynchos

REGION: A widespread resident across the whole of the region • SIZE: 50–60 cm (20–24 in) • FOOD: Omnivorous and opportunistic, taking plant shoots, seeds and invertebrates • CALL: Utters a familiar quacking call • SEX DIFFERENCES: Males are colourful while females have mottled brown plumage • JUVENILE: Similar to adult females but paler overall • FLIGHT: Rapid and direct; usually seen in pairs or flocks • NEST: Usually a depression on the ground, lined with downy feathers.

The mallard is the most common and widespread duck in the region. In addition to wild populations, many individuals are kept as pets, or have become so accustomed to people feeding them that they are tame. Consequently, it is usually extremely easy to get superb views of this species, even in towns and cities that have ornamental lakes and ponds.

The male mallard has a bright yellow bill and orange legs and feet. The iridescent green head and neck are separated from the reddish-chestnut breast by a well-defined white ring. In contrast, the female has rather subdued plumage but this is good camouflage when she is nesting on the ground among fallen leaves. During their summer moult, males resemble adult females. In flight, look for the shiny blue patch (called a 'speculum') on the upper surface of the innerwings. This species often hybridizes with ornamental duck species that are kept as pets, domesticated or in parks. The results can look extremely odd!

Mallards feed mainly by dabbling in the shallows, but occasionally birds will upend in order to reach a tasty morsel of submerged vegetation on the bottom of a pond or lake.

Habitat

Wetlands and ornamental ponds and lakes in both rural and suburban areas.

SIMILAR SPECIES

Wigeon

Anas penelope

LENGTH: 45–50 cm (18–20 in)

A distinctive duck of coasts and inland wetlands. Males have chestnut and yellow on the head, pink on the breast and fine, delicate barring on the back and flanks. Females are rather uniformly reddish-brown with a white belly. During their summer moult, males resemble adult females. Breeds in northern Europe, mainly Iceland, northern Britain and from Scandinavia eastwards. Seen around coasts of northwestern and southern Europe in winter and in other coastal areas (occasionally on inland water) on migration.

Teal

Anas crecca

LENGTH: 35–38 cm (14–15½ in)

The smallest duck in the region. Found on coasts and on inland wetlands. Males have chestnut, yellow and green on the head and fine vermiculations on the rest of the body. Females are mottled grey-brown. Breeds in northern Europe, mainly Iceland, northern Britain and from Scandinavia eastwards. Seen around coasts of northwestern and southern Europe in winter (sometimes on inland water) and in other coastal areas (occasionally on inland water) on migration.

Gadwall

Anas strepera

LENGTH: 45–55 cm (18–22 in)

A local resident in western Europe, with numbers boosted in winter by influxes of birds that breed in eastern and central Europe. Found on lakes and large ponds. Males have plumage with intricate fine markings and a striking black 'stern'; females are mottled brown. During their summer moult, males resemble adult females. The white patch on the wings can be seen in flight in both sexes.

Pochard

Aythya ferina

LENGTH: 42–48 cm (17–19 in)

A striking diving duck. Males have a red head, black neck and 'stern' and otherwise pale grey plumage. Females are subdued grey-brown but show a pale 'spectacle' around the eye. During their summer moult, males resemble adult females. A local resident in western Europe, with numbers boosted in winter by influxes of birds that bred in eastern and central Europe.

Wigeon

Tufted duck

Aythya fuligula

LENGTH: 40–47 cm (16–18½ in)

A diving duck that is often found on ornamental lakes where birds are fed. Males have striking black-and-white plumage and a 'tuft' on the head. Females are mainly brown with a white patch at the base of the bill. During their summer moult, males resemble adult females. Present year-round in much of central and northwest Europe; a summer visitor to east and northeast Europe and a winter visitor elsewhere.

Teal

Gadwall

Tufted duck

Pheasant

Phasianus colchicus

REGION: Widespread in many parts of Europe. In autumn, numbers are boosted by the release of captive-bred birds for shooting • SIZE: (including tail) male 65–90 cm (26–36 in); female 55–70 cm (22–28 in) • FOOD: Omnivorous, taking seeds, grain and berries as well as invertebrates • CALL: Territorial males utter a loud, shrieking call followed by loud, clattering wingbeats. A series of loud, disyllabic shrieking hiccups is uttered in alarm, as a bird takes to the wing • SEX DIFFERENCES: Males have colourful plumage and a striking red wattle on the face; females have mottled brown plumage and a shorter tail than males • JUVENILE: Plumage similar to adult females, but with a much shorter tail • FLIGHT: Takes to the wing explosively, on rapid, whirring wingbeats. Typically, birds only fly a couple of hundred metres at most before dropping into cover • NEST: A depression on the ground, sometimes lined with dead leaves.

It would be hard to confuse a male pheasant with any other European bird, partly because of its colourful plumage but also its extremely long tail. They are often bold and, in areas where they are not shot, indifferent to human observers. Female pheasants lead more unobtrusive lives and blend in with their surroundings. Their mottled brown plumage is particularly useful in the breeding season as extremely good camouflage when they are nesting among fallen leaves on the woodland floor.

At the start of the breeding season, a dominant male will gather a harem of a dozen or more females around him and fight off the attentions of any ardent rival suitors. Courting males perform elaborate displays in front of each female, dragging their wings, twisting their tails and inflating their facial wattles.

Above A female pheasant's plumage is designed for camouflage, although away from the woodland floor they are easy to spot.

Above Because most of the pheasants you will see will have been captive-bred, weird and wonderful colour variants may appear.

Habitat

Woodland, farmland and mature gardens.

How to attract this bird to your garden

If you live in a rural area, sooner or later they will visit your garden of their own accord. Scatter seed on the lawn and you will get regular visitors.

Can be mistaken for

Unmistakable when adult. Young birds (which have short tails) could be confused with partridge (right).

SIMILAR SPECIES

Red-legged partridge

Alectoris rufa

LENGTH: 32–34 cm (13–13½ in)

A gamebird that is resident in southwestern Europe but has been introduced to other parts of the region. Watch out for the red bill and legs, the black-bordered white throat and striking barring on the flanks. Found in agricultural land and sometimes visits rural gardens.

Grey partridge

Perdix perdix

LENGTH: 29–31 cm (11½–12½ in)

A similar size to a red-legged partridge but with an orange face and subtle grey and chestnut plumage markings. Males have a more striking dark patch on the belly than females. A declining resident.

Red-legged partridge

Grey partridge

Little grebe

Tachybaptus ruficollis

REGION: Resident across much of western and southern Europe; populations from eastern Europe are at least partially migrant, often forced to leave if the water freezes in winter • SIZE: 25–29 cm (10–11½ in) • FOOD: Fish and aquatic invertebrates • CALL: Utters a trilling, whinnying call • SEX DIFFERENCES: The sexes are similar although birds are much more colourful in summer than in winter • JUVENILE: Similar to a winter adult but with dark streaks on the face and an orange flush to the neck • FLIGHT: Low over the water, on weak, fluttering wingbeats • NEST: A mound of aquatic vegetation, often floating and anchored to a water plant.

You are only likely to see a little grebe on water. Their dumpy bodies are extremely buoyant and their legs and feet are designed for swimming (they are incapable of walking on land). At the rear end, note the powder-puff display of extremely fluffy feathers.

They are adept swimmers and spend much of their time diving in search of prey. If alarmed, a bird will hide among the vegetation. In desperation, it will submerge most of its body with only the bill and nostrils exposed to the air.

Above In winter, a little grebe has rather drab, buffish plumage.

Habitat

Freshwater ponds, canals and well-vegetated lakes.

How to attract this bird to your garden

If you have a large pond in the garden, with thriving populations of small fish and invertebrates, this species may visit occasionally. The larger your pond, the better your chances will be.

Can be mistaken for

Unmistakable on account of its dumpy shape, small size and habitat preference.

Water rail

Rallus aquaticus

REGION: Mainly a summer visitor to eastern Europe but present year-round locally elsewhere in the region with numbers boosted in winter by migrant visitors • SIZE: 23–28 cm (*c*. 9–11 in) • FOOD: Mainly insects and other invertebrates, but also seeds and berries in season • CALL: Utters an extraordinary pig-like squeal • SEX DIFFERENCES: The sexes are similar • JUVENILE: Similar to the adults but the underparts are mainly pale, not bluish • FLIGHT: Low and weak, on fluttering wingbeats and with dangling legs • NEST: A low mound of vegetation, sited at water level deep in a reedbed.

The body of a water rail is compressed laterally, which is a useful adaptation that allows it to slip with ease among the dense stems of reeds and other emergent aquatic plants. It also has remarkably long toes that allow it to spread its weight as it walks across vegetation floating at the water surface.

The water rail is a rather secretive bird and were it not for its piercing call would be easy to overlook. If you imitate its call, by making a squeaking sound through pursed lips, you may lure a curious individual out into the open. They are easiest to see during harsh winters, especially if forced to feed in the open when reedbeds and marshes freeze solid.

Habitat

Reedbeds and extensive marshes in the breeding season; often found in much smaller wetlands in winter.

How to attract this bird to your garden

If you have a well-vegetated pond, stream or ditch in your garden then this species may visit on migration, or during the winter months.

Can be mistaken for

Unmistakable on account of its plumage colours and long bill.

Adult

Moorhen

Gallinula chloropus

REGION: A widespread resident across much of Europe, although birds from eastern Europe tend to move west and south in winter • SIZE: 32–35 cm (13–14 in) • FOOD: Omnivorous, taking aquatic plants, seeds, fruits, invertebrates and small amphibians • CALL: Utters a loud, shrieking *kurrk* • SEX DIFFERENCES: The sexes are similar • JUVENILE: Mainly brown above and pale buffish on underparts • FLIGHT: Rather weak and usually low over the water with trailing legs • NEST: A floating mound of vegetation, usually anchored to emergent vegetation or the branches of a waterside bush.

In rural locations, moorhens tend to be shy and nervous birds. In contrast, however, where they occur on ornamental lakes in urban parks, they can become remarkably tame, especially if fed by people. If you see one walking on land, check out the extremely long toes.

Swimming moorhens are relatively easy to recognize, even at a distance, because they constantly flick their tails, revealing a flash of pure white feathers on the underside. At close range, you will see the white stripe along the flanks and strikingly colourful yellow-tipped red bill and frontal shield.

Above A juvenile moorhen lacks the adult's colourful bill and frontal shield.

Habitat

Freshwater wetlands but also ornamental ponds and lakes.

How to attract this bird to your garden

A well-vegetated pond is likely to attract this species.

Can be mistaken for

Adults are unmistakable but juveniles could perhaps be confused with female ducks, until you notice the pointed (not flattened) bill and absence of webbed feet.

Adult

Snipe

Gallinago gallinago

REGION: A summer visitor to much of central and northern Europe, and a winter visitor to the south; occurs year-round in northwestern Europe, but is most numerous in winter • SIZE: 25–28 cm (10–11 cm) • FOOD: Invertebrates • CALL: Utters a sneezing call when flushed • SONG: A much-repeated series of *chipa-chipa* phrases • SEX DIFFERENCES: The sexes are similar • JUVENILE: Similar to the adults • FLIGHT: Rapid and direct, often following a zigzag path when startled and flushed • NEST: A cavity created in a tussock of grass, sometimes lined with dry grass.

A motionless, roosting snipe can be extremely difficult to spot because its streaked plumage affords it superb camouflage among wetland vegetation. From time to time, a bird will move into the open and the extremely long bill becomes apparent. Feeding birds probe muddy ground for worms, moving their bills up and down in the manner of a sewing-machine needle.

Snipe are badly affected during harsh winters if their preferred wetland habitats freeze solid. At such times, they are forced to move to habitats and locations less suited to their needs and this is when they are most likely to turn up in gardens and parks.

Habitat

Wetland habitats.

How to attract this bird to your garden

You are only likely to find this species in your garden (as a winter visitor) if you have either a large pond or lake with shallow, vegetated margins.

Can be mistaken for

Unmistakable on account of the long bill.

Above A snipe's incredibly long bill is invaluable for feeding, and to observers.

Adult

Black-headed gull

Larus ridibundus

REGION: Present year-round in northwestern Europe; a summer visitor to northern and central Europe and elsewhere seen as a coastal winter visitor • SIZE: 35–38 cm (14–15½ in) • FOOD: Invertebrates, particularly worms, small fish and scavenged scraps of food • CALL: Utters a raucous, nasal *kaah* call • SEX DIFFERENCES: The sexes are similar but show seasonal differences: the dark hood is present in summer only • JUVENILE: Has marbled upperparts mottled with grey and yellowish buff • FLIGHT: Direct and buoyant, with rather long, pointed wings • NEST: A collection of twigs, water plants or seaweed, usually sited on a small island; breeds colonially.

The chocolate-brown hood is an adult black-headed gull's most distinctive feature during the summer months; in winter, all that remains are a few dark smudges behind and above the eye. Throughout the year, adult birds show a distinctive white leading edge to the upperwing in flight. Both the bill and legs in adult birds are reddish, although the colour is most intense during the summer.

The species is most numerous around the coast. Nevertheless, in winter, it is usually easy to find black-headed gulls in and around many towns and cities in northwest Europe. Birds usually concentrate in the vicinity of ornamental lakes and parks, and flocks will occasionally roost in seemingly unlikely places like supermarket car parks and school playing fields. The black-headed gull is a social bird throughout the year. You are unlikely to see a healthy individual on its own and flocks that are hundreds strong are a common sight in winter.

Habitat

During the breeding season, black-headed gulls favour coastal and freshwater habitats. At other times of the year, they can turn up almost anywhere.

How to attract this bird to your garden

If you live near the coast, or close to an urban park, then scraps of food on the lawn may attract this species, so long as the garden is not enclosed.

Can be mistaken for

Mediterranean gull (see opposite).

Above In winter, the underparts and back look clean while there are dark smudges on the head, the remains of the summer hood.

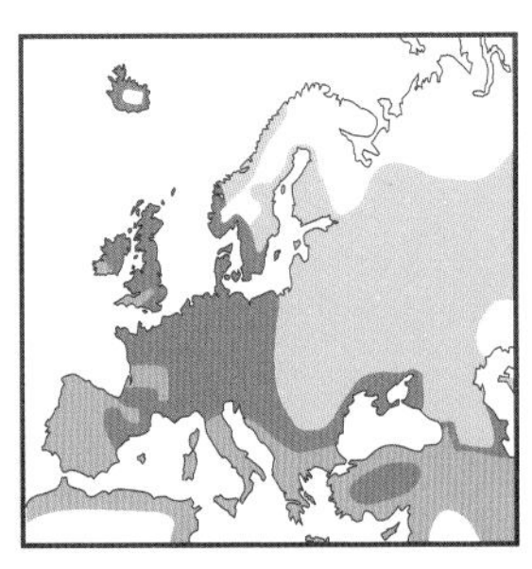

Black-headed gull

Mediterranean gull

Herring gull

Adult, summer

SIMILAR SPECIES

Mediterranean gull

Larus melanocephalus

LENGTH: 36–38 cm (14½–15½ in)

A similar size to a black-headed gull but the adults can be distinguished at all times by their pure white wings. Adults have black (not chocolate-brown) hoods in summer. The legs and bill are robust and reddish. The species has a patchy distribution in the Mediterranean but also occurs in good numbers in northwestern Europe. Most sightings are on the coast.

Summer adult

Winter adult

Herring gull

Larus argentatus

REGION: Occurs year-round in northwestern Europe although northern populations tend to move south outside the breeding season • SIZE: 56–62 cm (22½–25 in) • FOOD: Opportunistic and omnivorous, taking fish, birds' eggs and invertebrates, but also scavenges scraps of food • CALL: Utters a mewing *kyaoo* and an agitated *ga-ka-ka* • SEX DIFFERENCES: The sexes are similar • JUVENILE: Has marbled and mottled brown and buff plumage • FLIGHT: Direct and powerful; also capable of soaring and lengthy glides • NEST: A rudimentary structure of twigs, seaweed and debris. Usually nests colonially on cliffs but occasionally on coastal roofs too.

Adult

A combination of a silvery-grey back and pink legs is distinctive enough, for a bird of this size, to allow you to identify this bird easily. The herring gull has a robust bill and a personality to match – its bold and pugnacious character and adaptable behaviour allow it to live alongside people and make good use of discarded food. It is one of the most common scavengers at rubbish dumps.

Habitat

Mainly coastal habitats during the breeding season; in winter, it often visits rubbish dumps and ploughed fields.

Herring gull

Black-headed gull

Yellow-legged gull

Above Pink legs and a silvery-grey back are good identification features for an adult herring gull.

How to attract this bird to your garden

If you live near the coast, this species may nest on the roof of your house. Given its size and habits, you may not want to encourage visits to your garden.

Can be mistaken for

Yellow-legged gull (see page 248), but that species has yellow (not pink) legs and their geographical ranges seldom overlap.

Above Juvenile herring gulls have mottled brown plumage, quite unlike that of their parents. They acquire adult plumage through successive moults over a three-year period.

Yellow-legged gull

Larus cachinnans

REGION: Resident in coastal areas of southwestern Europe and the Mediterranean; a regular but rather scarce winter visitor to northwestern Europe • SIZE: Length 52–60 cm (20½–24 in) • FOOD: Opportunistic and omnivorous, taking fish, birds' eggs and invertebrates, but it also scavenges scraps of food • CALL: Utters a mewing *kyaoo* and an agitated *ga-ka-ka* • SEX DIFFERENCES: The sexes are similar • JUVENILE: Has marbled and mottled grey-brown and buff plumage • FLIGHT: Direct and powerful; also capable of soaring and lengthy glides • NEST: A rudimentary structure of twigs, seaweed and debris. Usually nests colonially on cliffs and islands.

In many ways, the yellow-legged gull is the southern counterpart of the herring gull: if it were not for the differences in leg colour it would be hard to tell the two species apart. Yellow-legged gulls are easiest to find in and around coastal towns, especially ones from which fishing boats operate. They will also visit nearby ploughed fields and areas of short coastal grassland in search of invertebrate food.

Unlike its close cousin the herring gull, this species almost always breeds on inaccessible cliffs and islands and you are unlikely to find one nesting on the roof of a house. Its association with people is more or less restricted to scavenging scraps of food discarded by fishing boats as they come into port.

Habitat

Found mainly around the coast but also on fields that are a short distance inland.

How to attract this bird to your garden

Scraps of food placed on the lawn may attract this bird, although typically it is more wary and nervous than other gull species.

Can be mistaken for

Herring gull (see pages 246–247), but that species has pink (not yellow) legs as an adult.

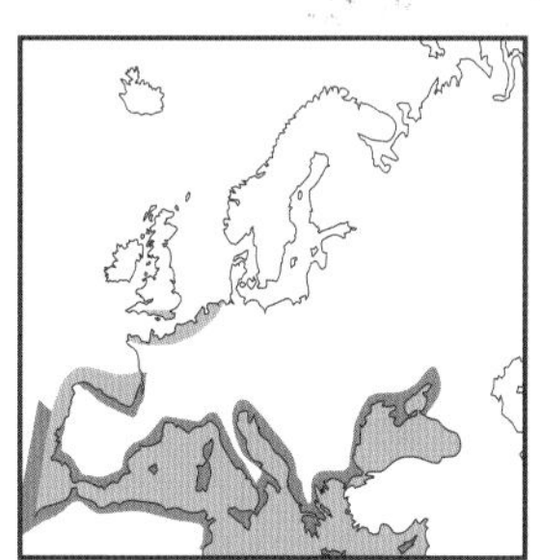

Adult, summer

Common tern

Sterna hirundo

REGION: A summer visitor to coastal parts of northwestern Europe, as well as inland freshwater locations both there and across central Europe. Present mainly May to August • SIZE: 33–35 cm (*c.*13–14 in) • FOOD: Mainly small fish, but sometimes eats insects • CALL: Utters harsh calls • SEX DIFFERENCES: The sexes are similar • JUVENILE: Has a gingery (not grey) back with a slightly 'scaly' appearance created by pale feather edges • FLIGHT: Buoyant and direct, on deep wingbeats • NEST: A rudimentary scrape in the ground, usually on shingle or sand, and often on an island.

On the wing, adult birds often look extremely white. However, at close quarters on the ground, the silvery-grey colour to the back and upper-wings is apparent. In addition, the black cap, the red legs and the black-tipped orange-red bill are even more striking.

Common terns are consummate aeronauts with a powerful and graceful flight. They are capable of flying in almost all weather conditions, are able to plunge-dive repeatedly in order to catch fish, and can even hawk for flying insects with aerobatic skill if the opportunity arises.

Above In flight, a common tern is streamlined, with dark-edged undersides.

Habitat

Inshore coastal seas and large inland bodies of fresh water, including lakes and flooded gravel pits.

How to attract this bird to your garden

If you live near the sea or a large lake then this species may fly over from time to time.

Can be mistaken for

Unmistakable, because of its dagger-like red bill and rather pale plumage.

Adult, summer

Checklist of birds

Heading	✓	Date	Location	Comments
Blue tit				
Great tit				
Coal tit				
Marsh tit				
Crested tit				
Long-tailed tit				
Sombre tit				
Penduline tit				
Nuthatch				
Treecreeper				
Short-toed treecreeper				
Swift				
Red-rumped swallow				
Swallow				
House martin				
Sand martin				
Meadow pipit				
Crested lark				
White/pied wagtail				
Wren				
Waxwing				
Dunnock				
Robin				
Bluethroat				
Nightingale				
Black redstart				
Redstart				
Rock thrush				
Blue rock thrush				
Blackbird				
Fieldfare				
Redwing				
Song thrush				
Mistle thrush				

Checklist of birds continued

Heading	✓	Date	Location	Comments
Woodpigeon				
Rock dove/feral pigeon				
Collared dove				
Turtle dove				
Stock dove				
Rose-coloured starling				
Starling				
Spotless starling				
Golden oriole				
Tree sparrow				
House sparrow				
Spanish sparrow				
Rock sparrow				
Chaffinch				
Brambling				
Goldfinch				
Linnet				
Twite				
Redpoll				
Bullfinch				
Siskin				
Greenfinch				
Hawfinch				
Serin				
Crossbill				
Pine grosbeak				
Cirl bunting				
Rock bunting				
Yellowhammer				
Reed bunting				
Ortolan bunting				
Cretzschmar's bunting				
Snow bunting				
Black-headed bunting				

Checklist of birds continued

Heading	✓	Date	Location	Comments
Corn bunting				
Sparrowhawk				
Buzzard				
Red kite				
Kestrel				
Lesser kestrel				
Red-footed falcon				
Barn owl				
Tawny owl				
Long-eared owl				
Scops owl				
Little owl				
Red-backed shrike				
Woodchat shrike				
Lesser grey shrike				
Masked shrike				
Cuckoo				
Bee-eater				
Hoopoe				
Kingfisher				
Ring-necked parakeet				
Wryneck				
Black woodpecker				
Grey-headed woodpecker				
Green woodpecker				
Great spotted woodpecker				
Lesser spotted woodpecker				
Middle spotted woodpecker				
Jay				
Magpie				
Azure-winged magpie				
Jackdaw				
Carrion crow				
Hooded crow				

Checklist of birds continued

Heading	✓	Date	Location	Comments
Rook				
Reed warbler				
Sedge warbler				
Melodious warbler				
Olivaceous warbler				
Lesser whitethroat				
Subalpine warbler				
Sardinian warbler				
Garden warbler				
Whitethroat				
Blackcap				
Barred warbler				
Willow warbler				
Chiffchaff				
Goldcrest				
Firecrest				
Collared flycatcher				
Pied flycatcher				
Spotted flycatcher				
Grey heron				
White stork				
Greylag goose				
Mallard				
Pheasant				
Little grebe				
Water rail				
Moorhen				
Snipe				
Black-headed gull				
Herring gull				
Yellow-legged gull				
Common tern				

Index

Executive Editor: Trevor Davies

Project Editor: Kate Tuckett

Executive Art Editors: Rozelle Bentheim, Darren Southern

Designer: Ginny Zeal

Production Manager: Ian Paton

Picture Acknowledgements:

All photographs were supplied by Nature Photographers Limited and were taken by Paul Sterry with the exception of:

Nature Photographers Ltd 9, 81; /Frank B. Blackburn 7 top left, 8, 20 bottom left, 190, 216, 222; /Mark Bolton 66; /T. D. Bonsall 105 top; /Colin Carver 55, 86, 88, 97 centre right, 99 top, 113, 150, 168, 207, 240 right; /Kevin Carlson 94, 100, 111, 147 left, 147 right, 219 inset; /Hugh Clark 7 top centre left, 25 top left, 38 left, 42 top, 69, 72 left, 185 bottom, 193 top, 235 bottom right; /Ron Croucher 47 top, 47 bottom; /Geoff Du Feu 145, 234; /Michael Gore 182, 210; /Phil Green 61 top, 117 top, 132; /Barry Hughes 5, 77 centre right, 95, 152, 191 top, 212; /E.A. Janes 24 left, 32, 41 left, 42 bottom, 48, 99 bottom centre, 135, 159 right, 170, 191 bottom, 239 bottom right; /Philip Newman 7 bottom right, 17 picture 3, 73, 79 right, 92, 93, 104, 144, 149 bottom, 151 left, 179, 213 centre, 214; /W.S. Paton 7 top centre right, 79 left; /Don Smith 166; /R.T. Smith 249 right; /Roger Tidman 20 top right, 21 bottom centre right, 71, 75 centre right, 103, 118, 131, 142, 143, 148, 159 left, 169, 202 inset, 206, 208, 213 bottom, 223, 239 centre right; /Patrick Whalley 54, 125, 194, 199.